Praise for *Rethinking C*
Theory Using Critical Frameworks

"My read of *Rethinking College Student Development Theory Using Critical Frameworks* generated one thought: "It's about time!" This must-read volume is a major contribution to the field of student affairs. The editors have assembled a book that not only unpacks and acknowledges the vast complexities that shape students' college experiences but also raises educators' critical consciousness in translating theory to practice. This book should be required reading in graduate programs, especially within advanced student development theory courses."—**Lori Patton Davis**, *Professor of Higher Education and Student Affairs and Chair, Department of Educational Studies, The Ohio State University*

"Framing development through the lens of emancipation will forever shift graduate preparation and professional practice in student affairs. Abes, Jones, Stewart, and chapter authors have transformed the theoretical foundation of student affairs into a more complex and liberatory understanding of student development, and for that I am eternally grateful."—**Jason C. Garvey,** *Associate Professor of Higher Education and Student Affairs Administration, University of Vermont*

"The field has been waiting for this book. It brings together in one place a host of the most thoughtful scholars working in, with, and through critical frameworks in student development theory. On their own, each chapter offers valuable insight; the volume as a whole takes the reader into the latest thinking using critical theory to understand and work with college students."—**Kristen A. Renn;** *Professor of Higher, Adult, & Lifelong Education; and Associate Dean of Undergraduate Studies for Student Success Research, Michigan State University*

"This book is exactly what we need to push our thinking about student development theory forward. As a field, we have been stymied for some time around student development theory, and the editors of this book give permission for educators to pursue new and different questions and practices through critical and poststructural lenses. I am excited to use this text in my courses and have already been inspired by the editors' ideas to create new assignments pushing students to better integrate critical praxis in their work as student affairs educators."—**Chris Linder,** *Assistant Professor, Higher Education, University of Utah*

RETHINKING COLLEGE STUDENT DEVELOPMENT
THEORY USING CRITICAL FRAMEWORKS

RETHINKING COLLEGE STUDENT DEVELOPMENT THEORY USING CRITICAL FRAMEWORKS

Edited by

Elisa S. Abes, Susan R. Jones, and

D-L Stewart

STERLING, VIRGINIA

Published by Stylus Publishing, LLC.
22883 Quicksilver Drive
Sterling, Virginia 20166-2012

Library of Congress Cataloging-in-Publication Data
Names: Abes, Elisa S., 1969- editor. | Jones, Susan R., 1955- editor. |
   Stewart, Dafina-Lazarus, 1973- editor.
Title: Rethinking college student development theory using critical
   frameworks / edited by Elisa Abes, Susan Jones, and D-L Stewart.
Description: First edition. | Sterling, Virginia : Stylus Publishing, LLC.,
   2019. | Includes bibliographical references and index.
Identifiers: LCCN 2018058251 (print) | LCCN 2019005543 (ebook) | ISBN
   9781620367650 (updf) | ISBN 9781620367667 (ePub, mobi) | ISBN
   9781620367636 (cloth : alk. paper) | ISBN 9781620367643 (pbk. : alk.
   paper) | ISBN 9781620367650 (library networkable e-edition) | ISBN
   9781620367667 (consumer e-edition)
Subjects: LCSH: College student development programs. | College
   students--Psychology. | Identity (Psychology)
Classification: LCC LB2343.4 (ebook) | LCC LB2343.4 .R47 2019 (print) |
   DDC 378.1/98--dc23
LC record available at https://lccn.loc.gov/2018058251

13-digit ISBN: 978-1-62036-763-6 (cloth)
13-digit ISBN: 978-1-62036-764-3 (paperback)
13-digit ISBN: 978-1-62036-765-0 (library networkable e-edition)
13-digit ISBN: 978-1-62036-766-7 (consumer e-edition)

Printed in the United States of America

All first editions printed on acid-free paper
that meets the American National Standards Institute
Z39-48 Standard.

Bulk Purchases
Quantity discounts are available for use in workshops and
for staff development.
Call 1-800-232-0223

First Edition, 2019

We dedicate this book to L. Lee Knefelkamp, brilliant and creative thinker, scholar, and champion of student development theory, who passed September 7, 2018. It was Lee's work that guided our initial knowledge of student development theories and no doubt planted the seeds for rethinking and reimagining what can be known not only about how all students develop but also about how all of who students are develops.

CONTENTS

PREFACE

As scholars of student development, we believe in the power of theory to transform not only individuals but also institutional practices and policies. Indeed, that is the impetus behind this book. College students bring to campuses increasingly complex and multifaceted ways of constructing identities and presenting themselves. We wanted to create a piece of work that would increase the likelihood of more equitable, inclusive, and respectful understandings of these college students and their development. In this book, we examine student development theory through the lens of critical and poststructural frameworks, because a goal of these theories "is to make it possible to think differently and thus to open the possibility for acting differently" (Gannon & Davies, 2007, p. 78). In emphasizing the power and potential of critical and poststructural frameworks, our intent is not to dismiss outright all student development theories that are not grounded in critical and poststructural theories but instead to rethink student development in ways that acknowledge, critique, and reconstruct core theoretical constructs. Just as Knefelkamp, Widick, and Parker suggested in 1978, we recognize that "important changes have occurred in the field" (p. vii). Among these changes is acknowledgment of the importance and role of integrating into conceptions of college student development an awareness of social constructions of identities and oppression based on minoritized identities. Also among these changes is the challenge to development as stable, fixed, and independent of structural systems. To this end, scholars and researchers are employing critical and poststructural perspectives to examine the assumptions underlying college student development theories and interrogating oppressive contextual influences at both societal and campus levels.

In a recent New Directions for Student Services volume titled *Critical Perspectives on Student Development Theory* (No. 154, 2016), the authors raised critical questions related to who students are, how students develop, intersectionality, individual agency, and the role of context. In that volume, guest editor Elisa S. Abes described how the chapters apply critical and poststructural theories, suggesting they "are applied in two ways: (1) to critique existing student development theories, illuminating how they marginalize oppressed students; and (2) to create new possibilities for student development theories that are more just and equitable" (p. 14). She went on to suggest,

The second task provides the next challenge for student development theorists and the one where there is much work to do. Theorists are not fully embracing the possibilities of critical and poststructural scholarship to re-envision student development theory, often centering the dominant while critiquing it. (Abes, 2016, p. 14)

In this book, *Rethinking College Student Development Theory Using Critical Frameworks*, we respond to this second task by examining the evolution of student development theories, presenting critical and poststructural theories relevant to understanding college student development, and providing examples of what these new possibilities might look like in theory and practice.

Before providing an overview of the organization and content of our book, we want to briefly introduce what is meant by the term *critical frameworks*, as it is this perspective that guided our approach to the entire book, as well as the language of critical perspectives. We use *critical theory* as an umbrella term that developed through the Frankfurt School of Social Research in Germany in the 1920s. Because critical theory has always been characterized by a diversity of thought and interdisciplinarity, it "should not be treated as a universal grammar of revolutionary thought objectified and reduced to discrete formulaic pronouncements or strategies" (Kincheloe, McLaren, & Steinberg, 2011, p. 164). However, critical theorists are united in putting forward philosophical reflections and social criticism on economic and sociocultural structures that reproduce systems of domination, with the goal of emancipation and liberation. According to Martínez-Alemán (2015),

Marxists, feminists, gender and queer theorists, structuralists, and poststructuralists all utilize critical theory to identify and locate the ways in which societies produce and preserve specific inequalities through social, cultural, and economic systems. The uninterrupted production and preservation of structures that reproduce social inequalities—whether material or cultural—are targeted by theory and research to increase the freedom of individuals. (p. 8)

Kincheloe et al. (2011) have also provided several basic assumptions that characterize a researcher, teacher, or theorist engaging critical theory. These included the following:

- All thought is fundamentally mediated by power relations that are social and historically constituted.
- The relationship between concept and object and between signifier and signified is never stable or fixed and is often mediated by the social relations of capitalist production and consumption.

- Certain groups in any society and particular societies are privileged over others, and although the reasons for this privileging may vary widely, the oppression that characterizes contemporary societies is more forcefully reproduced when subordinates accept their social status as natural, necessary, or inevitable.
- Oppression has many faces, and focusing on only one at the expense of others (e.g., class oppression versus racism) often elides the interconnections among them. (p. 164)

Implied in these assumptions is another unifying core tenet of critical theory, and that is the focus on social transformation, empowerment, and social justice through social action. The application of critical theory then is not the work of a dispassionate observer and social commentator but instead that of one committed to linking theory with practice directed toward the eradication of systems of domination and oppression.

For these reasons, throughout this book we use the term *critical frameworks* to include both critical and poststructural theories, while also recognizing what distinguishes these perspectives from one another—a discussion we take up in the Part One introduction. By grounding our theoretical inquiry into student development in critical frameworks, we are deliberately situating this work in a particular worldview or paradigmatic perspective. Theories reflect particular worldviews about the nature of reality and how we know what we know. They also reflect the assumptions, experiences, and identities of those who construct theories (Jones & Abes, 2017). We capture these influences on the evolution of student development theory by using the metaphor of theoretical waves (presented in chapter 1). For example, most early theories of student development can be located in positivist or postpositivist paradigms, resulting in theories that emphasize predictable, linear, and sequential stages along a developmental trajectory. By contrast, a critical paradigm foregrounds structures of power and inequality that pattern everyday life. Whereas student development theories anchored in positivist assumptions typically grew out of psychological inquiry into individual growth and change, critical theories emanated from scholars associated with the Frankfurt School who set out to extend the thinking of Karl Marx and critique capitalist structures that resulted in the subjugation of working people, minoritized populations, and women.

The language and vocabulary of critical frameworks comes directly from both historical and disciplinary origins, as well as the realities of contemporary life. Here our intent is not to try to oversimplify this vocabulary by providing definitional precision or a "universal grammar" but to offer some clarity about what these terms mean and how they are used. Clarifying language will then set the foundation for truly putting this vocabulary to work in rethinking college student development using critical frameworks. In addition to our considering language and vocabulary, capitalization of terms is not a neutral decision. Readers will note that we do not capitalize *white* when discussing racial categories and identities, which is consistent with the core tenets of critical frameworks and the associated commitments to social justice and emancipation; we do, however, capitalize *Black, Students of Color, Indigenous,* and other minoritized groups. In addition, as theoretical concepts, we do not capitalize terms such as *blackness* and *whiteness.* We adopted the guidance of Pérez Huber (2010), who made the case for

> rejecting the standard grammatical norm as a means to acknowledge and reject the grammatical representation of power capitalization brings to the term "white.". . . I do capitalize the terms People of Color, Communities of Color, and Immigrants of Color as a grammatical move towards empowerment and racial justice. (p. 93)

Just as the origins of critical theories were born in revolution and revolutionary ideas, the contemporary language of critical theories reflects current conditions of minoritized communities. This vocabulary not only describes those conditions but also provides a way out, such that theory may be seen as what bell hooks (1991) referred to as "liberatory practice." We introduce now a few concepts that are central to understanding critical frameworks and their applications to student development. Those we include are not anywhere close to an exhaustive list, nor is this a comprehensive discussion of any of them. We encourage readers to read deeply beyond this text to extend their understandings of these terms.

At the core of critical frameworks is the concept of *hegemony,* a concept often linked to the theorist Antonio Gramsci. Brookfield (2005) noted, "People learn to embrace as commonsense wisdom certain beliefs and political conditions that work against their interests and serve those of the powerful" (p. 43). Hegemony works because people come to accept what they consider "taken-for-granted" normative expectations and conditions of life. As Brookfield (2005) pointed out, hegemony hinges on consent, such that "people are not forced against their will to assimilate dominant ideology. They learn to do this, quite willingly, and in the process they believe that this ideology represents their best interests" (p. 94). Dominant ideologies are constructed in ways that are unrelenting, pervasive, and considered normative.

Understanding the process of hegemony as an overarching one, we then may see how normativity extends into domains such as patriarchy, white supremacy, heteronormativity, and cisheteropatriarchy or, stated differently, the hegemonic constructions of masculinities, race, heterosexuality, and gender (and their intersections) that operate on structural, political, institutional, organizational, and individual levels. Indeed, in this book we seek to expose the hegemonic assumptions that framed early student development theories. In doing so, we bring to light the new understandings that emerge when illuminating these assumptions and replacing them with emancipatory goals. We accomplish this both by focusing on taken-for-granted student development constructs and by foregrounding the experiences of students from minoritized communities.

In the end, our intent in *Rethinking College Student Development Theory Using Critical Frameworks* is to provide a sophisticated treatment of the complexities of student development in college by offering a set of theories applicable to understanding that development for practitioners who work with college students. We accomplish this through a theoretical examination that allows for the intersections of theoretical frameworks, lived experience, and practical applications.

Organization of the Book

This book is divided into three main parts. Every chapter in each part concludes with questions for reflection and discussion aimed to encourage the kind of rethinking we hope the chapters elicit. Serving as the theoretical foundation for what follows, the first part includes a chapter that provides an overview of the evolution of student development theories, as well as chapters describing the critical and poststructural theories that we consider most relevant to the next iteration of student development theory. These theoretical frameworks include critical race theory, intersectionality, critical feminist theories, decolonizing/Indigenous theories, queer theory, and crip theory. Recognizing that these critical frameworks are described more fully in other texts devoted to the specifics of each theory, these relatively brief chapters provide an overview of epistemic perspectives and point readers in the direction of further reading. These chapters also include a discussion of how each theory is relevant to the central questions of student development theory and how applying these frameworks enables both a rethinking and a reconstructing of theory and new understandings of student development. These critical frameworks are then put to work in Part Two.

Because "all critical inquiry is grounded in lived experience, and power relations and social justice are central concerns" (Martínez-Alemán, Pusser, & Bensimon, 2015, p. 3), chapters in Part Two provide an integrated analysis of personal narratives and theoretical frameworks through an exploration of constructs that continue to be important to understanding contemporary college students. These include the constructs of resilience, dissonance, socially constructed identities, authenticity, agency, knowledge and knowing, and context. Each chapter includes a personal narrative that centers a particular construct, followed by a reenvisioning of that construct using one or more critical and/or poststructural frameworks. This enabled a multivocal analysis that brings into dialogue individual narratives with theoretical constructs and critical and poststructural frameworks. We purposely organized this part around constructs rather than particular theories or social groups in order to provide a more robust and broader analysis of student development, which then led to a reimagining of each construct. Our approach permitted us to illuminate how critical frameworks, applied to inherently complex lived experiences, disrupt and reenvision our understanding of presumably core student development constructs.

The third part focuses on implications for practice. Specifically, these chapters consider possibilities for how student development constructs, as reenvisioned through critical perspectives, can be used in practice. We engage these questions of practical application through the analysis of three taken-for-granted "goods" in student affairs practice; that is, student involvement and engagement, principles of good practice, and high-impact practices. Finally, in the last chapter of the book and the fourth, concluding part, we return to the central topic of student development theory and offer a summative and integrative conclusion that points the field toward the future. In other words, what does rethinking look like and where does a rethinking of student development theory take us in terms of our understanding of college students today and our interest in promoting theoretical understandings that lead toward emancipation and social transformation?

Elisa S. Abes, Oxford, Ohio
Susan R. Jones, Columbus, Ohio
D-L Stewart, Fort Collins, Colorado

References

Abes, E. S. (2016). Situating paradigms in student development theory. In E. S. Abes (Ed.), *Critical perspectives on student development theory* (New Directions for Student Services, No. 154, pp. 9–16). San Francisco, CA: Jossey-Bass.

Brookfield, S. D. (2005). *The power of critical theory: Liberating adult learning and teaching.* San Francisco, CA: Jossey-Bass.

Gannon, S., & Davies, B. (2007). Postmodern, poststructural, and critical theories. In S. N. Hesse-Biber (Ed.), *Handbook of feminist research: Theory and praxis* (pp. 71–106). Thousand Oaks, CA: Sage.

hooks, b. (1991). Theory as liberatory practice. *Yale Journal of Law and Feminism*, 4(1), Article 2.

Jones, S. R., & Abes, E. S. (2017). The nature and uses of theory. In J. Schuh, S. R. Jones, & V. Torres (Eds.), *Student services: A handbook for the profession* (6th ed., pp. 137–152). San Francisco, CA: Jossey-Bass.

Kincheloe, J. L., McLaren, P., & Steinberg, S. R. (2011). Critical pedagogy and qualitative research: Moving to the bricolage. In N. K. Denzin & Y. S. Lincoln (Eds.), *The Sage handbook of qualitative research* (4th ed., pp. 163–177). Thousand Oaks, CA: Sage.

Knefelkamp, L. L., Widick, C., & Parker, C. A. (1978). *Applying new developmental findings* (New Directions for Student Services, No. 4). San Francisco, CA: Jossey-Bass.

Martínez-Alemán, A. M. (2015). Critical discourse analysis in higher education policy research. In A. M. Martínez-Alemán, B. Pusser, & E. M. Bensimon (Eds.), *Critical approaches to the study of higher education: A practical introduction* (pp. 7–43). Baltimore, MD: Johns Hopkins Press.

Martínez-Alemán, A. M., Pusser, B., & Bensimon, E. M. (2015). Introduction. In A. M. Martínez-Alemán, B. Pusser, & E. M. Bensimon (Eds.), *Critical approaches to the study of higher education: A practical introduction* (pp. 1–6). Baltimore, MD: Johns Hopkins Press.

Pérez Huber, L. (2010). Using Latina/o critical race theory (LatCrit) and racist nativism to explore intersectionality in the educational experiences of undocumented Chicana college students. *Educational Foundations*, 24(1–2), 77–96.

ACKNOWLEDGMENTS

This book represents the generosity, talent, and support of many, not all of whom we can name here but for whom we are grateful. However, we do want to acknowledge the efforts of some. First, we deeply appreciate the wonderful and insightful contributions of Antonio Duran, doctoral candidate in the higher education and student affairs (HESA) program at The Ohio State University. Antonio was not only a chapter contributor but also a wise consultant and reviewer who walked alongside us on this journey, offering suggestions and insights ranging from APA issues to complex ideas. We are extremely grateful for his enthusiasm for this project and the generosity of his time and talent. This book is stronger because of Antonio's contributions. We also want to acknowledge what is arguably the finest lineup of chapter authors ever to appear in HESA scholarship (okay, admittedly, we are a little biased here). We are grateful to these scholars who said yes to what we consider an innovative and novel approach to reimagining student development theory. Each of their chapters reflects intellectual acuity, vulnerability, and creative thinking that is sure to push our understanding of theorizing student development forward. We also thank our students, who challenge us to think in new ways about student development theory with wise insights from their own lived experiences and ways of making meaning. We truly learn alongside them in classes and through advising. We also want to acknowledge the enthusiastic support for our ideas and this book provided by David Brightman from Stylus. David made the publishing process seamless, and for that we are appreciative. Finally, we are grateful for one another and the opportunity to work on this book together. We all share some academic roots and a deep commitment to the emancipatory potential and power of theory. We have worked with one another before but never the three of us together. Putting our collective heads and hearts together to imagine what such a book might look like, and then to facilitate the process of making it happen, has been one of the most enriching scholarly projects in which we have engaged.

Elisa thanks Kathleen Knight-Abowitz, who as department chair crafted ways for her to have time to think and write; she appreciates how Kathleen has consistently been in her corner. Elisa is grateful to her partner, Amber Feldman, for being one of the biggest champions of her work. Amber selflessly finds ways to help Elisa write—or to tell her to stop and go for a run, which Amber lovingly insists makes everyone in the house happier. Elisa is also lucky that her kind, thoughtful, and funny children, Shoshana and Benjamin, ages 10 and 8 years, respectively, are simultaneously proud that their mom writes books and eager to remind her to close her computer and play. More so, both of her children's innate social justice sensibilities and respectful ways of moving through this world remind her of the importance of the work she is doing.

Susan thanks Eric Anderman, her department chair, for approving a sabbatical leave and a special research assignment (SRA), which resulted in a year's leave and, more important, the great gift of time for reflecting, reading, and immersing in this book project. Susan is fortunate to have her parents still alive, both of whom gave her the gift of words and using writing for self-expression. And she is especially thankful for her dad, who even in his end-of-life stage continuously asks, "What's that book about again?" And finally, thanks to Gretchen and the pups (Fritz Perls and Whitney). Our students refer to us as Dr. Theory and Dr. Practice, so Gretchen more than puts up with my great comfort in the world of ideas, providing a calm, patient, funny perspective on all things. And Fritz and Whitney never left my side during the long hours of writing.

D-L went through a major career and life transition since conversations about this book first began after an ASHE session in 2017, so he thanks his professional homes at Bowling Green State University and now Colorado State University for making sure he took time to write. D-L also thanks his chosen family, who have uplifted, affirmed, and nudged his growth and meaning making every step of the way. D-L also is grateful to his son Michael, now 20 years old and ending his sophomore college year, who accepted the fact that no matter where he went to college, about half a dozen student affairs professionals would know and be known by his parent. He has been a consistent source of support and inspiration for D-L's thinking. Finally, many thanks go to his sweet pittie Violet for always staying close as he wrote and nudging him to go outside.

PART ONE

STUDENT DEVELOPMENT ENTERING THE THIRD WAVE

As noted in the preface to this book, we are believers in the power of theory. And in particular, the potential of theory to point the way toward more emancipatory and inclusive policies and practices in higher education. In this first part of the book, six different theoretical perspectives are offered both as examples of critical and poststructural theories and for their utility in helping to rethink college student development. These six are not in any way meant to be an exhaustive or definitive set of examples; instead, we selected these six because several of them are almost completely missing from the theoretical landscape in higher education and because of what we see as their theoretical power in helping to scrutinize some more taken-for-granted student development constructs. Together, these theories offer new vantage points from which to understand student development, insights regarding the influence of inequitable power structures on the developmental processes of all students, and analytic tools that center minoritized populations of college students. More specifically, and by way of an example of our intent in showcasing each of these theoretical frameworks, the poststructural approach of crip theory carries specific relevance to students with disabilities, but importantly it also exposes the ableism in student development theories generally.

Before proceeding with an overview of the frameworks presented in this part and the approach taken by chapter authors, we want to briefly comment on critical and poststructural theories and what distinguishes them from one another. Although we took care to note in the preface that we use the term *critical frameworks* as an umbrella term that includes both critical and poststructural theories, there are some significant differences between these two schools of thought. Because some of these differences are evident in the chapters that follow, we thought it helpful to provide a mention of several distinguishing characteristics.

As introduced in the preface, critical theory emerged from scholars associated with the Frankfurt School in Germany and in response to the social, political, and cultural conditions of capitalist society. The term *critical theory* is attributed to Max Horkheimer, the director of the Institute for Social Research, which was founded in Frankfurt Germany in 1923 and is anchored in the philosophical views of those such as Immanuel Kant, Friedrich Hegel, and Karl Marx (Jessop, 2014). As Martínez-Alemán (2015) noted,

> According to Horkheimer . . . the goal of critical theory is to develop inter-disciplinary research that is both empirical and historical as a means for solving socio-philosophical problems, or more specifically, those problems that are the consequence of domination within and across human communities. (p. 7)

The *critical* in critical theory involves critique of "life as it is—within the practices, traditions, values and beliefs of a particular society" (Jessop, 2014, p. 194). A central aim of critical theory is social and political action leading to societally relevant practical solutions and transformation (Martínez-Alemán, 2015). In the area of student development, critical race theory (CRT) is a critical theory that is increasingly used in research and scholarship to expose the permanence and pervasiveness of racism in higher education. For examples of the application of CRT in student development research, see Harper (2009), Hernández (2016), and Patton (2014).

Whereas critical theory illuminates *life as it is*, poststructural perspectives suggest that structure to life cannot exist, hence the term *poststructuralism*. Poststructural thought emerged from scholars such as Jacques Derrida, Michel Foucault, and Judith Butler, who theorized the constructs of deconstruction, power, and performativity (Jackson & Mazzei, 2012). As suggested by Lather (2007),

> Poststructuralism refers more narrowly to a sense of the limits of Enlightenment rationality. It particularly foregrounds the limits of consciousness and intentionality and the will to power inscribed in sense-making efforts that aspire to totalizing explanatory frameworks, especially structuralism with its ahistoricism and universalism. (p. 5)

That is, poststructuralism pushes against the limitations of positivist constructions of truth and what Foucault (1984) referred to as "regimes of truth" (p. 73) or grand narratives. Deconstruction is a core strategy in poststructuralism and enables the "undoing, reversing, and displacing of taken-for-granted binary oppositions that structure discourse" (Schwandt, 2001, p. 204). Central themes characterizing poststructural theories include the decentering of the notion of an individual, the idea that everything is a text and all texts are interrelated, the idea that meaning is unstable and never fixed, and the emphasis on deconstruction as a strategy for displacing taken-for-granted texts and binary oppositions (Schwandt, 2001). In student development work, the poststructural school of thought of queer theory is put to use to expose normative assumptions associated with genders and sexualities, illuminate the performative nature of much of what is called student development, and open up possibilities. Examples in student development scholarship include the works of Abes and Kasch (2007), Denton (2016), Miller (2015), and Nicolazzo (2016).

In sum, most notable about what distinguishes critical theories from poststructural perspectives is that while critical theories hold up specific categories for interrogation using social, cultural, and historical critique, poststructural theories aim to deconstruct the very notion of categories. In fact, a lean interpretation of the application of poststructuralism to student development would suggest this is impossible; that is, development or identity is in constant motion with no predetermined end point and therefore impossible to hold up for scrutiny. This very tension is evident in several chapters, where the differences between critical and poststructural frameworks show up in, for example, the structural power analysis of intersectionality (critical theory) and the deconstruction of gender binaries in queer theory (poststructural).

In spite of these differences, there are some overlapping elements between these two theoretical frameworks, most notably a concern with marginalization, oppressive power structures, and emancipation. As noted in the preface, it is these common commitments that warrant the use of the term *critical framework* as an overarching umbrella to encompass both critical and poststructural theories. Specific to higher education theory and research, Tierney and Rhoads (2004) were among the first to advance a set of principles to consider when using critical theory. These interacting aspects of critical theory include emphasis on marginalization and emancipation, the role of culture, the role of power, a critique of positivism, and the union of theory and practice, or praxis (see pp. 319–324 for a more detailed discussion). Each of these elements, both individually and interconnected, may be seen in the critical theoretical frameworks presented in this text.

We want to note that the chapters that follow in this part are purposely brief. That is, each of the theoretical frameworks highlighted are book-length worthy in themselves. Chapter authors introduce these frameworks by illuminating core tenets or characteristics for each and point readers to the foundational and contemporary texts on these theories. Each chapter also includes discussion of the relevancy of critical frameworks to student development theory. That is, chapter authors take up the question of how student development theory might be different if reconsidered through a critical lens. For example, how might the developmental domains of self-authorship be conceptualized and experienced differently if a critical lens is applied? We want readers to leave these chapters with a basic understanding of the theories so as to grasp the application of them in the chapters that follow in Part Two and Part Three and also with a thirst to delve more deeply into them.

We begin this part on critical theoretical frameworks with an overview of the evolving theoretical developments in the field. Extending the metaphor of theoretical waves first introduced by Jones and Stewart (2016), Susan R. Jones explores the sociohistorical ways in which student development theories are created and viewed. Through the presentation of three waves of student development, Jones discusses the central theoretical contributions of each wave and suggests ways in which these contributions are both enduring and evolving. With the first wave broadly addressing earlier psychological theories and the second wave focusing on social identities, the introduction of the third wave, encompassing critical theoretical perspectives, paves the way for the theories that follow.

In chapter 2, Jessica C. Harris and OiYan A. Poon discuss the importance of accounting for racism and white supremacy in student development theory using the framework of CRT. In applying core tenets of CRT to student development, Harris and Poon both elevate the importance of race and racism and expose how systems of oppression operate with the goal of disrupting these systems. In chapter 3, Charmaine L. Wijeyesinghe provides an overview of intersectionality, addressing historical origins, as well as core tenets and assumptions. Wijeyesinghe then reexamines several central topics in student development by applying an intersectional analysis and emphasizing the importance of social location and social systems to students' development. Next, in chapter 4, Claire Kathleen Robbins introduces guiding definitions of *critical feminist theories* (FemCrit) and how these might be put to work as a framework for student development. Robbins also examines central questions of student development theory using FemCrit, encouraging thought-provoking reflections on the possibilities for understanding, deconstructing, and reconstructing student development. In chapter 5, Nicole Alia Salis Reyes and Maria Tauala present an overview of Indigenous and decolonizing paradigms, emphasizing the shared values in Indigenous paradigms of relationality, reciprocity, self-determination, and sovereignty. They then discuss how Indigenous and decolonizing paradigms shape Native college students' development and inform an understanding of non-Native students and existing structures of inequality (Indigenous erasure) in higher education.

J. Michael Denton, in chapter 6, delves into queer theory, highlighting foundational works and core tenets. Denton then more closely examines how the application of queer theory to student development domains provides new insights into ways of thinking about gender and sexualities. Last in this part, Elisa S. Abes advances an understanding of crip theory in chapter 7 through an exploration of its key ideas organized using the domains of holistic student development. Abes demonstrates how crip theory can be engaged to not only better understand college students with disabilities but also reconceptualize the meaning of student development and rethink student development theory.

We hope these critical theoretical frameworks, taken together, advance an understanding of the origins, core tenets, and applications to student development of individual theoretical frameworks, as well as provide a foundation for the analyses and applications that follow in Part Two and Part Three, respectively. We also hope that readers will (re)discover the power of theory to deepen our understanding of the complex issues facing higher education today and improve practices that stand to benefit all students.

References

Abes, E. S., & Kasch, D. (2007). Using queer theory to explore lesbian college students' multiple dimensions of identity. *Journal of College Student Development*, *48*(6), 619–636.

Denton, J. M. (2016). Critical and poststructural perspectives on sexual identity formation. In E. S. Abes (Ed.), *Critical perspectives on student development theory* (New Directions for Student Services, No. 154, pp. 57–69). San Francisco, CA: Jossey-Bass.

Foucault, M. (1984). Truth and power. In P. Rabinow (Ed.), *The Foucault reader* (pp. 51–75). New York, NY: Pantheon Books.

Harper, S. (2009). Niggers no more: A critical race counternarrative of Black male student achievement at predominantly white colleges and universities. *International Journal of Qualitative Studies in Education*, *22*(6), 697–712.

Hernández, E. (2016). Utilizing critical race theory to examine race/ethnicity, racism, and power in student development theory and research. *Journal of College Student Development*, *57*(2), 168–180.

Jackson, A. Y., & Mazzei, L. A. (2012). *Thinking with theory in qualitative research.* New York, NY: Routledge.

Jessop, S. (2014). Critical theory. In D. C. Phillips (Ed.), *Encyclopedia of educational theory and philosophy* (Vol. 1, pp. 193–196). Thousand Oaks, CA: Sage.

Jones, S. R., & Stewart, D-L. (2016). Evolution of student development theory. In E. S. Abes (Ed.), *Critical perspectives on student development theory* (New Directions for Student Services, No. 154, pp. 17–28). San Francisco, CA: Jossey-Bass.

Lather, P. (2007). *Getting lost: Feminist efforts toward a double(d) science.* Albany, NY: SUNY Press.

Martínez-Alemán, A. M. (2015). Critical discourse analysis in higher education policy research. In A. M. Martínez-Alemán, B. Pusser, & E. M. Bensimon (Eds.), *Critical approaches to the study of higher education: A practical introduction* (pp. 7–43). Baltimore, MD: Johns Hopkins Press.

Miller, R. A. (2015). "Sometimes you feel invisible": Performing queer/disabled in the university classroom. *The Educational Forum, 79*(4), 377–393.

Nicolazzo, Z. (2016). "It's a hard line to walk": Black non-binary trans* collegians' perspectives on passing, realness, and trans*normativity. *International Journal of Qualitative Studies in Education, 29*(9), 1173–1188.

Patton, L. D. (2014). Preserving respectability or blatant disrespect? A critical discourse analysis of the Morehouse College appropriate attire policy and implications for conducting intersectional research. *International Journal of Qualitative Studies in Education, 27*(6), 724–746.

Schwandt, T. A. (2001). *Dictionary of qualitative inquiry* (2nd ed.). Thousand Oaks, CA: Sage.

Tierney, W. G., & Rhoads, R. A. (2004). Postmodernism and critical theory in higher education: Implications for research and practice. In J. C. Smart (Ed.), *Higher education: Handbook of theory and research* (Vol. 9, pp. 308–343). New York, NY: Agathon Press.

WAVES OF CHANGE

The Evolving History of Student Development Theory

Susan R. Jones

Change? Yes, we must change, only show me the Theory . . . . Show me the words that will reorder the world, or else keep silent. (Kushner, 1994, p. 14)

I n this line from *Angels in America: Part Two: Perestroika*, we see the bold proclamation of the emancipatory potential of using theory to change the world. By definition, *theories* ought to expand our thinking and deepen our understanding of particular phenomena, in this case, college student development. As Jackson and Mazzei (2012) commented, "Thinking with theory . . . illustrates how knowledge is opened up and proliferated rather than foreclosed and simplified" (p. vii). Similarly, Coles (1989) described theory as an enlargement of observations but cautioned, "Remember, what you are hearing . . . is to some extent a function of *you*, hearing" (p. 15). When considering the evolution of student development theories in the context of critical and poststructural perspectives, this reminder that theories are products of their historical and sociocultural contexts, and the individuals developing them, is important to keep in mind as these shifting contexts shape the kinds of questions and concerns theories are intended to address (Jones & Stewart, 2016). Without this perspective, we may be too quick to dismiss older theories as irrelevant and distant from the realities of the issues faced by higher education in contemporary times, when in fact there may be aspects of these theories that continue to be useful.

The trajectory of moving toward more inclusive perspectives is evident in the evolution of student development theories; that is, both scrutinizing the samples and assumptions on which early theories were developed and bringing the experiences of those who have been excluded in theorizing to the center of analysis. According to Anderson and Collins (2007), this more inclusive view or "new angle of vision means actually seeing things differently, perhaps even changing the lens you look through—thereby removing the filters (or stereotypes and misconceptions) that you bring to what you see and think" (p. 4). In this introductory chapter, designed to provide an overview of the evolution of student development theories, I aim to briefly explore the historical lenses and filters through which we have viewed college student development, using the metaphor of theoretical waves (Jones & Stewart, 2016). In doing so, I identify several major (and perhaps enduring) theoretical contributions of each wave and set the stage for the chapters that follow, all in an effort to engage theory as a way to open up the possibilities for better understanding college students, to maximize their potential, eliminate barriers, and promote their success.

Theoretical Waves of Student Development

Borrowing the metaphor of waves from feminist scholars, Jones and Stewart (2016) charted the evolution of student development theories by their historical contexts and the kinds of questions addressed by different theories, the epistemological perspectives framing theories, and the methods used to investigate questions and concerns related to student development.

The metaphor of waves seemed apt as a way to capture shifting perspectives and questions because waves are not distinct entities; it is difficult to separate one wave from the next. Instead, waves ebb and flow and are overlapping. One wave contains both some of the wave that precedes and some of the waves that follow. Such is also the nature of theory evolution. What emerges as a new theoretical advance is often based somewhat on what came before and points the way to what is yet to arrive. In this overview, I highlight theoretical contributions reflective of each wave rather than identify actual theories (see Jones & Stewart, 2016, for specific theories that fit within waves), because it is these constructs that may continue to inform our understanding of student development more so than one theory in particular. Furthermore, although it appears in this "historical" overview that theory development implies a chronology, with first-wave theories coming first, I want to emphasize that these waves need not be only chronologically sequential. In other words, third-wave theoretical advances may become "foundational," and more recent theory development may be more characteristic of first-wave theorizing than third. In this way I also want to suggest that it is possible to hold two waves together (to extend the metaphor) in that we may see both developmental trajectories and attention to larger structures of inequality as central to what we call *student development*.

First-Wave Theoretical Contributions

Those theories often described as the foundations of student development theory are found in the first wave of theory development. These theories, and the theoretical constructs framing them, are largely drawn from psychology and developmental understandings of the experiences of college students. Typically organized into separate theoretical domains, such as psychosocial, cognitive, and moral, these theories advance the assumption that development progresses in a linear, somewhat sequential, and universal pattern. Furthermore, this developmental trajectory is characterized as individuals moving toward increasingly complex ways of making meaning of the issues that they face and in the areas of their concern, which are considered developmental tasks. These developmental tasks usually revolve around issues related to sense of self and identity, vocation, relationships, social identities, spirituality, and managing emotions, to name a few. In this first wave, it is assumed that developmental tasks are age related, so what rises to the level of concern changes over the life span. Furthermore, it is in the transition between stages of development where growth is experienced, most notably through a process of resolving discrepancies between existing ways of making sense of experiences and one's sense of self and the challenges posed by new contexts (Perry, 1968). This developmental process hinges on the experience of dissonance, or the "psychological discomfort associated with inconsistency in beliefs, expectations, and/or experiences" (Baker & Taylor, 2016, p. 10).

These psychological theories were not without attention to the contexts in which development occurred. For example, Lewin's (1936) claim that behavior is a function of the person in their environment set the stage for a number of theories that emphasize the role of the campus environment to development. For example, the importance of cultivating an optimal balance of challenge and support (Sanford, 1967), as well as a student's readiness as a condition for development (Sanford, 1966), depend on both internal processes and environmental factors. In addition, the important influence of peers and peer culture was introduced and is one of the most consistent findings from research on college student development (Feldman & Newcomb, 1969; Renn & Reason, 2013).

In sum, an enduring contribution of first-wave theoretical constructs is the assumption that college students should grow and develop as a result of their experiences in the college environment. In other words, as educators, we want students to be different as a result of their time on our campuses, and these constructs provide some scaffolding for thinking about how students develop and in what areas and how college environments can be designed to promote development. Because of their primary emphasis on mechanisms of development (e.g., dissonance, assimilation, accommodation), first-wave theories suggest that this developmental process was generally the same for all students and that the issues college students face are predictable ones, which is not meant to imply that the content of development is identical.

Second-Wave Theoretical Contributions

Central to second-wave theoretical contributions is an explicit focus on social identities and, in particular, the identities and experiences of students from nondominant groups. In response to growing recognition that these students were largely excluded and missing from earlier theoretical understandings, as well as to the growing diversity of students at colleges and universities, new theories were developed that foregrounded social identities such as race, culture, gender, sexuality, and ethnicity. A number of these theories retained the psychological and developmental focus of earlier theories by suggesting developmental trajectories, depicted via stages or statuses, for the development of racial identity or gender identity, for example. Because of the emphasis on minoritized identities, constructs such as power, privilege, oppression, and societal context were also incorporated in intersecting, rather than additive, ways. For example, it is impossible to understand a student's racial identity without grappling with racism in the United States or sexual identity without recognizing the powerful sociocultural force fields of heterosexism and homophobia.

However, although this larger context of, for example, racism is acknowledged (and the cultivation of a nonracist identity or achieved racial identity promoted) in these second-wave theories, context appears more static than dynamic. That is, because of the developmental emphasis of these theories, the implication is that there is an end point to the development of a particular social identity, and once it is achieved, one may always draw on that knowledge to deal with new experiences rather than emphasize the influence of shifting contexts on how one moves through the world (Jones & McEwen, 2000). Furthermore, although these theories treated individual social identities as discrete units of analysis (e.g., theories of racial identity, ethnic identity, sexual identity), they were less siloed by domain (e.g., cognitive and affective domains of development were considered together as instrumental to development). Focusing on race, Helms (1995) suggested racial identity development is based on "the dynamic cognitive, emotional, and behavioral processes that govern a person's interpretation of racial information in her or his environment" (p. 194).

Social identity theory is rooted in the importance attached to group memberships and how the sense of belonging gained from group memberships influences one's sense of self (Tajfel & Turner, 1979). Group memberships are also influenced by larger societal structures and thus reflect systems of dominance and oppression. What this means relative to student development is that how individuals perceive themselves is influenced by the groups to which they belong and in which they find meaning and also how those groups are perceived by others, thus reflecting structures of inequality. These dynamics then, in turn, affect intergroup relations and campus climate at colleges and universities. In addition to, and because of, the psychological approaches to the development of specific social identities, second-wave theories elevated the scrutiny of campus climates and the impact of inhospitable climates on student development.

An enduring contribution of second-wave theories is the emphasis on socially constructed identities, greater inclusion of diverse groups of students, and integration of sociocultural contexts into developmental understandings. Second-wave theories acknowledge the existence of larger structures of inequality but do not necessarily interrogate these relative to student development. Recognizing that student development is patterned by systems of oppression that are "complex, pervasive, variable, persistent, severe, and power based" (Weber, 2010, p. 23), second-wave theories elevate our understanding of the developmental dimensions related to specific social identities. Calling into question the presumed generalizability of the "holistic" theories characteristic of the first wave, second-wave theories necessarily brought into clearer focus the specificities of development along varying dimensions of social identity, thus contributing significantly to an understanding of the developmental journeys of those students previously excluded from student development theories.

Third-Wave Theoretical Contributions

The central contributions of the third wave are an emphasis on emancipation and societal transformation, required attention to larger structures of inequality, and the necessity of meaningfully integrating theory and practice through praxis to promote social change. These characteristics broadly capture what is referred to as *critical theory*. Space does not permit a full description of the intellectual traditions that inform critical perspectives or a delineation of the theories and worldviews that often get organized under a critical umbrella, including poststructural theories (see discussion in the preface and Part One introduction); however, it is important to note that many critical theories exist both generally and more specifically (e.g., there is no one critical feminist theory). Instead, here, I offer some scaffolding for understanding what makes theorizing *critical*, particularly in relation to student development theory and practice, and how these third-wave contributions are being used to reexamine student development theory.

Relative to the broad goals of critical theories to promote emancipation and societal transformation, Tierney and Rhoads (2004) wrote, "Fundamental to critical theory is the notion of freedom and justice. The goal of theory is not just to enlighten, but also to enable people to seek justice, freedom, and equality" (p. 319). Furthermore, Martínez-Alemán, Pusser, and Bensimon (2015) proposed, "Among Western theoretical frameworks, critical theory has uniquely positioned scholars and researchers to explain and decode inequitable social relations and actions in higher education" (p. 2). Some might be quick to dismiss emancipation and societal transformation as lofty goals that are impossible to accomplish. And in fact, many scholars claim these as their goals in research and practice but then fail to demonstrate how their work has moved toward reaching these goals. However, keeping these goals in the foreground of one's theorizing means being clear about what outcomes one is working toward and how one will get there. These goals may focus on more macro levels (e.g., changing policy to be more equitable) or micro levels (e.g., improving the daily lives of a group of students with minoritized identities through resource allocations or programming), but the hallmark of the third wave is the recognition of the inextricable relationship between the macro levels and the micro levels.

A second characteristic of critical theorizing is explicit attention to larger structures of inequality as the context in which development takes place. Again, bridging micro and macro levels, this means one's analysis and understanding simultaneously examine the individual domain and the sociocultural contexts in which all individuals move, whether they are aware of this or not. Given our interest in understanding student development, locating individuals within larger societal structures of privilege, power, and oppression requires foregrounding those with minoritized identities as well as implicating those from dominant identities, as oppression and privilege are inextricably connected; one cannot exist without the other. In fact, as Case, Iuzzini, and Hopkins (2012) pointed out, "Research on privilege brings dominant group advantages into sharp focus, making this unrecognized element of oppression and internalized domination visible" (p. 3). And because these larger structures are intertwined and mutually reinforced in what Collins (1990) termed the *matrix of domination*, interrogating domains of power becomes central to understanding the lived experiences of college students and their development. This means that in the third wave it will never be enough to simply *describe* students' experiences or the meaning they make of those experiences; instead, this perspective of a holistic view requires critical analysis of the intersecting domains of power and structures of inequality that frame development in the first place.

Finally, the critical theorizing characteristic of the third wave should bridge the gap between theory and practice and keep us focused on the question of "theorizing to what end?" The answer to this question draws on the element of praxis and suggests that theories must be practical, useful, applicable, and directed toward transformation of structures (Freire, 1993). In fact, Freire (1998) went on to suggest, "Critical reflection on practice is a requirement of the relationship between theory and practice. Otherwise theory becomes simply 'blah, blah, blah' and practice, pure activism" (p. 30). This important element of the third wave calls on student development educators to scrutinize the assumptions and lenses they bring to understanding students' development and their own practice and to ensure that theory and practice are linked in applicable and meaningful ways.

In summary, third-wave theorizing calls into sharper focus questions about the nature of student development itself. Because of the need for emphasizing societal transformation and emancipation, larger structures of inequality, and praxis, third-wave theorizing challenges the central assumptions undergirding much of what anchors the first and second waves of theorizing. As Jones and Stewart (2016) suggested, the third wave prompts us to reconsider both the foci of student development theory and practice (e.g., student development in relation to social identities, constructivist developmentalism, and assumptions about who students are) and knowledge in the field (e.g., the role of context, intersectionality, and individual agency). Doing so gets us closer to freedom, justice, and liberatory practice—the overarching goals of third-wave theorizing.

Conclusion: Using Theory as Liberatory Practice

Theory is not inherently healing, liberatory, or revolutionary. It fulfills this function only when we ask that it do so and direct our theorizing towards this end. (hooks, 1994, p. 61)

In her treatise on the necessity of using theory to bridge practice and to ensure that practice is indeed liberatory, bell hooks (1994) called on educators to elevate what we expect of theories to incorporate the critical goals of emancipation and societal transformation. As educators in higher education interested in promoting the success of all students, we must both scrutinize the theories available to us and use theories to open up possibilities to understand complexity rather than reduce it. Indeed, as Perry (1968) pointed out long ago, no one theory is ever enough to explain the complexity of students' lives. What has been enduring, when taking a longer view on the evolution of student development theories, is a commitment to understanding the whole student, recognizing that approaches to understanding what constitutes wholeness have been different over the years. For example, limitations in first-wave conceptualizations of the "whole" student led researchers and theory generators to focus on the importance of social identities to wholeness. Similarly, third-wave theorizers suggested that isolating individual social identities did not present a complete picture of the ways in which social identities are mutually constituted and intersect. As noted, theoretical constructs from the third wave were not created with student development in mind. However, it is possible to put into theoretical dialogue third-wave theorizing, such as the primary influence of inequitable power structures, with a first-wave construct, such as developmental change, to deepen our understanding of student development.

This is the primary reason, as presented in the preface to this book, that we focus this text on theoretical constructs rather than on specific theories. Although specific theories may ebb and flow in their relevance to contemporary issues in student development, constructs such as resilience, dissonance, social construction of identities, authenticity, agency, knowledge and knowing, and context are lasting in their application to understanding the tasks, dilemmas, challenges, and realities characteristic of individuals' lives and development. However, and importantly, they are multifaceted constructs and can (and should) be examined from different vantage points and theoretical perspectives. We cannot keep silent when it comes to the development of theories about student development. Using theory to "reorder the world" (Kushner, 1994, p. 14) and promote liberatory practice is possible if we ask theory to do so and also ask that of ourselves.

Discussion Questions

1. As you think about the evolution of student development theory, what theoretical constructs are enduring? How do you know? (e.g., What filters might you be employing when thinking about theory? How is what you know influenced by your own experiences?)
2. Design three sets of research questions for a study related to student development that reflect first-wave questions, second-wave questions, and third-wave questions. What shifts (in addition to the questions) as you change the central assumptions and characteristics of each approach?

3. What are a few strategies you can employ to more meaningfully bridge the gap between third-wave theories and practice?

4. Think about specific situations you dealt with in the past year and how student development theories might help you. What contributions from first-wave, second-wave, and third-wave theories are useful in responding to these situations?

References

Anderson, M. L., & Collins, P. H. (2007). Why race, class, and gender still matter. In M. L. Anderson & P. H. Collins (Eds.), *Race, class, and gender: An anthology* (6th ed., pp. 1–16). Belmont, CA: Thomson/Wadsworth.

Baker, A. R., & Taylor, K. B. (2016, November). *Examining the role of discomfort in collegiate learning and development.* Paper presented at the Association for the Study of Higher Education conference, Columbus, OH.

Case, K. A., Iuzzini, J., & Hopkins, M. (2012). Systems of privilege: Intersections, awareness, and applications. *Journal of Social Issues, 68*(1), 1–10.

Coles, R. (1989). *The call of stories: Teaching and the moral imagination.* Boston, MA: Houghton Mifflin.

Collins, P. H. (1990). *Black feminist thought: Knowledge, consciousness, and the politics of empowerment.* New York, NY: Routledge.

Feldman, K. A., & Newcomb, T. M. (1969). *The impact of college on students* (2 vols.). San Francisco, CA: Jossey-Bass.

Freire, P. (1993). *Pedagogy of the oppressed.* New York, NY: Continuum. (Original work published 1970).

Freire, P. (1998). *Pedagogy of freedom: Ethics, democracy, and civic courage.* Lanham, MD: Rowan & Littlefield.

Helms, J. E. (1995). An update on Helms's white and People of Color racial identity models. In J. G. Ponterotto, J. M. Casas, L. A. Suzuki, & C. M. Alexander (Eds.), *Handbook of multicultural counseling* (pp. 181–198). Thousand Oaks, CA: Sage.

hooks, b. (1994). *Teaching to transgress: Education as the practice of freedom.* New York, NY: Routledge.

Jackson, A. Y., & Mazzei, L. A. (2012). *Thinking with theory in qualitative research: Viewing data from multiple perspectives.* New York, NY: Routledge.

Jones, S. R., & McEwen, M. K. (2000). A conceptual model of multiple dimensions of identity. *Journal of College Student Development, 41*, 405–414.

Jones, S. R., & Stewart, D-L. (2016). Evolution of student development theory. In E. S. Abes (Ed.), *Critical perspectives on student development theory* (New Directions for Student Services, No. 154, pp. 17–28). San Francisco, CA: Jossey-Bass.

Kushner, T. (1994). *Angels in America: Part two: Perestroika.* New York, NY: Theatre Communications Group.

Lewin, K. (1936). *Principles of topological psychology*. New York, NY: McGraw-Hill.

Martínez-Alemán, A. M., Pusser, B., & Bensimon, E. M. (2015). Introduction. In A. M. Martínez-Alemán, B. Pusser, & E. M. Bensimon (Eds.), *Critical approaches to the study of higher education: A practical introduction* (pp. 1–6). Baltimore, MD: Johns Hopkins Press.

Perry, W. G., Jr. (1968). *Forms of intellectual and ethical development in the college years: A scheme*. New York, NY: Holt, Rinehart, & Winston.

Renn, K. A., & Reason, R. D. (2013). *College students in the United States: Characteristics, experiences, and outcomes*. San Francisco, CA: Jossey-Bass.

Sanford, N. (1966). *Self and society*. New York, NY: Atherton Press.

Sanford, N. (1967). *Where colleges fail: The study of the student as a person* San Francisco, CA: Jossey-Bass.

Tajfel, H., & Turner, J. C. (1979). An integrative theory of intergroup conflict. In W. G. Austin & S. Worchel (Eds.), *The social psychology of intergroup relations* (pp. 33–37). Monterey, CA: Brooks/Cole.

Tierney, W. G., & Rhoads, R. A. (2004). Postmodernism and critical theory in higher education: Implications for research and practice. In J. C. Smart (Ed.), *Higher education: Handbook of theory and research* (Vol. 9, pp. 308–343). New York, NY: Agathon Press.

Weber, L. (2010). *Understanding race, class, gender, and sexuality* (2nd ed.). New York, NY: Oxford University Press.

CRITICAL RACE THEO

Interrogating Race and Racism in College Students' Development

Jessica C. Harris and OiYan A. Poon

R ace matters. Although race is a social construction that has no biological basis, it is a social, political, economic, and historical invention that allows racism to reproduce material inequities, privileging
whiteness through the systemic oppression of People of Color (Delgado &
Stefancic, 2012; Delgado, 1992; Harris, 1993). Often thought of as idyllic
places of enlightenment, colleges and universities are not immune to racism and systemic white supremacy, which remain pervasive and persistent in
postsecondary contexts (Patton, 2016). From blatant incidents of racial violence and bigotry (Garcia & Johnston-Guerrero, 2015) to implicit structures
of white dominance and racial microaggressions (Solórzano, Ceja, & Yosso,
2000), race matters in higher education. Therefore, student development
theory, research, and praxis must account for white supremacy and racism.

Critical race theory (CRT) offers a lens through which to focus scholarly
inquiries on how racism and white supremacy shape student development.
Legal scholars originally theorized CRT to advance critical analyses of racism
in the law, providing a "useful critical compass for negotiating the treach-
erous terrain of American racial politics" (Crenshaw, Gotanda, Peller, &
Thomas, 1995, p. xxxii; also see Lawrence, 1987; Matsuda, 1987). Applied
to student development theory, it is imperative for CRT research in education to intentionally engage in the scholarly tradition's central tenets, of
which there are several (see Delgado & Stefancic, 2012; Dixson & Rousseau,
2006; Harris, 1993; Ladson-Billings & Tate, 1995; Ledesma & Calderón,
2015; Solórzano, 1998). In this chapter, we focus on four tenets of CRT,

uding racism as endemic, whiteness as property, challenging ahistorical narratives, and differential racialization.

First, CRT scholars understand racism as a fundamental, endemic organizing force embedded within U.S. society, including higher education (Patton, Harper, & Harris, 2015). Racism is also normalized and common, making it hard to identify, address, and redress. CRT foregrounds race and racism throughout the research process but also acknowledges that other systems of domination intersect with race and racism (Solórzano & Yosso, 2002; see chapter 3 for more information on intersectionality and student development theory).

Second, in CRT scholarship whiteness as property is a defining notion of racism in education (Ladson-Billings, 1998). Originally theorized by Harris (1993), whiteness is a form of property that transmits material and other benefits to white people in ways similar to tangible forms of property (e.g., land or money). The four property functions include the right to use and enjoy white privileges, reputation and status property, the absolute right to exclude, and the rights of disposition (Harris, 1993). Detailed definitions of the four property functions, connected to college students' developmental processes, are offered in the next section.

Third, without historically accurate analyses of race and racism in higher education, color-evasive racist explanations for racial inequalities persist, reproducing systemic racial inequities (Annamma, Jackson, & Morrison, 2017; Poon et al., 2016). CRT research interrogates ahistorical majoritarian interpretations of history and centers the histories of People of Color (Solórzano & Yosso, 2002). Fourth, the CRT tenet of differential racialization recognizes "that each disfavored group in this country has been racialized in its own individual way and according to the needs of the majority group at particular times in its history" (Delgado & Stefancic, 2012, p. 77). Taken together, these final two tenets of CRT encourage a focus on how race and racism are in a perpetual state of social re/construction by and for white supremacy.

Student Development Theory and CRT

CRT scholarship offers valuable analytical tools to unveil and understand the effects of racial domination in shaping college student development. In recent years, higher education and student affairs (HESA) scholars have adapted CRT to advance the field's theorizing of race and racism (Harper, 2012; Patton et al., 2015). The remainder of this chapter provides an in-depth exploration of how specific CRT tenets can advance practitioners' and scholars' uses of and approaches to student development theory.

Racism as an Endemic Influence in College Students' Development

Guided by Harper's (2012) review of the mis/use of race and racism in higher education scholarship, we contend that educators, including scholars and practitioners, often obscure the influence of racism in student development in two central ways. First, educators often do not name the role of racism in the lives of Students of Color (Harper, 2012). Instead, semantic substitutes are used, such as "chilly," "harmful," and "isolating," to describe racism in higher education. Second, racism, including institutionalized racism, is often not viewed as signficant in students' developmental processes, racial and otherwise. The discounting of racism not only falls short in acknowledging the pervasiveness of white supremacy in postsecondary contexts but also renormalizes racism and upholds the status quo (Harper, 2012).

Scholars must connect students' collegiate experiences to the ways in which racism always operates and influences individuals' developmental processes in U.S. higher education. For example, Hernández (2016) used CRT to reconsider how racism and racial power may influence students' self-authoring processes, shifting the developmental conversation "from the individual, to the individual in relation to her political, racialized, environment" (p. 172).

It is also important to expose and account for the different forms and types of racisms and racialization that influence students' developmental processes. The use of one singular racism, as opposed to racisms, may hinder educators' understandings of how various forms of racisms differently structure some students' developmental processes (Delgado & Stefancic, 2012). Because racism can manifest in multiple forms including racist nativism (Pérez Huber, Lopez, Malagon, Velez, & Solorzano, 2008), monoracism (Johnston & Nadal, 2010), and anti-blackness (Patton, 2016), educators must acknowledge different forms and types of racisms affecting students' development.

Finally, racism does not only manifest in students' development of their racial identities and thus should not just be explored while teaching, researching, and supporting students' racial identity development. Racism is a pervasive problem that systematically seeps into all facets of students' lives and developmental processes, including ethical, psychosocial, gender, and ability. Racism influences the development of all individuals on campus, including white students. Conversations and theorizing concerning racism should not be exclusively reserved for racial identity development theories and/or the developmental processes of Students of Color.

Whiteness as Structuring Property for College Students' Development

Whiteness is a social location and an ideological and "political construct of power" (Gusa, 2010, p. 468) that structurally allows white people to gain unearned material privileges over People of Color. At many historically white institutions, whiteness acts as a "structuring property" that "systematically deforms—and informs—every aspect of the social world" (Owen, 2007, p. 208). Through a lens of whiteness as property, educators can explore how whiteness functions as a form of structuring property in higher education that influences students' developmental processes.

The Rights to Use, Enjoy, and Exclude

The exclusionary nature of whiteness influences all students' individual identities and strengthens the collective boundaries related to who is white and who may access white privileges in higher education. Educators must ask questions that interrogate how individual interactions re/construct larger understandings of who is white and thus privy to material benefits of whiteness. How does the use, enjoyment, and exclusion of white privilege influence students' developmental processes? For instance, Renn (2003) explored how the permeability of boundaries around campus peer culture influenced students' multiracial identity development. Yet, the property functions of whiteness encourage educators to interrogate how this exclusionary nature of whiteness re/constructs racialized peer group boundaries. Furthermore, educators must examine how white-constructed peer boundaries might strengthen and privilege the individual and collective identities of white students while subordinating Students of Color. Reaching beyond racial identity development, educators can use these first two property functions to explore how students' cognitive and psychosocial identity development is influenced by their subordination of others/being subordinated by the right of exclusion from whiteness and the use and enjoyment of white privileges.

The Rights of Disposition

Scholars and practitioners must explore how a legacy of whiteness, passed down generationally, may influence students' development both on campus and prior to arriving on campus. The rights of disposition can be used to address wealth in terms of students' cultural wealth or cultural capital. How does intergenerational student cultural knowledge influence students' navigation of higher education and their identity development processes? In what ways might educational systems and practices center marginalized students' cultural knowledge, or community cultural wealth (see Yosso, 2005), in ways that empower students and challenge whiteness and its right to disposition?

Educators can also use this property function to frame how whiteness is passed down through faculty members' and/or campus professionals' relationships with white students. For example, research has suggested that faculty interactions influence students' developmental processes (Chang, Astin, & Kim, 2004). However, white faculty are more likely to interact with and mentor white students (Hurtado et al., 2011), reproducing whiteness and exclusionary ownership of its material benefits (Harris, 1993).

Reputation and Status Property
Scholars must interrogate how white students are presumed to be trustworthy and innocent on the basis of white racial status. For example, white reputation and status property allow white students to claim and be believed as inherently *not* racist despite their racism (Davis & Harris, 2015). Subsequently, the reputation and status of whiteness allows for the perpetuation of white innocence (Poon, 2018) in the enactment of racist behaviors, such as racist theme parties and performing blackface, with minimal to no consequences that might challenge and support students' moral, racial, or psychosocial development. Scholars must also examine how institutional structures continue to dehumanize Students of Color and the influence this reputation and status, or lack thereof, has on their developmental processes. For instance, bceause of their socially constructed reputations, Students of Color are often under surveillance on their own campus (Ray, 2013) or invisible (Garland, 2013; Poon et al., 2016), limiting their developmental opportunities in some campus spaces.

Differential Racialization and Challenging Ahistoricism Throughout Development

Students' racial identities are not static, because meanings of race change over time (Delgado & Stefancic, 2012). Students' identities are temporal and ever changing and must be placed in sociohistorical and contemporary contexts that "reexamine America's historical record" (Delgado & Stefancic, 2012, p. 24). For instance, throughout the 2016 U.S. presidential campaign, the reification of whiteness and white supremacy have differentially racialized minoritized groups like Latinxs and Muslims, shaping how these students may make meaning and develop their racial, ethnic, religious, and intersecting identities on campus. The Trump Muslim ban, for example, was rooted in, and justified, legalized Islamophobia (Ali, 2017). Educators must acknowledge heightened Islamophobia that may influence Muslim students' racial, ethnic, and/or religious identity. Educators must also square this differential racialization within U.S. history, as this is not the first time that bans on travel and immigration have been used to exclude People of Color and secure white supremacy (see the Chinese Exclusion Act of 1882 and the Immigration Act of 1924). Thus, contemporary theories of student development should be positioned in both historical and contemporary contexts to be effective. For example, educators must consider the sociohistorical context in which theories were developed and how this might influence uses of theory in a contemporary context.

Moving forward, scholars and practitioners must be knowledgeable about contemporary events, issues, and contexts and how they are entangled in histories of racism and colonization in the United States and beyond. In an attempt to connect how race, racism, and power have shifted over time, educators should explore how other fields like American studies and ethnic studies, and even other education scholars, have theorized race and racism and how their theorizing may interrogate the operationalization of race and racism in higher education. Faculty members who teach student development theory must present historical perspectives in the HESA classroom and encourage students to connect and critique theory through historical understandings of race and racism. Using texts like Wilder's (2013) *Ebony and Ivy: Race, Slavery, and the Troubled History of America's Universities* can move HESA programs to more deeply interrogate the role of racism in higher education through interdisciplinary understandings. Annual conferences and HESA-centered journals must solicit for the inclusion of historical research and encourage contemporary research to be placed in a historical context. Researchers should build theories across institutions and regions, interrogating the ways in which race is differentially constructed across contexts. Longitudinal research designs may expose differential racialization across time. For example, scholars might follow multiracial students' development across a six-year period, noting how policies, procedures, and movements influence their identity development in various ways at various time points. Finally, theories should never be seen as complete or static. Students' development, as well as student development theory, should always be thought of as in flux and incomplete, mirroring the nature of race and racism in U.S. society.

Discussion Questions

Educators must continue to explore the possibilities of student development theory through critical frameworks, such as CRT, in order to disrupt systems of oppression that are woven throughout postsecondary contexts and influence students' development. We encourage educators to use CRT to ask critical questions of student development theory.

1. How might CRT be used to focus on white students' development?
2. How can CRT aid practitioners in their self-reflection of race and racism in challenging and supporting students?
3. How can CRT be coupled with other critical or poststructural theories to disrupt normative assumptions about student development?

References

Ali, A. I. (2017). Trumpal fears, anthropological possibilities, and Muslim futures. *Anthropology and Education Quarterly, 48*(4), 386–392.

Annamma, S. A., Jackson, D. D., & Morrison, D. (2017). Conceptualizing color-evasiveness: Using dis/ability critical race theory to expand a color-blind racial ideology in education and society. *Race Ethnicity and Education, 20*(2), 147–162.

Chang, M. J., Astin, A. A., & Kim, D. (2004). Cross-racial integration among undergraduates: Some consequences, causes, and patterns. *Research in Higher Education, 45*(5), 529–553.

Crenshaw, K., Gotanda, N., Peller, G., & Thomas, K. (1995). Introduction. In K. Crenshaw, N. Gotanda, G. Peller, & K. Thomas (Eds.), *Critical race theory: The key writings that formed the movement* (pp. xiii–xxxii). New York, NY: New Press.

Davis, S., & Harris, J. C. (2015). But we didn't mean it like that: A critical race analysis of campus responses to racial incidents. *Journal of Critical Scholarship on Higher Education and Student Affairs, 2*(1), Article 6. Retrieved from http://ecommons.luc.edu/jcshesa/vol2/iss1/6/

Delgado, R. (1992). The imperial scholar revisited: How to marginalize outsider writing: Ten years later. *University of Pennsylvania Law Review, 140*(4), 1349–1372.

Delgado, R., & Stefancic, J. (2012). *Critical race theory: An introduction* (2nd ed). New York, NY: New York University Press.

Dixson, A. D., & Rousseau, C. K. (2006). And we are still not saved: Critical race theory in education ten years later. In A. D. Dixson & C. K. Rousseau (Eds.), *Critical race theory in education: All God's children got a song* (pp. 31–56). New York, NY: Taylor & Francis Group.

Garcia, G. A., & Johnston-Guerrero, M. (2015). Challenging the utility of a racial microaggressions framework through a systematic review of racially biased incidents on campus. *Journal of Critical Scholarship on Higher Education and Student Affairs, 2*(1), Article 4. Retrieved from http://ecommons.luc.edu/jcshesa/vol2/iss1/4

Garland, J. L. (2013). Foreword. In H. J. Shotton, S. C. Lowe, & S. J. Waterman (Eds.), *Beyond the asterisk: Understanding Native students in higher education* (pp. xv–xvi). Sterling, VA: Stylus.

Gusa, D. L. (2010). White institutional presence: The impact of whiteness on campus climate. *Harvard Educational Review, 80*(4), 464–489.

Harper, S. R. (2012). Race without racism: How higher education researchers minimize racist institutional norms. *The Review of Higher Education, 36*(1), 9–29.

Harris, C. I. (1993). Whiteness as property. *Harvard Law Review, 106*(8), 1707–1791.

Hernández, E. (2016). Utilizing critical race theory to examine race/ethnicity, racism, and power in student development theory and research. *Journal of College Student Development, 57*(2), 168–180.

Hurtado, S., Eagan, M. K., Tran, M. C., Newman, C. B., Chang, M. J., & Velasco, P. (2011). "We do science here": Underrepresented students' interactions with faculty in different college contexts. *Journal of Social Issues, 67*(3), 553–579.

Johnston, M. P., & Nadal, K. L. (2010). Multiracial microaggressions: Exposing monoracism in everyday life and clinical practice. In D. W. Sue (Ed.), *Microaggressions and marginality: Manifestations, dynamics, and impact* (pp. 123–144). New York, NY: Wiley & Sons.

Ladson-Billings, G. (1998). Just what is critical race theory and what's it doing in a nice field like education? *International Journal of Qualitative Studies in Education, 11*(1), 7–24.

Lawrence, C. R. (1987). The id, the ego, and equal protection: Reckoning with unconscious racism. *Stanford Law Review, 39*(2), 317–388.

Ladson-Billings, G., & Tate, W. G. (1995). Toward a critical race theory of education. *Teachers College Record, 97*(1), 47–68.

Ledesma, M. C., & Calderón, D. (2015). Critical race theory in education: A review of past literature and a look to the future. *Qualitative Inquiry, 21*(3), 206–222.

Matsuda, M. J. (1987). Looking to the bottom: Critical legal studies and reparations. *Harvard Civil Rights–Civil Liberties Law Review, 22*(2), 323–400.

Owen, D. S. (2007). Towards a critical theory of whiteness. *Philosophy and Social Criticism, 33*(2), 203–222.

Patton, L. D., Harper, S. R., & Harris, J. (2015). Using critical race theory to (re)interpret widely studied topics related to students in U.S. higher education. In pp. A. M. Martínez-Alemán, B. Pusser, & E. M. Bensimon (Eds.), *Critical approaches to the study of higher education: A practical introduction* (pp. 193–219). Baltimore, MD: Johns Hopkins University Press.

Patton, L. D. (2016). Disrupting postsecondary prose: Toward a critical race theory of higher education. *Urban Education, 51*(3), 315–342.

Poon, O. A. (2018). Ending white innocence in student affairs and higher education. *Journal of Student Affairs, 27*, 13–23.

Pérez Huber, L., Lopez, C. B., Malagon, M. C., Velez, V., & Solorzano, D. G. (2008). Getting beyond the "symptom," acknowledging the "disease": Theorizing racist nativism. *Contemporary Justice Review, 11*(1), 39–51.

Poon, O., Squire, D., Kodama, C., Byrd, A., Chan, J., Manzano, L., Furr, S., & Bishundat, D. (2016). A critical review of the model minority myth in selected literature on Asian Americans and Pacific Islanders in higher education. *Review of Educational Research, 86*(2), 469–502.

Ray, R. (2013). Fraternity life at predominantly white universities in the U.S.: The saliency of race. *Ethnic and Racial Studies, 36*(2), 320–336.

Renn, K. A. (2003). Understanding the identities of mixed-race college students through a developmental ecology lens. *Journal of College Student Development, 44*(3), 383–403.

Solórzano, D., Ceja, M., & Yosso, T. (2000). Critical race theory, racial microaggressions, and campus racial climate: The experiences of African American college students. *Journal of Negro Education, 69*(1–2), 60–73.

Solórzano, D. G. (1998). Critical race theory, race and gender microaggressions, and the experience of Chicana and Chicano scholars. *International Journal of Qualitative Studies in Education, 11*(1), 121–136.

Solórzano, D. G., & Yosso, T. J. (2002). Critical race methodology: Counter-storytelling as an analytical framework for education research. *Qualitative Inquiry, 8*(1), 23–44.

Wilder, C. S. (2013). *Ebony and ivy: Race, slavery, and the troubled history of America's universities.* New York, NY: Bloomsbury Press.

Yosso, T. J. (2005). Whose culture has capital? A critical race theory discussion of community cultural wealth. *Race Ethnicity and Education, 8*(1), 69–91.

3

INTERSECTIONALITY AND STUDENT DEVELOPMENT

Centering Power in the Process

Charmaine L. Wijeyesinghe

Intersectionality links identity to interlocking systems of oppression and foregrounds the impact of social systems and power on how individuals experience the world, interact with other people, and are treated in society. The significant impact of intersectionality on knowledge and practice related to student development is evident in the incorporation of several of its central themes into identity models (Jones & Abes, 2013; Wijeyesinghe, 2012), research methodology (Choo & Ferree, 2010; Griffin & Museus, 2011; Tillapaugh & Nicolazzo, 2014), and student affairs practice (Jones & Abes, 2013; Wijeyesinghe, 2017). Intersectionality offers a lens for reexamining assumptions and concepts underlying theories of student development (Abes, 2016; Jones & Stewart, 2016), even as its historical roots and core assumptions extend beyond individual moral, intellectual, emotional, or relational development or identity development based on singular, socially constructed identities such as race, gender, sexual orientation, and faith. By foregrounding interrelated systems of power and inequality, intersectionality reveals a more complex and complicated understanding of student development and the contexts in which identity evolves and is lived.

Intersectionality offers a broader understanding of identity, intergroup dynamics, systems of oppression, and efforts to address social inequality. However, employing intersectionality within the same evolving systems of power that it centers in the analysis of these areas can result in fundamental aspects of the framework being ignored or overlooked and a muddying of intersectionality's definition and intent (Cho, Crenshaw, & McCall, 2013; Collins, 2015). As Collins and Bilge (2016) noted, "Intersectionality's travels from social movements into the academy enable some dimensions of inter-sectionality to flourish, leaving others to languish, if not disappear" (p. 7). Attending to foundational themes, rooted in its history and sustained over time, is essential to effectively using intersectionality as a tool for evaluating existing theory and informing emerging developmental models. This chapter draws on the work of several authors to highlight core tenets and assumptions of intersectionality and to present examples of how they enhance, complicate, and challenge concepts within student development theory.

Central Themes

Collins (2015) defined *intersectionality* as "the critical insight that race, class, gender, sexuality, ethnicity, nation, ability, and age operate not as unitary, mutually exclusive entities, but as reciprocal constructing phenomena that in turn shape complex social inequalities" (p. 2). Embedded within this overarching definition are interconnected and reinforcing relationships between the experiences of people within socially constructed groups and systems of social inequality. These relationships inform several themes that are essential to intersectionality's historical foundations and analytic power and that are briefly reviewed in this section of the chapter.

The Nature of Identity

Intersectionality frames identity as a complex intertwining of socially constructed categories such as race, gender, age, gender identity, economic status, sexual orientation, ability, and nationality. The meaning and experience of one's membership in any of these groups is always affected by others so that, for example, a person's experience of race cannot be understood in isolation from their identities based on, for instance, ability, age, nationality, and economic status. However, the focus of intersectionality is "not exclusively or even primarily preoccupied with categories, identities, and subjectivities" (Cho et al., 2013, p. 797) but on how people as members of social groups are influenced by structures and systems that create or deny opportunities and privileges (Holvino, 2012; Wijeyesinghe & Jones, 2014; Yuval-Davis, 2009). Linking identity to interconnected manifestations of oppression illuminates how social locations (based on access to power and privilege within any socially constructed group) affect how people are treated on multiple levels, including the personal, interpersonal, organizational, and societal. Holvino (2012) and Weber (2010) described identity and social systems as so intertwined that one could not be examined independently from the other. Such relationships were evident in some of the earliest writing associated with intersectionality, such as when the Lesbians of Color from the Combahee River Collective (1978) wrote, "We also often find it difficult to separate race from class from sex oppression because in our lives they are most often experienced simultaneously" (p. 213). Their Black Feminist Statement underscored the critical role of interlocking systems of oppression in framing their experiences, analysis of social inequality, and approaches to social justice projects—years before Crenshaw was credited with introducing the term *intersectionality* into general discourse.

In considering how intersectionality informs the representation of identity in psychosocial models of development, Wijeyesinghe and Jones (2014) asked,

> Can identity truly be an individual experience when people embody social identities that carry meaning in society and result in differential access to resources and control of various domains that fundamentally influence a person's life, regardless of whether he or she acknowledges the existence or influence of those identities? (p. 14)

Because it creates an essential connection between individual understanding or meaning-making and evolving systems of power, intersectionality challenges conceptualizations of development where individuals "construct an individual identity *separate* from external influences" within contextual environments (Baxter Magolda, 1999, p. 12, emphasis added). Put more succinctly, intersectionality questions the extent to which there is a personal, individual "I" in identity. Relatedly, it complicates the concept of salience, represented as the ability of individuals to attribute differential levels of significance to various social categories in response to different contexts (Cross & Fhagen-Smith, 2001; Goodman, 2014; Jones & Abes, 2013; Wijeyesinghe, 2012). Collins and Bilge (2016) indicated, "Individuals can be seen as having multiple 'subjectivities' that they construct from one situation to the next. In other words, people have many choices and considerable *agency* about who they choose to be" (p. 125, emphasis added). Examining salience in light of intersectionality raises for examination how such agency relates to privilege when individuals selectively identify with only certain social locations.

By describing all of a person's social locations as being present at all times and in all situations, intersectionality asks questions related to conceptualizations of identity and development, such as the following: Is it possible for people to experience one social location or set of group memberships in total isolation from others? Can individuals choose which identities or social locations influence their lives in given situations and times, while ignoring the impact of others? And if so, how might the concept of choice be discussed in models of student development? Are salience and intersectionality compatible topics within the same model of development? Using the more holistic conceptualization of identity put forward by intersectionality complicates concepts such as self-definition, salience, privilege, and context but also informs how these areas may be addressed in future student development theories.

Centering Marginalized Groups

The historical underpinnings and tenets of intersectionality are deeply rooted in the lived experiences of Women of Color and movements to remedy complex disparities affecting them based on institutionalized social systems related to race, class, and gender (Collins, 1991; Crenshaw, 1989; Dill & Zambrana, 2009). The voices of these women and other multiply oppressed people reveal "counterhistories and counternarratives to those based primarily on the experience of social elites" (Dill & Zambrana, 2009, p. 6). When placed at the forefront of inquiry, the experiences of groups that are overlooked, discounted, or assumed to be included in knowledge based on the lives of "social elites" illuminate ways that oppression appears in theory and practice. By validating and focusing on "multiple interpretive communities" (Collins, 2015, p. 4), new ways of understanding social problems, forms of systemic oppression, and movements for social justice are created.

Intersectionality reveals how constructs and assumptions drawn from the experiences, needs, and privileges of dominant social locations inform representations of identity and development and illuminates how power underlies the uncritical extension of these representations to people from marginalized social locations. Butler (2017) noted, "The relationship between identity and power—sometimes called the politics of identity or identity politics—arguably shapes what is taught and to whom; whose histories are told and not told; who is defined as object and not subject" (p. 43). Social power also legitimizes sets of knowledge while isolating others, such as when models based on experiences of individuals targeted by systems of inequality (e.g., Black identity theories) are positioned as caveats to the main, overarching body of knowledge on so-called universal student development. According to Abes (2016), foregrounding interconnected relationships of power "avoids problematizing the student's development" (p. 9) and not only reveals "the ways in which some student development theories silence underrepresented students but also create[s] possibilities for new ways to conceptualize student development theory" (p. 10). Placing the lives of Students of Color; gay, lesbian, bisexual, transgender, and queer students; first-generation college students; students who are veterans; disabled students; and students from other marginalized social locations at the center of inquiry and analysis expands the understanding of how *all* students experience college life. In addition, the experiences of these students highlight the diversity within socially constructed categories and the reality that most people inhabit social locations of marginality *and* privilege. For example, veterans are understood to represent cisgender, transgender, and gender-variant people; People of Color and whites; and people who are gay, lesbian, bisexual, and heterosexual. Considering how privilege and marginalization interconnect and affect the experiences of individuals is another layer of complexity that intersectionality adds to theoretical and practical approaches to student development.

The Nature of Systems of Power

Intersectionality unveils how social structures work together to support and maintain differential access to power, influence, and privilege across evolving social, political, and historical contexts (Collins & Bilge, 2016; Dill & Zambrana, 2009; Warner, 2008; Weber, 2010). Therefore, for example, "within intersectional frameworks, there is no pure racism or sexism. Rather, power relationships of racism and sexism gain meaning in relation to one another" (Collins & Bilge, 2016, pp. 26–27). While intersectionality frames social systems as intertwined, it does not erase or discount the unique ways that forms of oppression are manifested and experienced (Luft, 2009; Yuval-Davis, 2009). For example, intersectionality exposes how homophobia and sexism work together to affect the experiences of transgender women, while acknowledging that these experiences will be mediated by differences in the women's races, ages, socioeconomic positions, and faith traditions.

Interlocking, mutually supporting systems of oppression are embedded in the environments where identity develops, experiences are lived, and knowledge about self and others is created. They also influence the histories, standards, and practices of the disciplines from which theories emerge. Wijeyesinghe and Jones (2014) noted, "Although the social world and its contexts have always been considered in identity theories, exactly what constitutes context has evolved to also include larger structures of inequality" (p. 9). As these systems and the issues that arise from them change in response to evolving social pressures, norms, and perspectives, theorists, researchers, and practitioners will have to address questions such as the following: How will evolving definitions or representations attached to social categories, such as race, gender identity, or nationality, affect the content of student development theories? Are there key components to development that remain stable over time, and if so, do they reflect experiences of diverse social groups and social locations? Is it possible to research the effect of one form of oppression, such as Islamophobia, on development without attending to racism, sexism, classism, and other systems of inequality and their influence on how Islamophobia is understood and experienced by students? The number and nature of the connections among systems of inequality, and between these systems and the experiences of social groups, can seem overwhelming. Although intersectionality presents challenges to both theory and practice, it offers promises for a fuller representation of how identities develop and are experienced in a complex world.

Informing and Promoting Social Justice

Intersectionality draws strong and essential connections between knowledge production informed by more integrated and holistic understandings of identity and social systems and practices that seek to confront social inequities. Weber (2010) described intersectionality as deepening "our understanding of oppression by opening up new ways of looking at social institutions, raising new questions, and suggesting more effective ways of addressing seemingly intractable systems of social inequality" (p. 215). The creation of both a more complex understanding of social problems and a more informed way of resolving them were essential aspects of Crenshaw's foundational, intersectional legal analysis of employment discrimination (Crenshaw, 1989) and domestic violence (Crenshaw, 1991). Inherent in intersectional practice is an understanding of and a desire to change relationships of power as they affect the day-to-day lives of individuals and social groups.

Because intersectionality shifts the focus of personal identity from a position of self as individual to self as member of social groups affected by social systems related to power and privilege, students and the people working with them can develop a more sophisticated understanding of their experiences, systems of inequality, and how their social locations affect social justice work in different communities and on different issues (Kendall & Wijeyesinghe, 2017; Mitchell, 2017; Wijeyesinghe & Jones, 2014). Social justice is also promoted when core tenets of intersectionality are used to examine the assumptions, content, and context of historical and emerging student development theories and foreground the analysis of power, social systems, and privilege in the production, research, and application of these theories.

Concluding Thoughts

In describing intersectional praxis in higher education, Collins and Bilge (2016) wrote, "College classrooms may be the place where students first learn about intersectionality, yet their experiences in dormitories, dining halls, libraries, sporting events, and, for those who must work to pay for their education, their jobs become places where intersectionality is lived" (p. 47). Intersectionality's historical and central themes, and the lives of people reflected in them, enhance the understanding of how social locations and social systems affect the development of all students. Employing an intersectional lens to reflect, reconsider, and reenvision student development theory and concepts central to these theories is not only an intellectual undertaking but also work that advances social justice. Because student development theories often inform practice, intersectional evaluation of theory deeply influences the day-to-day lives of students. Such work requires scholars and practitioners to evaluate and challenge how overarching systems of power inform their assumptions, knowledge, and disciplines.

Discussion Questions

1. What underlying assumptions are revealed when core themes of intersectionality are applied to key concepts within student development literature, such as self-authorship, context, and the nature of development?
2. Should increases in knowledge of social location, power, and privilege be essential indicators of development in student development theories? Why or why not? How would you measure this variable in research?
3. Using more complex and interrelated understandings of identity and social systems to address social inequality is a central tenet of intersectionality. How might the requirement to engage in actions to promote social justice be addressed by theories of student development?
4. What strategies might teachers, researchers, and practitioners use to increase their ability to access, interpret, and use experiences of multiply marginalized students?

References

Abes, E. S. (2016). Situating paradigms in student development theory. In E. S. Abes (Ed.), *Critical perspectives in student development theory* (New Directions for Student Services, No. 154, pp. 9–16). San Francisco, CA: Jossey-Bass.
Baxter Magolda, M. B. (1999). *Creating contexts for learning and self-authorship: Constructive-developmental pedagogy.* Nashville, TN: Vanderbilt University Press.

Butler, J. E. (2017). Intersectionality and liberal education. *Liberal Education*, *103*(3–4), 38–45.

Cho, S., Crenshaw, K. W., & McCall, L. (2013). Toward a field of intersectional studies: Theory, application, and praxis. *Signs*, *38*(4), 785–810.

Choo, H. Y., & Ferree, M. M. (2010). Practicing intersectionality in sociological research: A critical analysis of inclusion, interactions, and institutions in the study of inequalities. *Sociological Theory*, *28*(2), 129–149.

Collins, P. H. (1991). *Black feminist thought: Knowledge, consciousness, and the politics of empowerment*. New York, NY: Routledge.

Collins, P. H. (2015). Intersectionality's definitional dilemma. *Annual Review of Sociology*, *41*(1), 1–20.

Collins, P. H., & Bilge, S. (2016). *Intersectionality*. Malden, MA: Polity Press.

Combahee River Collective. (1978). A Black Feminist Statement. In Z. Eisenstein (Ed.), *Capitalist patriarchy and the case for socialist feminism* (pp. 210–218). New York, NY: Monthly Review Press.

Crenshaw, K. (1989). Demarginalizing the intersections of race and sex: A Black feminist critique of antidiscrimination doctrine, feminist theory, and antiracist politics. *University of Chicago Legal Forum*, *140*, 139–167.

Crenshaw, K. (1991). Mapping the margins: Intersectionality, identity politics, and violence against Women of Color. *Stanford Law Review*, *43*(5), 1241–1299.

Cross, W. E., Jr., & Fhagen-Smith, P. (2001). Patterns in African American identity development: A life span perspective. In C. L. Wijeyesinghe & B. W. Jackson III (Eds.), *New perspectives on racial identity development: A theoretical and practical anthology* (pp. 243–270). New York, NY: New York University Press.

Dill, B. T., & Zambrana, R. E. (2009). Critical thinking about inequality: An emerging lens. In B. T. Dill & R. E. Zambrana (Eds.), *Emerging intersections: Race, class, and gender in theory, policy, and practice* (pp. 1–21). New Brunswick, NJ: Rutgers University Press.

Goodman, D. J. (2014). The tapestry model: Exploring social identities, privilege, and oppression from an intersectional perspective. In D. Mitchell, C. Y. Simmons, & L. A. Greyerbiehl (Eds.), *Intersectionality and higher education: Theory, research, and praxis* (pp. 99–108). New York, NY: Peter Lang.

Griffin, K. A., & Museus, S. D. (Eds.). (2011). *Using mixed methods approaches to study intersectionality in higher education* (New Directions in Institutional Research, No. 151). San Francisco, CA: Jossey-Bass.

Holvino, E. (2012). The "simultaneity" of identities: Models and skills. In C. L. Wijeyesinghe & B. W. Jackson III (Eds.), *New perspectives on racial identity development* (2nd ed., pp. 161–191). New York, NY: New York University Press.

Jones, S. R., & Abes, E. S. (2013). *Identity development of college students: Advancing frameworks for multiple dimensions of identity*. San Francisco, CA: Jossey-Bass.

Jones, S. R., & Stewart, D-L. (2016). Evolutions of student development theory. In E. S. Abes (Ed.), *Critical perspectives in student development theory* (New Directions for Student Services, No. 154, pp. 17–28). San Francisco, CA: Jossey-Bass.

Kendall, F. E., & Wijeyesinghe, C. L. (2017). Advancing social justice work at the intersections of multiple privileged identities. In C. L. Wijeyesinghe (Ed.), *Enacting intersectionality in student affairs* (New Directions for Student Services, No. 157, pp. 91–100). San Francisco, CA: Jossey-Bass.

Luft, R. E. (2009). Intersectionality and the risk of flattening difference: Gender and race logics, and the strategic use of antiracist singularity. In M. T. Berger & K. Guidroz (Eds.), *The intersectional approach: Transforming the academy through race, class, and gender* (pp. 100–117). Chapel Hill, NC: University of North Carolina Press.

Mitchell, T. D. (2017). Teaching community on and off campus: An intersectional approach to community engagement. In C. L. Wijeyesinghe (Ed.), *Enacting intersectionality in student affairs* (New Directions for Student Services, No. 157, pp. 35–44). San Francisco, CA: Jossey-Bass.

Tillapaugh, D., & Nicolazzo, Z. (2014). Backward thinking: Exploring the relationship among intersectionality, epistemology, and research design. In D. Mitchell, C. Y. Simmons, & L. A. Greyerbiehl (Eds.), *Intersectionality and higher education: Theory, research, and praxis* (pp. 111–122). New York, NY: Peter Lang.

Warner, L. R. (2008). A best practices guide to intersectional approaches in psychological research. *Sex Roles, 59*(5-6), 454–463.

Weber, L. (2010). *Understanding race, class, gender, and sexuality* (2nd ed). New York, NY: Oxford University Press.

Wijeyesinghe, C. L. (2012). The intersectional model of multiracial identity: Integrating multiracial identity theories and intersectional perspectives on social identity. In C. L. Wijeyesinghe & B. W. Jackson III (Eds.), *New perspectives on racial identity development* (2nd ed., pp. 81–107). New York, NY: New York University Press.

Wijeyesinghe, C. L., & Jones, S. R. (2014). Intersectionality, identity, and systems of power and inequality. In D. Mitchell, C. Y. Simmons, & L. A. Greyerbiehl (Eds.), *Intersectionality and higher education: Theory, research, and praxis* (pp. 9–19). New York, NY: Peter Lang.

Wijeyesinghe, C. L. (Ed.). (2017). *Enacting intersectionality in student affairs* (New Directions for Student Services, No. 157). San Francisco, CA: Jossey-Bass.

Yuval-Davis, N. (2009). Intersectionality and feminist politics. In M. T. Berger & K. Guidroz (Eds.), *The intersectional approach: Transforming the academy through race, class, and gender* (pp. 44–60). Chapel Hill, NC: University of North Carolina Press.

4

(RE)FRAMING STUDENT DEVELOPMENT THROUGH CRITICAL FEMINIST THEORIES

Claire Kathleen Robbins

In her 1990 essay on feminist critical theories in the *Stanford Law Review*, Deborah L. Rhode described an invitation to contribute a chapter on feminist theory to a critical legal studies anthology. Rhode had two critiques of this invitation. First, it was tokenizing; the authors seemed to want to include women without critiquing gender as a basis for exclusion in the first place. Second, the invitation was daunting because "almost any systematic statement about these two bodies of thought [feminism and critical legal studies] risks homogenizing an extraordinarily broad range of views" (p. 617). Happily, tokenization was absent from my invitation to contribute this chapter on critical feminist theories nearly 30 years later, because this volume centers minoritized and marginalized scholars, students, social identities, ways of knowing, and theoretical perspectives. Yet, I relate to Rhode's other concern, in that any analysis of critical feminist and college student development theories risks omissions and oversimplifications.

Accordingly, this chapter offers an introduction to critical feminist theories (hereafter, FemCrit) and their possibilities for understanding, critiquing, deconstructing, and reimagining the development of students attending U.S. postsecondary institutions. I present guiding definitions and tenets of FemCrit, use these tenets to construct one possible FemCrit (re)imagining of student development theory, and offer discussion questions to guide those seeking to enact future possibilities for FemCrit and student development theory.

Defining *FemCrit*

Because FemCrit theorists reject the notion of a theoretical canon, any claim to present an exhaustive grouping of these theorists would, by definition, misrepresent their work. Scholars seeking theoretical perspectives that are both "critical" and "feminist" frequently cite Chris Weedon's (1987) *Feminist Practice and Poststructural Theory,* Gloria Anzaldúa's (1999) *Borderlands: La Frontera,* Chela Sandoval's (2000) *Methodology of the Oppressed,* or Adrien Wing's (2003) *Critical Race Feminism: A Reader,* yet these texts diverge as much as they overlap. Critical scholars such as bell hooks, Sandra Harding, Donna Haraway, Judith Butler, Karen Barad, and Sara Ahmed "theorize from a specifically feminist perspective" (C. Labuski, personal communication, October 5, 2017), yet this perspective eludes a single definition. Thus, I have selected not 1 but 3 definitions from a 30-year period that illustrate the range of academic disciplines, guiding assumptions, and ideological commitments reflected in theories under the FemCrit umbrella:

1. A way to "understand social and cultural practices which throw light on how gender and power relations are constituted, reproduced, and contested" (Weedon, 1987, p. vii);
2. "Feminist critical theory begins from gender issues to understand and challenge all forms of contemporary subordination, domination and oppression" (Mills, 1994, p. 211); and
3. "In investigating gender relations (in schooling or otherwise), one must look at how all manifestations of gender and power, usually unspoken, are evident within relationships, discourse, and individual decisions" (Smith & Niemi, 2017, p. 111).

Together, these definitions reveal that FemCrit, as a theoretical perspective, foregrounds gender as the starting point for understanding, critiquing, and ultimately dismantling the multiple, interlocking, patriarchal systems of oppression through which inequitable power relations shape everyday life in relationships, virtual and physical spaces, organizations, and communities.

Tenets of FemCrit as a Framework for College Student Development

In this section I present three tenets as a framework for (re)theorizing the development of college students from a FemCrit perspective. These tenets—reimagining ways of knowing, being, and doing; enacting differential consciousness; and engaging the art of failure—were not drawn from a canonical text but from my review of approximately 25 books, book chapters, and articles written in the past 3 decades by critical feminist scholars across multiple disciplines. The 13 works cited in these tenets include those most frequently cited in higher education scholarship (Ropers-Huilman & Winters, 2011) plus pieces that expand on the previous definitions. Not an exhaustive list, these works illustrate how scholars have engaged FemCrit perspectives in other theoretical "homes" with the hope of inspiring new possibilities for college student development theory. I elaborate on these possibilities after describing the three tenets.

Reimagining Ways of Knowing, Being, and Doing

FemCrit scholars have (re)conceptualized *knowing, being,* and *doing* as mutually constitutive processes that are produced by everyday life in relationships, spaces, organizations, and communities; embedded in multiple systems of oppression; and held in place by inequitable power relations. Ways of *knowing* have been reimagined by scholars committed to critical feminist pedagogy, which "is concerned with emancipation and the full development" of knowers in inequitable, patriarchal educational systems (Caldwell, 1998, p. 3). Feminist pedagogy recognizes the interdependence of knowers who must "rely on one another in the development of knowledge" and "as a means of survival" (Caldwell, 1998, p. 3). Annette Baier (1985) described this interdependence as second-person knowing. Also discussed by Lorraine Code (1991) in *What Can She Know? Feminist Theory and the Construction of Knowledge,* one key assumption of second-person knowing is that "every cognitive act takes place at a point of intersection of innumerable relations, events, circumstances, and histories which make the knower and the known what they are at that time" (Caldwell, 1998, p. 3).

Importantly, this ecologically informed assumption recognizes the inextricability of knowing, being, and doing—an epistemological and methodological challenge for FemCrit scholars across disciplines. The relationship between knowing and being—in other words, experience (as a collective source of knowledge) and identity (as a result of accumulative experiences)—is particularly contested. As Joan Scott, a feminist historian, argued in her influential 1992 article "The Evidence of Experience," "when the evidence offered is the evidence of 'experience,' the claim for referentiality is further buttressed—what could be truer, after all, than a subject's own account of what he or she [*sic*] has lived through?" (p. 777). Yet, the danger of treating "experience as uncontestable evidence and as an originary point of explanation" is that such analyses "take as self-evident the identities of those whose experience is being documented and thus naturalize their difference," which leaves "those assumptions and practices that excluded considerations of difference in the first place" unexamined (p. 777). In other words, the assumptions and practices of patriarchal systems are what produce gender differences, and the identities associated with those differences, in the first place.

Recognizing the inextricability of knowledge (knowing) and identity (being), many FemCrit scholars have reimagined both by turning their attention to ways of doing. For example, according to Judith Butler (1990) and Julia Kristeva (1981), gender is not a stable or "natural" characteristic of one's identity but instead an ever-changing product of one's imagination, everyday practices, and embodiment in response to relentless, powerful messaging about sex, sexuality, desire, and success. In other words, gender is something people *do*. As Cooks and Simpson (2008) explained, Butler conceptualized gender performance as "a marked act with a beginning and an end," while gendered performatives are "everyday (re)iterative acts that sediment" (p. 17). Some "marked acts" are discrete, whereas others "sediment" in daily life and are both reinforced and resisted in institutional settings, such as higher education. Conceptualizing gender as performative allows FemCrit scholars to identify both structural constraints (like reinforcement) and agentic possibilities (like resistance) (Butler, 1990; Cosgrove, 2003).

Enacting Differential Consciousness

In her foundational text *Methodology of the Oppressed* Sandoval (2000) argued that feminists and other social actors routinely engage in forms of resistance that, while effective in isolated instances, ultimately undermine the kind of coalition building necessary for achieving radical, lasting political and social transformation. In response, Sandoval imagined a differential consciousness to "gather up the modes of ideology-praxis represented within previous liberation movements" (p. 54) into a distinct paradigm. Unlike those enacting prior modes of resistance, the oppositional actor must peacefully and lovingly collaborate with people in multiple social locations to cocreate a shared ideological perspective that resists domination. According to Sandoval, the practices necessary for being an oppositional actor constitute a methodology for developing and sustaining an oppositional consciousness. Such consciousness refuses "the apartheid of theoretical domains dividing academic endeavors by race, sex, class, gender, and identity" (p. 4). In other words, for Sandoval, uprooting sexism requires members of feminist social movements to learn and practice the methodology of the oppressed. Unlike other feminist approaches, Sandoval's methodology requires feminist actors to develop and sustain (a) an unwavering, collective commitment to uprooting colonialism, racism, classism, and all forms of oppression and (b) meaningful coalitions with other social movements committed to the same. Sandoval's approach offers many possibilities for critical educators (DeSaxe, 2012).

Engaging the Art of Failure

In *Fictions of Feminist Ethnography*, Kamala Visweswaran (1994) presented the story of a "failed" attempt at an interview during her ethnographic fieldwork in India to "illustrate a particular moment when feminist intentions 'fail'" (p. 97). Feminist ethnographers have long sought (appropriately) to represent women's lives using gender as an analytic tool. Yet, feminist ethnographers also recognize that gender is inextricable from race, class, and sexuality. As a result, the question of "*how* to consider these 'multiple axes of oppression'" remains unresolved, illustrating not only a methodological challenge but also "the displacement of the very epistemological center of feminism (gender)" (p. 99). Rather than responding to this so-called failure with despair, Visweswaran drew on the work of prior ethnographers and feminist theorists to argue "for a suspension of the feminist faith that we can ever wholly understand and identify with other women" (p. 100). As Visweswaran explained, "This requires a trickster figure who 'trips' on, but is not tripped up by, the seductions of a feminism that promises what it may never deliver: full representation on the one hand, and full comprehension on the other" (p. 100).

Methodologically, "tripping on" the seductions of full representation and full comprehension requires feminist ethnographers to acknowledge that their accounts are always already partial in both senses: incomplete and biased. Because those who encounter partial descriptions demand fuller ones, Visweswaran (1994) encouraged feminist ethnographers to account more fully for their partiality by doing "homework, not fieldwork" (p. 101)—in other words, through critical reflexivity on one's own positionality. Illustrating how this approach constituted her own engagement with failure, Visweswaran summarized her ethnographic text this way:

> My own narrative has begun with the "field" and worked its way steadily homeward. If I have not told you anything of the women with whom

I have worked, I have at least told you something of why it was that I attempted to work with them. (p. 112)

Nearly 20 years later, Elisabeth Anker (2012), a critical and cultural political theorist, engaged the art of failure as part of a feminist analysis of post-9/11 U.S. political discourse about freedom. Anker's analysis relied on the work of Jack Halberstam, a queer theorist who advocates for "'the art of failure' as a feminist and queer strategy that refutes celebratory stories of progress and heroism in order to thematize the failure of current governing systems and social norms to enable lived experiences of freedom" (Halberstam, 2011, p. 4, as cited in Anker, 2012, p. 208). While Visweswaran (1994) suggested patriarchal systems make it impossible for feminist researchers to "ever wholly understand and identify with other women" (p. 100), Anker demonstrated how the same systems seduce us to discount evidence of enduring inequities and embrace the illusion that things are getting better. Although written at different points in time and from different disciplinary contexts, Visweswaran's, Anker's, and Halberstam's work all used the notion of failure as a critical feminist analytic to expose "progress" as a fictional metanarrative encouraging faith in systems, norms, and practices that serve patriarchal interests.

(Re)Imagining College Student Development Theory From a FemCrit Perspective

Numerous higher education and student development scholars have engaged perspectives that are both critical and feminist (e.g., Robbins & McGowan, 2016; Ropers-Huilman & Winters, 2011). Kelli Zaytoun's (2006) use of standpoint theory and social location to reconceptualize adult psychosocial development is particularly thoughtful. Still, much of this work engages a *single* critical feminist perspective (e.g., intersectionality or standpoint theory) and/or a single *domain* of development (e.g., cognitive or psychosocial). Few resources exist for those seeking to reframe college student development theory through tenets that cut across multiple critical feminist perspectives. To that end, in this section I offer one FemCrit (re)imagining of college student development theory using the three tenets described earlier.

A FemCrit perspective foregrounds gender as the starting point for understanding, critiquing, and ultimately dismantling the multiple, interlocking, patriarchal systems of oppression through which inequitable power relations shape everyday life in relationships, virtual and physical spaces, organizations, and communities. Thus, a FemCrit perspective on college student development must unapologetically center gender as the starting point for (re)imagining who college students are (and are not), what development is (and is not), and what constitutes theory (and who decides). With this in mind, a student development researcher guided by a FemCrit perspective might construct an ethnographic study of historically and predominantly white fraternity and sorority recruitment practices. Data could reveal how, over time, students' interactions, attire, and use of physical space (among other practices) "sedimented" (Cooks & Simpson, 2008, p. 17) into gendered performatives (Butler, 1990) that serve intersecting systems of oppression (e.g., white supremacy, capitalism, and cisheteropatriarchy) and institutional interests (i.e., ensuring students form positive connections to the institution so they will engage in alumni giving).

In this study, gender would be the starting point for (re)imagining college students not as individual makers of meaning (Robbins & McGowan, 2016) but as actors who have agency and are constrained by inequities (e.g., fraternity and sorority life as an inequitable and patriarchal system). Development would not necessarily or exclusively mean increased meaning-making capacity among college women (Robbins & McGowan, 2016) but instead foreground the performance, sedimentation, and reproduction of gender in all students' everyday lives in college environments. Theory would refer not solely to the constructivist-developmental tradition but to the use of FemCrit as a theoretical perspective guiding the conceptualization and design of the study and interpretation of findings.

This example illustrates one possibility for researchers interested in (re)imagining college student development theory from a FemCrit perspective. Yet, there are deeper implications. Student affairs educators have long argued that the holistic development of individual students should be central to the mission of U.S. higher education, but this preoccupation with individual development may constitute a grand narrative serving patriarchal, capitalist, white supremacist interests (e.g., the "development" of an educated workforce rife with disparities even among college graduates). This preoccupation may divert attention from cissexism, transphobia, homophobia, and the other interlocking systems of oppression through which inequitable gendered power relations shape college access, college-going practices, and students' everyday lives in higher education settings. FemCrit offers a perspective through which more radical possibilities might be imagined and enacted in theory, research, practice, and policy. To conclude, I offer the following cautionary words from Rhode (1990):

> The point of this approach is neither to develop some unifying Grand Theory nor simply to compare feminism with other critical frameworks. Rather it is to underscore the importance of multiple frameworks that

avoid universal or essentialist claims and that yield concrete strategies for social change. (pp. 618–619)

Similarly, this chapter and the following discussion questions illustrate only a few of the many transformative possibilities FemCrit might offer.

Discussion Questions

1. In 1978, Knefelkamp, Widick, and Parker posed four questions to guide the study of college student development, including "*Toward what end should development in college be directed?*" (p. x, emphasis added). Might Sandoval's (2000) skills for oppositional actors constitute one possible "end" for college student development from a FemCrit perspective? If so, how might the development of these skills help us reimagine student affairs practice? For example, how might such an approach embolden college educators to coalesce around a more radical and emancipatory set of commitments to guide their practice? Or does the notion of directing development toward any particular end reflect exactly the sort of grand, patriarchal progress narrative that FemCrit would ask us to disrupt?

2. *Development* is frequently defined as increasing complexity in a student's meaning-making capacity (Baxter Magolda & King, 2012). In what ways might this definition exemplify the "celebratory stories of progress and heroism" that obfuscate "the failure of current governing systems and social norms to enable lived experiences of freedom" (Halberstam, 2011, p. 4, as cited in Anker, 2012, p. 208)?

3. To what extent are student development theorists seduced by the fictions of full comprehension and full representation (Visweswaran, 1994) such that we mask the partiality—the incompleteness and the unfairness—of our work? In what ways might engaging the art of failure open up new possibilities for using gender as an analytic for understanding and representing college students' lives?

4. FemCrit scholars have argued that knowing, being, and doing are inextricable from one another, produced by everyday life, embedded in multiple systems of oppression, and held in place by inequitable power relations. How, then, might we deconstruct and/or blur the boundaries between domains of development (e.g., cognitive, interpersonal, and intrapersonal) previously imagined as distinct?

References

Anker, E. (2012). Feminist theory and the failures of post-911 freedom. *Politics and Gender, 8*(2), 207–215.

Anzaldúa, G. (1999). *Borderlands/La Frontera: The New Mestiza* (2nd ed.). San Francisco, CA: Aunt Lute Books.

Baier, A. (1985). *Postures of the mind: Essays on mind and morals*. Minneapolis, MN: University of Minnesota Press.

Baxter Magolda, M. B., & King, P. M. (2012). Nudging minds to life: Self-authorship as a foundation for learning. In *Assessing meaning making and self-authorship: Theory, research, and application* (ASHE Higer Education Report, Vol. 3, pp. 1–19). San Francisco, CA: Jossey-Bass.

Butler, J. (1990). *Gender trouble: Feminism and the subversion of identity*. New York, NY: Routledge.

Caldwell, K. M. (1998). All that jazz talk: Possibilities for collaborative conversation in the college classroom. *Transformations, 9*(1), 1–9.

Code, L. (1991). *What can she know? Feminist theory and the construction of knowledge*. Ithaca, NY: Cornell University Press.

Cooks, L. M., & Simpson, J. S. (Eds.). (2008). *Whiteness, pedagogy, performance: Dis/placing race*. Lanham, MD: Lexington.

Cosgrove, L. (2003). Feminism, postmodernism, and psychological research. *Hypatia, 18*(3), 85–112.

DeSaxe, J. (2012). Conceptualizing critical feminist theory and emancipatory education. *Journal for Critical Education Policy Studies, 10*(2), 173–201.

Halberstam, J. (2011). *The queer art of failure*. Durham, NC: Duke University Press.

Knefelkamp, L. L., Widick, C., & Parker, C. A. (1978). Editors' notes: Why bother with theory? In L. L. Knefelkamp, C. Widick, & C. A. Parker (Eds.), *Applying new developmental findings* (New Directions for Student Services, No. 4, pp. vii–xvi). San Francisco, CA: Jossey-Bass.

Kristeva, J. (1981). Women's time (Alice Jardine and Harry Blake, Trans.). *Signs: Journal of Women in Culture and Society, 7*(1), 13–35.

Mills, P. J. (1994). Feminist critical theory: *Unruly practices: Power, discourse, and gender in contemporary social theory* and *Justice and the politics of difference* [Review of the books]. *Science and Society, 58*(2), 211–217.

Rhode, D. L. (1990). Feminist critical theories. *Stanford Law Review, 42*(3), 617–638.

Robbins, C. K., & McGowan, B. L. (2016). Intersectional perspectives on gender and gender identity development. In E. S. Abes (Ed.), *Critical perspectives on student development theory* (Vol. 154, pp. 71–83). San Francisco, CA: Jossey-Bass.

Ropers-Huilman, R., & Winters, K. T. (2011). Feminist research in higher education. *The Journal of Higher Education, 82*(6), 667–690.

Sandoval, C. (2000). *Methodology of the oppressed*. Minneapolis, MN: University of Minnesota Press.

Scott, J. W. (1992). The evidence of experience. *Critical Inquiry, 17*(4), 773–797.

Smith, J. B., & Niemi, N. (2017). Otherwise occupied: The complex relationships between gender and college attendance in late adolescence. *Gender Issues, 34*(2), 105–128.

Visweswaran, K. (1994). *Fictions of feminist ethnography.* Minneapolis, MN: University of Minnesota Press.

Weedon, C. (1987). *Feminist practice and poststructuralist theory.* New York, NY: Basil Blackwell.

Wing, A. (2003). *Critical race feminism: A reader* (2nd ed). New York, NY: New York University Press.

Zaytoun, K. (2006). Theorizing at the borders: Considering social location in rethinking self and psychological development. *NWSA Journal, 18*(2), 52–72.

5

INDIGENOUS PARADIGMS

Decolonizing College Student Development Theory Through Centering Relationality

Nicole Alia Salis Reyes and Maria Tauala

L iterature has suggested that higher education remains a contested terrain for Indigenous peoples (e.g., Brayboy, Fann, Castagno, & Solyom, 2012; Huffman, 2010; Kamehameha Schools, 2014; Kanaʻiaupuni, Malone, & Ishibashi, 2005). Despite high college-going aspirations, postsecondary enrollment and completion for Native Americans, Alaska Natives, and Native Hawaiians continue to lag behind other racial and ethnic groups (Brayboy et al., 2012; Kamehameha Schools, 2014; Kanaʻiaupuni et al., 2005). Wright (1991) argued that, given the ways that institutions of higher education have been used historically as vehicles for assimilation, it is no wonder that Native students do not enter higher education in large numbers. Within the halls of academia, Native students may find themselves in what Scott (1986) and Huffman (2010) called *a difficult situation*, feeling the pressure to adopt institutional norms through experiences of cultural discontinuity. These difficult experiences uncover differences not only in outward cultural practices but also between underlying white and Indigenous ways of being and of knowing.

Any steps taken toward transforming institutions of higher education in ways that are more supportive of the development of Native students must begin with a better understanding of Indigenous and decolonizing paradigms. With knowledge of such paradigms, postsecondary educators may gain new perspectives regarding who Native students are, what they hope to achieve, and how they might be better supported in remaining their authentic selves through the pursuit of their postsecondary goals. Moreover, these paradigms call attention to the ways in which colonization has shaped common conceptions of what college student development should entail. This attention may help to denaturalize the Eurocentric assumptions that often undergird student development theories, leaving room for more varied considerations of how all students, Native and non-Native, may be supported in their development through college.

In this chapter, we offer an overview of Indigenous and decolonizing paradigms, how they shape Native student development within higher education, and how they critically call into question the primacy of the individual that has been infused into dominant understandings of college student development.

What Are Indigenous and Decolonizing Paradigms?

Before describing Indigenous and decolonizing paradigms, it is important to recognize that they originate from and continue both to influence and be influenced by Indigenous peoples. Indigenous peoples are just that, *peoples*. They do not compose a monolithic group. Rather, they originate from diverse places and represent diverse nations, cultural systems, and languages (Cannon, 2011; Smith, 1999). The term *Indigenous peoples* emerged in the 1970s as a means for bringing together and empowering the collective voices of peoples who have experienced and continue to experience colonization (Smith, 1999). On this note, Dei (2011) suggested that the term is "about a political reclamation and self-definition to challenge Eurocentric dominance" (p. 23). In many ways, then, the term *Indigenous peoples* is inherently political, as it was developed through and as a means for enabling collective action against the hegemonic forces of colonization. Such action centers around processes of decolonization and Indigenization. Smith (1999) indicated that these processes may involve "a 'knowingness of the colonizer' and a recovery of ourselves, an analysis of colonialism, and struggle for self-determination" (p. 7). Processes of decolonization and Indigenization are about "rejection, resistance, subversiveness, pragmatism, ambivalence, accommodation, participation [and] cooperation" (Nakata, 2002, p. 285).

Considering the vast diversity that exists among Indigenous peoples, it follows then that there is no one Indigenous or decolonizing paradigm. Rather, there are many Indigenous paradigms, which are all grounded by distinct places, cultural knowledges, and experiences. Still, while there is great diversity among Indigenous paradigms, there are also some shared values, such as those of relationality, reciprocity, self-determination, and sovereignty, that ground many Indigenous paradigms. These values provide the foundation for interests in the maintenance of communal well-being and the dismantling of colonialism.

Relationality and Reciprocity

Perhaps more than any other concept, relationality seems to be at the heart of Indigenous and decolonizing paradigms. It emphasizes wholeness and balance through healthy connections with the surrounding world. These connections go far beyond interpersonal relationships (Wilson, 2008). To this end, Chilisa (2012) acknowledged that Indigenous peoples connect in many ways with many things: "They have connections with the living and the nonliving, with land, with the earth, with animals, and with other living beings" (p. 21). In his discussion of the nature of the production of knowledge, Wilson (2008) acknowledged "a relationship with all of creation. It is with the cosmos; it is with the animals, with plants, with the earth that we share this knowledge" (p. 56). Meyer (2008), in her review of Hawaiian epistemology, further offered,

> Existing in relationships triggers everything: with people, with ideas, with the natural world. . . . It marked a consciousness of the dialectic, a reckoning with what one brought to other. Relationship gave mentors opportunities to practice generosity with others, harmony with land, and ways to develop their own pathway to an idea. (p. 221)

In other words, from the perspective of Indigenous paradigms, we are, we know, and we do through our relationships with not only other people but also the natural and spiritual worlds. Our relationships root us and provide us with direction for growth. Thus, although a Western paradigm may tend to emphasize the centrality of the individual, Indigenous paradigms tend to emphasize the vitality of I–we relationships (Chilisa, 2012).

A value of reciprocity is closely tied to this concept of relationality. It suggests that when we benefit from the relationships that we share with others, then we too are responsible for paying those benefits forward to others. However, rather than quid pro quo, reciprocity, from the perspective of Indigenous paradigms, might entail "a sense that individuals must act outside of their self-interests for those of the community and work toward their own betterment for the community's sake" (Brayboy et al., 2012, p. 16). Engaging in reciprocity then becomes the act of actively and purposefully joining into cycles of interdependence with the end goal of continued communal *survivance*, which, more than mere survival, entails an active presence and resistance to erasure (Vizenor, 2008).

Self-Determination and Sovereignty

Furthermore, in a related way, Indigenous and decolonizing paradigms emphasize that Indigenous survivance relies on self-determination and sovereignty. This is because, though Indigenous peoples are often thought of as racial or ethnic groups, they also compose political entities that have governed themselves since time immemorial. Thus, they are connected through shared senses of nationhood (Brayboy, 2005; Salis Reyes, 2014).

Sovereignty has been conceptualized in many ways. Within what is now widely known as the United States, the status of Native nations' political relationships with the U.S. federal government often circumscribes notions of sovereignty. Federally recognized Native nations to some extent have the rights to maintain independent authority and to govern themselves while not being beholden to state laws (Brayboy et al., 2012). Cornell and Kalt (1998) argued that this political sovereignty is vital to the healthy economic development of Native nations. However, pointing to the tentative nature of a domestic dependent status that is circumscribed by U.S. federal authority, some argue more for the importance of cultural sovereignty (Coffey & Tsosie, 2001). Coffey and Tsosie (2001) defined *cultural sovereignty* as "the effort of Indian nations and Indian people to exercise their own norms and values in structuring their collective futures" (p. 196), regardless of the status of their formalized relationships with the U.S. government. In this case, the form that sovereignty takes will depend on the people themselves. *Ea*, which has multiple meanings but is often translated as *sovereignty* in ʻōlelo ʻŌiwi (Hawaiian language), provides an example of a specific, people-based understanding of sovereignty. Goodyear-Kaʻōpua (2014) suggested, "Ea is based on the experiences of people on the land, relationships forged through the process of remembering and caring for wahi pana, storied places" (p. 4). She further explained, "Like breathing, ea cannot be achieved or possessed; it requires constant action day after day, generation after generation" (p. 4). For Kānaka ʻŌiwi, then, ea cannot be taken away through law or politics because ea is about being. As long as we live and continue to carry out our *kuleana* (responsibilities) to our people, our lands, and our waters, we will always have our ea, and our ea, in turn, will always be strengthened through our living.

Brayboy et al. (2012) suggested that self-determination can be thought of as the operationalization of sovereignty. In other words, Indigenous peoples exercise sovereignty through their acts of self-determination. When viewed in relation to a political sovereignty that relies on the maintenance of trust relationships between Native nations and the federal government, self-determination is predicated on providing greater control to tribal citizens and their governments (Brayboy et al., 2012). More broadly, though, Indigenous peoples participate in processes of self-determination as they decide for themselves how best to move forward in thriving as nations (Salis Reyes, 2016).

How Do Indigenous and Decolonizing Paradigms Relate to College Student Development?

Although student development theories no longer explicitly emphasize individual autonomy as the end goal of development, they do still centralize it as a part of the developmental process. For example, although Chickering and Reisser (1993) revised their model of student development in an effort to acknowledge the importance of interdependence, a revised vector, "Moving Through Autonomy Toward Interdependence," still suggests that individual autonomy must be realized in order for further growth to be enabled. Emotional independence, which is a prerequisite for moving into this vector, first demands separation from familial ties, working under the assumption that "greater autonomy enables healthier forms of interdependence" (Chickering & Reisser, 1993, p. 47). Other theories (e.g., Astin, 1984; Baxter Magolda, 2009; Tinto, 1993) also similarly centralize the individual in the developmental process. Moreover, some (e.g., Astin, 1984; Tinto, 1993) suggest that college students are best able to realize their full potential when they spend as much time as possible on college campuses. All of this suggests that students must come to know themselves as individuals and in isolation from outside influences before coming to understand their interrelatedness with others in a positive way. This conceptualization may align with individualistic cultural orientations but may clash with collectivistic cultural orientations (Guiffrida, Kiyama, Waterman, & Museus, 2012).

Indigenous and decolonizing paradigms, for example, highlight how Indigenous peoples make sense of themselves *through* the world around them. When Indigenous students set foot on college campuses, this sensemaking does not change. Indigenous and decolonizing paradigms continue to shape Indigenous college students' understandings of their experiences and objectives for participating in higher education. Knowledge of these paradigms can help disrupt normative notions of what college student development should look like and suggest other possibilities of how college students may develop.

Home-going behaviors, defined "as returning home frequently while attending a residential post-secondary institution" (Waterman, 2012, p. 194), provide an example of how caring for familial and communal relationships can be instrumental in some students' journeys through college. Waterman (2012) found that Haudenosaunee students who attended school away from home engaged in home-going behaviors in order to fulfill their familial responsibilities and to participate in traditional ceremonies. Some might expect that home-going behaviors would hinder academic success and development by pulling students away from the college environment and thereby increasing their time to graduation or even leading them to drop out. However, for the Haudenosaunee students in Waterman's study, home-going was essential for maintaining a strong sense of self. It empowered them to persevere in their studies in the face of challenges (Waterman, 2012).

Giving back provides another example of how some students may come to gain a sense of purpose through the roles that they take in serving others. In previous work, I (Salis Reyes, 2016) spoke to Native college graduates who represented various nations, educational backgrounds, and fields about how they gave back and what giving back meant to them. Participants recognized the opportunity to attend college as a great gift that many had a hand in making possible. That being the case, participants also felt a responsibility to use the skills, knowledge, and networks that they developed during college to contribute to the health and well-being of their home communities and/or to Indigenous peoples more broadly. In many ways, then, these Native college graduates attended college not only for themselves but also for their families and their peoples. They completed college so that they could be better or differently equipped to serve others and help (re)build their and other Native nations (Salis Reyes, 2016).

These examples highlight how Native college students continue to see themselves as inextricably linked to others even when higher education is often constructed as a tool that might be leveraged toward individual consumerism and competition rather than democratic participation (Giroux, 2002). In many ways, such a neoliberal construction of higher education and the developmental aims of higher education may by and large serve to (re)produce social inequities. If students are coaxed and prodded to become highly independent individuals through isolated developmental processes, then they may be inadequately prepared to see their full potential in contributing to a greater good beyond their own upward mobility. In conceptualizing the process of student development as requiring movement toward individual autonomy and away from reliance on connections outside of the college or university, student development theory overlooks that Indigenous students, who often are centered by relationships and driven by interests in Indigenous sovereignty, often develop through the relationships that they share with others, including many who are outside the ivory towers of academia. Others who come from collectivist cultures may be driven in similar ways.

Indeed, this conceptualization of student development theory in many ways may maintain higher education's role as a tool for assimilation and perpetuate colonization, thus maintaining a rigid understanding of development to which all students are held subject. Indigenous ways of knowing and being can clash with underlying assumptions of college student development theory, creating campus environments in which Native and perhaps other students' ways of knowing are understood not only as less than but also as impediments to development and success. Thus, to fall in line with such notions of student development, "collectivist students may be required to abandon salient elements of their cultural identities and traditions if they wish to become successful at PWIs" (Guiffrida et al., 2012, p. 70) and possibly other kinds of institutional environments as well.

Indigenous and decolonizing paradigms point to the need to decolonize and Indigenize the ways in which we think about college student development. They call us to reconceptualize and broaden our understanding of development by considering home-going behaviors as valid pathways to development rather than barriers and to support giving back as a valid motivation to enter and succeed within higher education. Indigenous paradigms call us to involve much more than individual cognitive growth in our practice. Instead, developmental goals may also be tied to maintaining and contributing to the values and relationships that students bring with them to higher education. Actively involving students' families and communities in the developmental process rather than encouraging or requiring separation from these groups might serve to recognize and engage interpersonal strengths that would otherwise go unrecognized or be considered inconsistent with Eurocentric values and norms (Champagne, 2004; Guiffrida et al., 2012; Guillory & Wolverton, 2008). This and similar shifts in practice, rooted in a broader understanding of development, may serve to create space for Native students and students from other collectivistic cultural orientations to succeed in higher education. They may also help students from individualistic cultural orientations to realize earlier the importance of relationships and interdependence in their development. Thus, they may also contribute to increased capacities for Native nation-building, broader democratic participation, and social justice.

Discussion Questions

1. How can student development theories better account for the ways that students may develop not in isolation but through their relationships with others?
2. How can the end goals of student development be reconceptualized to align more with values of relationality, reciprocity, self-determination, and sovereignty?
3. How could a more decolonized/Indigenized conception of student development theory differently shape common practices in student and academic affairs?

References

Astin, A. W. (1984). Student involvement: A developmental theory for higher education. *Journal of College Student Personnel, 25,* 297–308.

Baxter Magolda, M. B. (2009). *Authoring your life: Developing an internal voice to navigate life's challenges.* Sterling, VA: Stylus.

Brayboy, B. M. J. (2005). Toward a tribal critical race theory in education. *The Urban Review, 37*(5), 425–446.

Brayboy, B. M. J., Fann, A. J., Castagno, A. E., & Solyom, J. A. (2012). Postsecondary education for American Indian and Alaska natives: Higher education for nation building and self-determination. *ASHE Higher Education Report, 37*(5).

Cannon, M. (2011). Ruminations on red revitalization: Exploring complexities of identity, difference and nationhood in Indigenous education. In G. J. S. Dei (Ed.), *Indigenous philosophies and critical education: A reader* (pp. 125–141). New York, NY: Peter Lang.

Champagne, D. (2004). Education for nation-building. *Cultural Survival Quarterly, 27*(4).

Chickering, A. W., & Reisser, L. (1993). *Education and identity* (2nd ed.). San Francisco, CA: Jossey-Bass.

Chilisa, B. (2012). *Indigenous research methodologies.* Thousand Oaks, CA: Sage.

Coffey, W., & Tsosie, R. (2001). Rethinking the tribal sovereignty doctrine: Cultural sovereignty and the collective future of Indian nations. *Stanford Law and Policy Review, 12*(2), 191–221.

Cornell, S., & Kalt, J. P. (1998). Sovereignty and nation-building: The development challenge in Indian Country today. *American Indian Culture and Research Journal, 22*(3), 187–214.

Dei, G. J. S. (2011). Revisiting the question of "Indigenous." In G. J. S. Dei (Ed.), *Indigenous philosophies and critical education: A reader* (pp. 21–33). New York, NY: Peter Lang.

Giroux, H. (2002). Neoliberalism, corporate culture, and the promise of higher education: The university as a democratic public sphere. *Harvard Educational Review, 72*(4), 425–463.

Goodyear-Kaʻōpua, N. (2014). Introduction. In N. Goodyear-Kaʻōpua, I. Hussey, & E. K. Wright (Eds.), *A nation rising: Hawaiian movements for life, land, and sovereignty* (pp. 1–33). Durham, NC: Duke University Press.

Guiffrida, D. A., Kiyama, J. M., Waterman, S. J., & Museus, S. D. (2012). Moving from cultures of individualism to cultures of collectivism in support of Students of Color. In S. D. Museus & U. M. Jayakumar (Eds.), *Creating campus cultures: Fostering success among racially diverse student populations* (pp. 68–87). New York, NY: Routledge.

Guillory, R. M., & Wolverton, M. (2008). It's about family: Native American student persistence in higher education. *Journal of Higher Education, 79*(1), 58–87.

Huffman, T. E. (2010). *Theoretical perspectives on American Indian education: Taking a new look at academic success and the achievement gap.* Lanham, MD: Altamira Press.

Kamehameha Schools. (2014). *Ka huakaʻi: 2014 Native Hawaiian educational assessment.* Honolulu, HI: Kamehameha Publishing.

Kanaʻiaupuni, S. K., Malone, N., & Ishibashi, K. (2005). *Ka huakaʻi: 2005 Native Hawaiian educational assessment.* Honolulu, HI: Kamehameha Schools, Pauahi Publications.

Meyer, M. A. (2008). Indigenous and authentic: Hawaiian epistemology and the triangulation of meaning. In N. K. Denzin, Y. S. Lincoln, & L. T. Smith (Eds.), *Handbook of critical and Indigenous methodologies* (pp. 217–232). Thousand Oaks, CA: Sage.

Nakata, M. (2002). Indigenous knowledge and the cultural interface: Underlying issues at the intersection of knowledge and information systems. *IFLA Journal, 28*(5-6), 281–291.

Salis Reyes, N. A. (2014). The multiplicity and intersectionality of Indigenous identities. In D. Mitchell Jr., C. Y. Simmons, & L. A. Greyerbiehl (Eds.), *Intersectionality in higher education: Theory, research, and praxis* (pp. 45–54). New York, NY: Peter Lang.

Salis Reyes, N. A. (2016). *"What am I doing to be a good ancestor?" An Indigenized phenomenology of giving back among Native college graduates* (Doctoral dissertation). Retrieved from ProQuest Dissertations and Theses database. (ProQuest No. 10127227).

Scott, W. J. (1986). Attachment to Indian culture and the "difficult situation": A study of American Indian college students. *Youth and Society, 17*(4), 381–395.

Smith, L. T. (1999). *Decolonizing methodologies: Research and Indigenous peoples.* New York, NY: Zed Books.

Tinto, V. (1993). *Leaving college: Rethinking the causes and cures of student attrition.* Chicago, IL: University of Chicago Press.

Vizenor, G. (Ed.). (2008). *Survivance: Narratives of Native presence.* Lincoln, NE: University of Nebraska Press.

Waterman, S. J. (2012). Home-going as a strategy for success among Haudenosaunee college and university students. *Journal of Student Affairs Research and Practice, 49*(2), 193–209.

Wilson, S. (2008). *Research is ceremony: Indigenous research methods.* Winnipeg, Manitoba, Canada: Fernwood.

Wright, B. (1991). The "untamable savage spirit": American Indians in colonial colleges. *The Review of Higher Education, 14*(4), 429–452.

6

QUEER THEORY

Deconstructing Sexual and Gender Identity, Norms, and Developmental Assumptions

J. Michael Denton

What might change and be possible if sex, sexuality, and gender are not, in fact, natural or biologically determined states of being but rather the result of societal institutions? In what ways do cultural and institutional norms and representations (i.e., discourses) of sex, sexuality, and gender constrain, regulate, and make possible various ways of life for people? Although the body of work commonly called *queer theory* has existed for decades, these kinds of questions are still relatively new and underutilized in student development theory. Understanding poststructuralism is helpful in understanding queer theory. Poststructuralism and constructivism (the paradigm for much student development theory) both claim that reality is socially constructed. However, while constructivism seeks to understand the world, poststructuralism seeks to critique the world (Lather, 2006). Constructivists understand that multiple truths exist, but poststructuralists take that idea further, viewing supposed truths as inherently flawed, relative, arbitrary, and rooted in false binaries (Lather, 2006). Abes and Kasch (2007) were the first to apply ideas from queer theory to student development theory. Since then, only a few others have rethought student development using queer theory (see Denton, 2016). As such, research and practice about college student sexuality and gender have not grappled with the challenges presented by queer theory.

Foundational Ideas in Queer Theory

The influence of Foucault's (1990) first volume of *The History of Sexuality* on queer theory cannot be understated. Foucault revealed how, in the wake of seeming sexual repression, social institutions have produced an abundance of thought about sex and (arbitrarily) positioned sexuality as an essential truth of the self. As multiple social institutions (e.g., medicine, government, law, education) increasingly focused on sexuality as a central, crucial dimension of human life, they produced certain new categories. One of these categories was the homosexual. Although individuals have engaged in same-sex sex and relationships throughout history, the identity of *homosexual* did not previously exist. This new category allowed for new and different forms of violence, stigma, and oppression but also enabled individuals to form communities and organize politically around this identity category.

Following Foucault's work, Rubin (2011) described the sex hierarchy that exists in U.S. society. In this hierarchy, certain forms of sexuality and relationships are elevated as ideal and normal (e.g., private, married, heterosexual, monogamous, procreative, nonkinky sex). Same-sex, promiscuous, kinky, nonprocreative, paid, public, and other forms of sex that differ from the privileged forms are marginalized and labeled abnormal. What forms of sex and desire are privileged and valued change over time within a society, but Rubin reminded us to question *why* certain kinds of sex are considered healthy and normal and others are not. Sedgwick (1990) took Foucault's ideas even further, examining and exploding various binaries around sexuality. Sedgwick demonstrated that heterosexuality is as much of a construct as homosexuality, reliant on the suppressed existence of homosexuality to maintain its legitimacy as the natural, normal, and preferred form of relationships in society. Butler's (2006) concept of *performativity* is another foundational concept of queer theory, which I cover later.

Queer theory has often been criticized for failing to interrogate whiteness. Queer of Color critique is "made up of women of color feminism, materialist analysis, poststructural theory, and queer critique" that directly addresses issues of race, class, gender, and sexuality (Ferguson, 2004, p. 149). Queer of Color critique includes specific strands of thought such as quare theory, or Black queer studies (Johnson, 2005), and jotería studies, inquiry that "centers on . . . mestiza/o subjectivities" (Pérez, 2014). At the heart of Queer of Color critique is that race and class differences among queers must be of paramount importance in analysis and political action (Cohen, 2005). For example, Cohen (2005) strongly criticized the concept of identity fluidity as it is steeped in class privilege and appears "to ignore the ways in which some traditional social identities and communal ties can, in fact, be important to one's survival" (p. 34). Following Hames-García (2001), who argued that distinguishing Queer of Color critique from queer theory marginalizes the contributions of Queers of Color to queer theory, I draw no further distinctions between these bodies of thought.

Queer theoretical writing can be dense and complicated. As one student put it, trying to understand queer theory can be like trying to nail Jell-O to a tree. Although primary texts should be read, the overviews of Jagose (1996), Turner (2000), Sullivan (2003), and Wilchins (2014) may prove helpful.

Queering Student Development

Student development theory is often framed using three developmental domains (i.e., epistemological, interpersonal, and intrapersonal) identified by Baxter Magolda (2001). Baxter Magolda, Abes, and Torres (2008) represented these domains with these questions: How do I know? How do I relate to others? Who am I? Queer theorists ask different questions. Through the lens of queer theory, "How do I know?" becomes "What kind of exercise of power are certain truth and knowledge claims?" Interpersonally, queer theorists do ask questions about desire and relationships but often ask, "What kinds of citizens should queer folks be?" Finally, queer theorists ask, "What cultural, historical, and institutional discourses (i.e., modes of representation through language or image) produce certain identities?" The following sections briefly describe major themes in how queer theorists have approached these questions. First, I overview Foucault's notion of knowledge as an exercise of power. Next, I introduce the various ways queer citizenry in a heteronormative society is theorized. Finally, I look at the way queer theory corrodes the concept of identity. Student development theory tends to foreground individuals and their inner psychological processes. Queer theory places more focus on how institutions, society, and culture police and shape people's sexuality and gender. Inner psychological processes are eschewed in favor of queer people's outward expressions, cultural practices (e.g., drag balls, diva worship, artistic works), and relationship to larger society.

Power/Knowledge and the Construction of Sexuality and Gender

Foucault (1980) framed truth and knowledge as an exercise of power within specific sociopolitical contexts. To oversimplify, truth is a political product of various institutions, and the effects of our societal truths need to be understood. Foucault's focus on the invention of sexuality and its prominence in human life by modern Western institutions provided a key insight into denaturalizing heterosexuality and homosexuality. Sedgwick (1990) elaborated that attempting to establish coherent taxonomies or identities around sexuality or gender, even for antihomophobic purposes, ignores "overlapping, contradictory, and conflictual definitional forces" (p. 45) present in modern society. Creating knowledge is an act of power that can have damaging effects on individuals whose sexualities and genders are excluded. Consequently, queer analysis shifts the focus from individuals to institutions and societal values that position some people as normal and others as deviant (Eng, Halberstam, & Muñoz, 2005).

Heteronormative Culture and Queer Citizens

Queer theorists often focus on the cultural, national, and societal context in which queer people live. Foundational to queer theory is a challenge to *heteronormativity*, or heterosexual culture (Cohen, 2005; Warner, 1993). Heteronormative culture "thinks of itself as the elemental form of human association, as the very model of intergender relations, as the indivisible basis of all community, and as the means of reproduction without which society wouldn't exist" (Warner, 1993, p. xxi). The presence or lack of (safe) public space for queer people and activities in heteronormative society is another concern of queer theorists (Warner, 1993, 1999). For example, Namaste (1996) examined the often-violent policing of perceived gender transgressions in public spaces. Berlant and Warner (1998) examined the material (e.g., urban gentrification) and discursive (e.g., representing immigrants as threats) ways public space has been denied or taken away from queer people in the name of protecting heteronormative values.

Queer theory also concerns itself with the ways in which queer people perpetuate and assimilate into heteronormative culture and other oppressive and violent activities of society. Duggan (2003) called gay assimilation into heteronormative and corporate consumerist culture *homonormativity*. The queer collective Against Equality (Conrad, 2014) asserted that assimilation may advantage a few queer people but leaves oppressive heteronormative culture and institutions fundamentally unchanged. Similarly, *homonationalism* is when queer liberal politics are complicit with the United States' exploitation of other nations, along with xenophobic national policies and treatment of immigrants and foreign nationals (Puar, 2007).

Another line of thought theorizes broader questions about the responsibilities of queer citizens. Some theorists have developed what is often called the "antisocial thesis" (Caserio, Edelman, Halberstam, Muñoz, & Dean, 2006), which emphasizes the ethical imperative of queer people to reject assimilation and resist conforming to forms of "good" citizenship, heteronormative culture, and ideals of future progress. Conversely, Muñoz (1999) asserted that queerness is about futurity and collectivity. This rejection of the antisocial thesis asserts that queer people have a "responsibility to democratic, anti-capitalist, and anti-imperialist progress" (Caserio et al., 2006, p. 820). Questions about queers' social positioning often bleed into questions about identity, because queer theorists understand identity as a product of institutional and societal discourses.

Identity Corrosion

As mentioned previously, queer thought questions essentialized claims about sexual and gender identity. Queer theorists challenge political and medical discourses that sexual and gender identity are products solely of biological factors. Although individuals often experience their sexual and gender identities as innate, unchosen, and ingrained, these feelings and identities exist within a specific historical period that limits and/or provides access to certain ways (e.g., categories, nomenclature, cultural norms) for making meaning of feelings, desires, fantasies, and identities. As Foucault (1990) pointed out, prior to Victorian-era concerns about family and reproduction, same-sex sex acts occurred, but the identity *homosexual* did not. This new discourse asserted that sexuality was an important aspect of people's lives that required intensive study and investigation. A change occurred where sexuality was newly understood as expressing a fundamental truth about an individual, a perspective that retains dominance in Western society today.

Butler (1993, 2004, 2006) introduced the concept of *performativity*. Performativity means that individuals repeat actions, movements, gestures, and other stylistic choices in ways that society genders and sexes. In the documentary *Examined Life* (Mann, Basmajian, & Taylor, 2008), Butler recounted the case of Charlie Howard, a young man killed for walking down the street with a "swish." Butler asked, "How could it be that somebody's gait, somebody's style of walking, could engender the desire to kill that person?" Layered in Butler's question are several important ideas: the ways we use and move our bodies convey or—more precisely—are imbued with gendered meanings, certain uses of the body are limited based on a person's (perceived and self-identified) gender, and transgression of dominant prescriptions of masculinity and femininity will often result in various social sanctions, including deadly violence. Performativity does not mean that people's stylistic acts are inauthentic or even chosen but rather describes how those actions communicate gender, as interpreted through societal norms. The inability to repeat the ways in which we gesture, walk, move, dress, groom, or talk with exactitude points to the arbitrary markers and norms society imputes to gender. If gender is then arbitrarily defined and substantially incoherent, then socially sanctioned opportunities for multiple genders and expressions of gender should open, and oppression and violence based on gender should end. As gender categories are disrupted, so too are categories of sexual identification (e.g., gay–straight).

The implication of Butler's (and Foucault's) thesis is that appeals to identity as inborn, natural, and beyond societal influence obscure the oppressive social and institutional contexts in which identity definitions and categories are formed (Talburt, 2000). Queer theorists understand queerness as exceeding identity categories. As Halperin (2012) explained, "Same-sex desire alone does not equal gayness . . . gayness [is] . . . a mode of perception, an attitude, an ethos; in short, it is a practice" (pp. 12–13). Muñoz conceptualized the self-fashioning practice of Queers of Color as *disidentification*, a navigation of the "cultural logics of heteronormativity, white supremacy, and misogyny" (Muñoz, 1999, p. 5). To disidentify is neither to identify with available cultural identity discourses nor to oppose them. To resist dominant identity discourses legitimizes those identities; disidentification tries to transform shameful aspects of the self into something "sexy and glamorous" (Muñoz, 1999, p. 3). Disidentification is one theory about how Queers of Color navigate identity discourses; more broadly, queer theorists deconstruct identity categories, making much of queer theory "identity corrosive" (M. Detloff, personal communication, 2014).

The Challenges and Possibilities of Queer Theory

Queer theory is not one line of unified thought and covers much more ground than permitted here. In summary, queer theory deviates significantly from developmental theory. Queer theory challenges the epistemological and theoretical assumptions of student development theory yet offers new domains and horizons of focus (e.g., society, the nation). Queer critique can help scholars and practitioners consider how even well-intentioned knowledge production (e.g., scholarship, programs) exercises power in ways that may exclude students who do not fit current hetero- and homonormative binaries of sexual and gender identity. In short, queer theory challenges linear and stable notions of development and opens up possibilities for thinking beyond identity categories. Given these challenges and possibilities, I pose the following questions.

Discussion Questions

1. Although some scholars of student development have used queer theory, what are the tensions, contradictions, and challenges in using queer theory to theorize student development? What are the advantages or possibilities for using queer theory?

2. How can the concept of heteronormativity inform sexual and gender identity development research and higher education programming and policies?

3. How do identity-focused studies reify oppressive social and institutional discourses? How does centering identity fail to capture the complexity of sexual and gender experiences? Which students remain unintelligible when identity is the unit of inquiry?

4. How might practitioners' and scholars' cultural biases result in oppressive, normative judgments about students' sexual and gender behaviors and practices?

References

Abes, E. S., & Kasch, D. (2007). Using queer theory to explore lesbian college students' multiple dimensions of identity. *Journal of College Student Development*, *48*(6), 619–636.

Baxter Magolda, M. B. (2001). *Making their own way: Narratives for transforming higher education to promote self-authorship*. Sterling, VA: Stylus.

Baxter Magolda, M. B., Abes, E., & Torres, V. (2008). Epistemological, intrapersonal, and interpersonal development in the college years and young adulthood. In M. C. Smith & N. Defrates-Densch (Eds.), *Handbook of research on adult learning and development* (pp. 183–219). New York, NY: Routledge.

Berlant, L., & Warner, M. (1998). Sex in public. *Critical Inquiry*, *24*(2), 547–566.

Butler, J. (1993). *Bodies that matter: On the discursive limits of sex*. New York, NY: Routledge.

Butler, J. (2004). *Undoing gender*. New York, NY: Routledge.

Butler, J. (2006). *Gender trouble*. New York, NY: Routledge. (Original work published 1990).

Caserio, R. L., Edelman, L., Halberstam, J., Muñoz, J. E., & Dean, T. (2006). The antisocial thesis in queer theory. *PMLA*, *121*, 819–828.

Cohen, C. (2005). Punks, bulldaggers, and welfare queens: The radical potential of queer politics? In E. P. Johnson & M. G. Henderson (Eds.), *Black queer studies* (pp. 21–51). Durham, NC: Duke University Press.

Conrad, R. (Ed.). (2014). *Against equality: Queer revolution, not mere inclusion*. Oakland, CA: AK Press.

Denton, J. M. (2016). Critical and poststructural perspectives on sexual identity development. In E. S. Abes (Ed.), *Critical perspectives on student development theory* (New Directions for Student Services, No. 154, pp. 57–69). San Francisco, CA: Jossey-Bass.

Duggan, L. (2003). *The twilight of equality? Neoliberalism, cultural politics, and the attack on democracy*. Boston, MA: Beacon Press.

Eng, D. L., Halberstam, J., & Muñoz, J. E. (2005). Introduction: What's queer about queer studies now? *Social Text, 3–4*(84–85), 1–17.

Ferguson, R. A. (2004). *Aberrations in black: Toward a Queer of Color critique.* Minneapolis, MN: University of Minnesota Press.

Foucault, M. (1980). *Power/knowledge.* New York, NY: Vintage Books.

Foucault, M. (1990). *The history of sexuality: An introduction.* New York, NY: Vintage Books.

Halperin, D. M. (2012). *How to be gay.* Cambridge, MA: Harvard University Press.

Hames-García, M. (2001). Can queer theory be critical theory? In W. S. Wilkerson & J. Paris (Eds.), *New critical theory: Essays on liberation* (pp. 201–222). Lanham, MD: Rowman & Littlefield.

Jagose, A. (1996). *Queer theory: An introduction.* New York, NY: New York University Press.

Johnson, E. P. (2005). Quare studies, or (almost) everything I know about queer studies I learned from my grandmother. In pp. E. P. Johnson & M. G. Henderson (Eds.), *Black queer studies* (pp. 124–157). Durham, NC: Duke University Press.

Lather, P. (2006). Paradigm proliferation as a good thing to think with: Teaching research in education as a wild profusion. *International Journal of Qualitative Studies in Education, 19*(1), 35–57.

Mann, R., Basmajian, S. (Producers) & Taylor, A. (Director). (2008). *Examined life.* Canada: Zeitgeist Films.

Muñoz, J. E. (1999). *Disidentifications: Queers of Color and the performance of politics.* Minneapolis, MN: University of Minnesota Press.

Namaste, K. (1996). Genderbashing: Sexuality, gender, and the regulation of public space. *Environment and Planning D: Society and Space, 14*(2), 221–240.

Pérez, D. E. (2014). Jotería epistemologies: Mapping a research agenda, unearthing a lost heritage, and building "quer Aztlán." *Aztlán: A Journal of Chicano Studies, 39*(1), 143–154.

Puar, J. K. (2007). *Terrorist assemblages: Homonationalism in queer times.* Durham, NC: Duke University Press.

Rubin, G. S. (2011). Thinking sex. In G. S. Rubin (Ed.), *Deviations: A Gayle Rubin reader* (pp. 137–181). Durham, NC: Duke University Press (Original work published 1984).

Sedgwick, E. K. (1990). *Epistemology of the closet.* Berkeley, CA: University of California Press.

Sullivan, N. (2003). *A critical introduction to queer theory.* New York, NY: New York University Press.

Talburt, S. (2000). *Subject to identity: Knowledge, sexuality and academic practices in higher education.* Albany, NY: SUNY Press.

Turner, W. (2000). *A genealogy of queer theory.* Philadelphia, PA: Temple University Press.

Warner, M. (Ed.). (1993). *Fear of a queer planet: Queer politics and social theory.* Minneapolis, MN: University of Minnesota Press.

Warner, M. (1999). *The trouble with normal: Sex, politics, and the ethics of queer life.* Cambridge, MA: Harvard University Press.

Wilchins, R. (2014). *Queer theory, gender theory.* New York, NY: Magnus Books.

7

CRIP THEORY

Dismantling Ableism in Student Development Theory

Elisa S. Abes

D isabled college students who make their way to ableist college campuses are necessarily resilient. Yet, little is known about the nature of their development while in college, because disability has received limited attention in the first and second waves of student development theory literature, as described in chapter 1 of this book. Not surprising, then, as the field moves into a third wave, crip theory, a poststructural theory that critiques the dominant discourses that shape the meaning of disability (Kafer, 2013; McRuer, 2006), is nearly absent from the emerging literature about critical perspectives on student development theory.

To reveal the potential of using crip theory to reimagine student development theory that centers disabled students, I review in this chapter crip theory's key ideas. With an eye on how crip theory can reshape the theoretical constructs described in the next part of this book, these key ideas are organized using the domains of holistic student development: intrapersonal, cognitive, and interpersonal (Baxter Magolda, 2001). Organizing the ideas in this way shows how crip theory can be used to not only critique existing student development theories but also, more important, open up new possibilities for the meaning of development that are not centered in ableist norms, as well as to understand and support disabled students. This chapter concludes with questions to consider when reimagining student development theory using crip theory. Above all, I urge in this chapter strong consideration of how crip theory, a perspective critiqued by some as too "academic," can be applied in a way that is liberatory and empowering for disabled students.

Before I proceed with this chapter, it is important to clarify why I use the identity-first language *disabled college students* rather than the more typical person-first language *college students who are disabled*. Person-first language emphasizes personhood rather than disability. This phrasing is the preference of many individuals and is often considered the language that should be used when addressing a disabled person who has not expressed a language preference (Linton, 1998). Identity-first language, which is growing in preference, emphasizes disability as a social construction. In doing so, it highlights how ableist norms rather than medical impairment determine who is disabled (Brown, 2011; Linton, 1998). Given crip theory's aim to expose and dismantle ableist discourse, as described in the following, I use identity-first language to reinforce that ableism assigns meaning to reality.

Poststructuralism, Crip Theory, and Queer Theory

Poststructuralism reveals how the language and symbols, or discourse, of social institutions, such as government, education, and religion, construct and maintain power (Lather, 2007). Poststructural analysis deconstructs these dominant discourses, exposing and critiquing how they structure reality (Lather, 2007). Within poststructuralism, Sandahl (2003), McRuer (2006), and Kafer (2013) have written much of the scholarship on crip theory. These three scholars explain that crip theory grew out of queer theory, also a poststructural theory, and it shares ideas with queer theory related to its challenges to dominant discourses that define who and what are normal and to the fluid and contested nature of identity. Crip theory highlights the interrelationship between disability and queerness. For example, disabled people and queer people share histories of being demonized by religion and pathologized by medicine and generally are considered abnormal (Sandahl, 2003). "'Defective,' 'deviant,' and 'sick' have been used to justify discrimination against people whose bodies, minds, desires, and practices differ from the unmarked norm" (Kafer, 2013, p. 17). Ableist and heterosexist systems are bound together not only in their shared history of injustice but also because people who do not fit heterosexual norms have often been deemed disabled. Deviating from normative sexuality and gender, their bodies are rendered abnormal (Kafer, 2013; McRuer, 2006; Sandahl, 2003).

Compulsory Able-Bodiedness and Able-Mindedness

A central concept of crip theory is compulsory able-bodiedness and able-mindedness (Kafer, 2013; McRuer, 2006). Just as heterosexism maintains "compulsory heterosexuality," which is the systemic assumption and enforcement of heterosexuality that renders abnormal and erases nonheterosexual identities (Rich, 1980), ableism maintains compulsory able-bodiedness

(McRuer, 2006) and able-mindedness (Kafer, 2013). Compulsory able-bodiedness and able-mindedness are the dominant discourses that constantly push people toward a normalcy that few can achieve and determines who is disabled and therefore less worthy (Kafer, 2013; McRuer, 2006).

Crip theory critiques the discourses of compulsory able-bodiedness and able-mindedness and the resulting disabled–nondisabled binary that deems disability abnormal (Kafer, 2013; McRuer, 2006). By critiquing this push toward an idealized normality, crip theory reveals the "plethora of unruly possibilities for thinking about the body outside normative restrictions about what a body should be" (Erevelles, 2013, p. 35). To "crip" is to expose discourses of compulsory able-bodiedness and able-mindedness, not only in contexts where disability is purposefully explored but also in contexts not explicitly focused on disability (McRuer, 2006). Cripping "spins mainstream representations or practices to reveal able-bodied assumptions and exclusionary effects" (Sandahl, 2003, p. 37). To crip student development theory, then, is to expose theoretical discourses that privilege able bodies and minds, pushing students toward an idealized normal. To consider how crip theory reshapes student development theory, I describe crip theory's key ideas in the next three sections in relationship to domains of holistic development: identity, knowledge, and relationships identified by Baxter Magolda (2001).

Contested Crip Identity

By critiquing the normative discourses that create an oppressive disabled–nondisabled binary, crip theory destabilizes the meaning of disability, presenting it as a contested, fluid identity. Crip theory explores the tension between "claiming crip" as an identity and perpetuating oppressive narratives associated with categorizing disability as an identity (Kafer, 2013; McRuer, 2006; Sandahl, 2003). To "claim crip" means to identify as disabled regardless of a specific diagnosis. Doing so purposefully blurs the boundaries between disabled and nondisabled categories. Claiming crip is an act of resistance, sometimes done, for instance, by children of deaf adults, friends of disabled people, or others who identify with the cultural aspect of disability such as dance and shared community (Brown, 2002). This form of resistance pushes back against the dominant discourses that define disability and maintain compulsory able-bodiedness and able-mindedness. Claiming crip is "a way of acknowledging that we all have bodies and minds with shifting abilities, and wrestling with the political meanings and histories of such shifts" (Kafer, 2013, p. 13).

At the same time, claiming crip risks categorizing disability, which feeds into ableist discourses that insist on and place value on the categories of disabled and nondisabled. Claiming crip also runs the risk of erasing the line between disabled and nondisabled that can be necessary to challenge disability-based discrimination (Kafer, 2013). Kafer explained that "to claim crip critically is to recognize the ethical, epistemic, and political responsibilities behind such claims: deconstructing the binary between disabled and able-bodied/able-minded requires more attention to how different bodies/minds are treated differently, not less" (Kafer, 2013, p. 13). Using a slightly different approach, Schalk (2013), who described herself as a "fat, Black, queer woman," identified "with" crip rather than "as" crip to encourage coalition-building among multiple marginalized identities who resist normality.

Further adding to the tension regarding the nature of disability identity, crip theory destabilizes the meaning of disability but does not "dematerialize disability identity" (McRuer, 2006, p. 35). That is, crip theory simultaneously contests the meaning of disability identity and recognizes that identity politics are necessary for survival for those with marginalized identities (Schalk, 2013). This both–and approach is similar to the Quare of Color poststructural critique of identity, briefly discussed in chapter 6 of this book, that destabilizes without dematerializing identity (Ferguson, 2004). Regardless of the position on the nature of disability as identity, crip theory consistently challenges how compulsory able-bodiedness and able-mindedness are at the root of these tensions. Contesting the meaning of identity by challenging ableist and value-laden binaries opens up new ways of thinking about the meaning of disability identity and development.

Knowledge Through Cripistemology

In addition to contesting the nature of disability identity, crip theory offers perspectives on the nature of knowledge. Johnson and McRuer (2014a) described a crip epistemology they called "cripistemology." Drawing on the lineage of Black feminist scholars' standpoint theory (e.g., Collins, 1990), cripistemology is the critical, social, and personal knowledge production from the perspectives of disabled people. Cripistemology requires "thinking the unthinkable" based on disabled "knowledge of bodies" and "bodies of knowledge" previously invisible and unknowable using ableist norms (Erevelles, 2013, p. 37). Likewise, cripistemology embraces the multiple ways that minds produce and make sense of knowledge (Johnson & McRuer, 2014b).

Cripistemology embraces crip failure and crip time. Drawing from Halberstam's (2011) queer art of failure, described also in chapter 4 of this book, crip failure makes visible the productive potential in failing ableist, normalizing cultural and educational practices (Mitchell, Snyder, & Ware,

2014). Crip failure transforms failure within ableist norms into a meaningful way to introduce nonnormative ways of knowledge production. Related to crip failure is the notion of crip time. Drawing from Halberstam's (2005) notion of queer temporalities that reimagine the order and time lines of life, crip time challenges the normalized and disabling pace of life (Kafer, 2013; Samuels, 2017). Crip time means more than an extension that allows disabled people more time—rather it is "a challenge to normative and normalizing expectations of pace and scheduling. Rather than bend disabled bodies and minds to meet the clock, crip time bends the clock to meet disabled bodies and minds" (Kafer, 2013, p. 27). By opening up new ways of knowledge production, cripistemology, including crip failure and crip time, challenges the neoliberal practice of making disabled identities undesirable because they are unproductive (McRuer, 2006). These new possibilities for knowledge production lend themselves to reshaping student development theory.

The Intimacies of Crip Relationships

Although crip theory speaks less directly to relationships than to identity and knowledge, cripistemology does suggest rethinking relationships from the perspective of disabled people rather than assuming a normative way of developing mature relationships. Disability often mutes agency in relationships. Describing power and dependency in relationships, Mingus (2017) spoke to *forced intimacy* as a disabled person. She explained,

> "Forced Intimacy" is . . . the common, daily experience of disabled people being expected to share personal parts of ourselves to survive in an ableist world. This often takes the form of being expected to share (very) personal information with able bodied people to get *basic* access, but it also includes forced physical intimacy, especially for those of us who need physical help that often requires touching of our bodies. (para. 1)

In addition to this physical intimacy, Mingus (2017) explained that forced intimacy also includes the requirement that disabled people create emotional intimacy with others, an intimacy that is often not genuine, in order to have their accessibility needs met.

Mingus (2017) observed that ableism prevents this forced intimacy from realizing its potential to lead to genuine intimacy and the resulting personal transformation. She noted that there is a "magnificent vulnerability" (para. 9) and interdependence in forced intimacy that is typically unrealized because ableism portrays disabled people as dependent, burdens, and tragic. As a result, forced intimacy replaces authentic relationships grounded in genuine connections. Because forced intimacy is dependent on ableist assumptions about disabled people, Mingus's relationships with people on whom she depends for accessibility are often a "constant oppressive reminder of domination and control" (para. 9).

Forced intimacy is starkly different from what Mingus (2011) termed *access intimacy*, which is the sense that someone genuinely understands and cares about the access needs of a disabled person. The closeness associated with access intimacy is a critical component of Mingus's most meaningful relationships. Access intimacy, which is typically elusive, is especially important for her as a queer, Transnational adoptee from a racially minoritized group seeking community that is difficult to find. Mingus's intersectional focus is a reminder of the ways in which ableism is redefined through other systems of oppression, which shapes the ways in which disabled people form relationships. Crip theory, specifically through the ways in which Mingus extends its reach, therefore encourages rethinking the normative standards of mutual relationship that have dominated student development theory.

Limitations of Crip Theory

Although crip theory offers meaningful insights into new possibilities for the meaning of development when ableism and disabled students are centered, it has limitations. One critique of crip theory is that it privileges physical disability over other forms of disability (Bone, 2017). Despite Kafer's (2013) addition of compulsory able-mindedness, much of the literature in this chapter supports Bone's claim. A notable exception is Löfgren-Mårtenson's (2013) crip analysis of the sexuality of people with intellectual disabilities. Crip theory has also been critiqued for not adequately considering intersections with other social identities (Schalk, 2013), the importance of which is seen through Mingus's (2011, 2017) lived experiences. An exception to this criticism, Kafer (2013) aimed to "address how disability is figured in and through . . . other categories of difference" (p. 17) such as gender, race, and class rather than as an additive identity category.

Connected to these critiques, crip theory has been challenged as an academic theory that does not benefit the lives of disabled people but instead "continues a cycle of silencing and marginalization" (Bone, 2017, p. 1298). Bone (2017) explained that being disabled often results in poverty, a lack of health care, and inaccessibility to education, realities that crip theory does not address. Related, Sherry (2013) claimed that *crip* is a fashionable term among academics, but using crip theory and reclaiming a derogatory word in "the safety of academia masks enormous embodied, classed, gendered, sexualized, and racialized privilege" (para. 5). Considering the limitations of crip theory, Löfgren-Mårtenson (2013) asked if it is only academically "hip" to be crip (p. 421). She responded, however, just as I do, that it is not merely "hip" but rather necessary to expose how ableism determines who is normal and abnormal and assigns people to limiting and power-laden relationships, identity categories, and belief systems.

Conclusion

Although crip theory has limitations, as do all theories, Bone (2017) noted that crip theory has the potential to change oppressive systems, including the culture of higher education. Crip theory can indeed change higher education broadly and student development theory specifically. To do so, the right questions need to be posed about applying crip theory in a liberatory and empowering way for diverse disabled students. To conclude this chapter, I propose discussion questions as a starting place for considering how crip theory can be applied to reimagine student development theory such that ableism no longer shapes how educators understand college students.

Discussion Questions

1. How might diverse disabilities be conceptualized when identity is simultaneously contested and claimed? How do the intersections of other social identities mediate these understandings of disability? How can educators support diverse students' fluid yet material disability identities in order to foster student success?
2. How does embracing disabled ways of knowing (cripistemology) reimagine the meaning of knowledge and knowers? How can educators design and enact practice grounded in cripistemology?
3. How does a critique of compulsory able-bodiedness and able-mindedness, and resulting forced intimacy, redefine the meaning of mature relationships? How can educators seize the transformative potential of the "magnificent vulnerability" of forced intimacy when supporting disabled students' relationships?
4. How does a critique of compulsory able-bodiedness and able-mindedness reimagine the assumptions of development toward complexity and the assumptions regarding the pace of development that result in disabling educational contexts?

References

Baxter Magolda, M. B. (2001). *Making their way: Narratives for transforming higher education to promote self-development.* Sterling, VA: Stylus.

Bone, K. M. (2017). Trapped behind the glass: Crip theory and disability identity. *Disability and Society, 32*(9), 1297–1314.

Brown, L. X. Z. (2011, August 4). The significance of semantics: Person-first language: Why it matters [Blog post]. Retrieved from http://www.autistichoya.com/2011/08/significance-of-semantics-person-first.html

Brown, S. E. (2002). What is disability culture? *Disability Studies Quarterly, 22*(2), 34–50.

Collins, P. H. (1990). *Black feminist thought: Knowledge, consciousness, and the politics of empowerment.* New York, NY: Routledge.

Erevelles, N. (2013). "What. . . [thought] cannot bear to know": Crippin' the limits of "thinkability." *Review of Disability Studies, 8*(3), 35–44.

Ferguson, R. A. (2004). *Aberrations in Black: Toward a Queer of Color critique.* Minneapolis, MN: University of Minnesota Press.

Halberstam, J. (2005). *In a queer time and place: Transgender bodies, subcultural lives.* New York, NY: New York University Press.

Halberstam, J. (2011). *The queer art of failure.* Durham, NC: Duke University Press.

Johnson, M. L., & McRuer, R. (2014a). Cripistemologies: Introduction. *Journal of Literary and Cultural Disability Studies, 8*(2), 127–147.

Johnson, M. L., & McRuer, R. (2014b). Proliferating cripistemologies: A virtual roundtable. *Journal of Literary and Cultural Disability Studies, 8*(2), 149–169.

Kafer, A. (2013). *Feminist, crip, queer.* Bloomington, IN: Indiana University Press.

Lather, P. (2007). *Getting lost: Feminist efforts toward a double(d) science.* Albany, NY: SUNY Press.

Linton, S. (1998). *Claiming disability: Knowledge and identity.* New York, NY: New York University Press.

Löfgren-Mårtenson, L. (2013). "Hip to be crip?" About crip theory, sexuality and people with intellectual disabilities. *Sexuality and Disability, 31*(4), 413–424.

McRuer, R. (2006). *Crip theory: Cultural signs of queerness and disability.* New York, NY: New York University Press.

Mingus, M. (2011, May 5). Access intimacy: The missing link [Blog post]. Retrieved from https://leavingevidence.wordpress.com/2011/05/05/access-intimacy-the-missing-link/

Mingus, M. (2017, August 6). Forced intimacy: An ableist norm [Blog post]. Retrieved from https://leavingevidence.wordpress.com/2011/05/05/access-intimacy-the-missing-link/

Mitchell, D. T., Snyder, S. L., & Ware, L. (2014). "[Every] child left behind": Curricular cripistemology and the crip/queer art of failure. *Journal of Literary and Cultural Disability Studies, 8*(3), 295–313.

Rich, A. (1980). Compulsory heterosexuality and lesbian existence. *Signs: Journal of Women in Culture and Society, 5*(4), 631–660.

Samuels, E. (2017). Six ways of looking at crip time. *Disability Studies Quarterly*, *37*(3).

Sandahl, C. (2003). Queering the crip or cripping the queer: Intersections of queer and crip identities in sole autobiographic performance. *GLQ: A Journal of Lesbian and Gay Studies*, *9*(1–2), 25–56.

Schalk, S. (2013). Coming to claim crip: Disidentification with/in disability studies. *Disability Studies Quarterly*, *33*(2).

Sherry, M. (2013, November 23). Crip politics? Just . . . no. *The Feminist Wire*. Retrieved from http://www.thefeministwire.com/2013/11/crip-politics-just-no

PART TWO

LIVING AND THINKING WITH THEORY

In this second part of the book, we rethink the meaning and nature of student development theory using the critical and poststructural theoretical perspectives described in Part One. We do so by critically rethinking a few of the key constructs of student development. We selected seven constructs: resilience, dissonance, socially constructed identities, authenticity, agency, knowledge and knowing, and context. Recognizing that this is not an exclusive list of relevant constructs, we chose these seven because they are among the central ideas of student development as reflected in the literature and are relevant to all students in some capacity. We chose to rethink student development through constructs rather than specific theories, because we believe this approach better allows us to reconstruct and not only deconstruct student development. In our experiences and as noted in the preface to this book, when we use critical and poststructural theories to rethink existing student development theories, the dominant narratives often remain centered (Abes, 2016). The reconceptualized theories tend to only critique existing theories rather than offer new ideas that foreground the lived experiences of marginalized students. Constructs, on the other hand, have multiple meanings and interpretations that are not wedded to a theory rooted in dominant norms. Although the seven constructs we selected represent particular meanings in first- and second-wave theorizing, third-wave theorizing is able to offer fresh interpretations not tied to normative assumptions.

Each chapter in this part is coauthored and includes at least one of the author's personal narratives and a critical and/or poststructural analysis of the narrative. These critical analyses focus on a student development theory construct. Most of these analyses are grounded in at least one of the critical and/or poststructural theories described in the first part of this book; some also use additional critical and poststructural theories. We include personal narratives at the center of the chapters, because lived experiences can be an entryway to understand how systems and discourses shape the lives of marginalized populations. Critical and poststructural theories illuminate people's lived experiences and seek to resist the discourses shaping their experiences within systems of oppression. Through the use of story, we want these theoretical perspectives to be understood as deeply relevant to students' lives and experiences in higher education. To minimize power differentials, including the wielding of power that exists when those with privileged identities retell the stories of marginalized individuals, the chapter coauthors jointly analyze the personal narratives through their own positionality and coconstruction. The presentation and format of these collaborative analyses differ in each of the chapters. Each, however, arrives at a reconceptualized view of a student development theory construct.

We begin this section with Z Nicolazzo and Riss Carter's chapter 8 on the construct of resilience. Applying crip theory, queer theory, and critical trans politics, and their experiences as trans* people across racialized and disability identities, Nicolazzo and Carter rethink resilience by analyzing a song Carter wrote and performed about Carter's experiences. Using a duoethnographic approach with the song as their artifact, they propose that resilience is a community-based practice.

In chapter 9, Kari B. Taylor and Danyelle J. Reynolds rethink the construct of dissonance. Using a Black feminist theoretical perspective to analyze Reynolds's narrative, they reconceptualize dissonance as the phenomenon of recognizing lies that societal systems and authorities tell. This reconceptualization acknowledges how Women of Color and other marginalized communities experience psychological inconsistency within college environments.

In chapter 10, D-L Stewart and Shaunda Brown rethink the construct of social construction of identities. Using a critical-poststructural perspective and high-density theorizing, they apply QueerCrit, quare theories, and post-humanism to demonstrate how Brown's narrative reveals the social construction of identities as rejecting dehumanization and destabilizing identity. They explain how social construction is facilitated by mentoring as othermothering and through community-engaged praxis.

Next, in chapter 11, V. Leilani Kupo and Symphony Oxendine rethink the construct of authenticity. They raise the question of whether it is possible to decolonize authenticity, and to respond to this inquiry, they apply decolonization, TribalCrit, and Indigenous Knowledge Systems to analyze their stories through dialogue with each other. They propose that authenticity is not only fluid and contextual but also grounded in history, community, geopolitical context, storytelling, and, at times, blood.

In chapter 12, Wilson Kwamogi Okello and Kiaya Demere White use Black feminism to rethink the construct of agency. They present the concept of embodied agency through an analysis of White's narrative. Richly described in the chapter as an existential practice involving the body, mind, spirit, and voice, embodied agency uses all aspects of one's self to move through and give meaning to the world.

Next, in chapter 13, Stephanie J. Waterman and Cori Bazemore-James rethink the construct of knowledge and knowing. To do so, they write a letters to each other in which they discuss the ways in which their Indigenous ways of knowing have been discounted in higher education. They propose that higher education and student development must embrace the collectivist, relational ways of knowing central to Indigenous Knowledge Systems, valuing knowledge grounded in lived experiences and stories.

Antonio Duran and Susan R. Jones conclude Part Two in chapter 14 by using critical theory to rethink the construct of context based on their analysis of Duran's narrative. They make the case that context, which is tied to systems of power and inequality, must always be presumed to be a significant influence on development. They consider four questions: Who gets privileged in current assumptions of context? How does context affect developmental dimensions differently? How do you measure context? And who can shape context?

Our hope is that individually each of these chapters provides a critical understanding of a particular student development construct and that taken together the chapters offer a rethinking of student development theory more broadly. We also hope that the compelling narratives bravely shared by the chapter authors encourage readers to consider their own stories and their students' stories through the lens of multiple critical perspectives. By engaging theory and stories together, we can have our collective eyes on how to apply critical perspectives on student development theory in practice, a task taken up in Part Three of this book.

Reference

Abes, E. S. (2016). Situating paradigms in student development theory. In E. S. Abes (Ed.), *Critical perspectives on student development theory* (New Directions for Student Services, No. 154, pp. 9–16). San Francisco, CA: Jossey-Bass.

8

RESILIENCE

Z Nicolazzo and Riss Carter

Higher education researchers have begun using the construct of resilience to explore individuals' abilities to recover from hardships and overcome stress. With roots in psychopathology and psychology, resilience has also been considered an individualistic construct (Greene, Galambos, & Lee, 2004), leading to its conflation with the notion of grit. As a result, previous conceptions of resilience invest in deficit perspectives of student development in college; either one has resilience or one does not, and it is on the individual to be resilient rather than focus on the ways college environments are toxic for marginalized populations. Although likely not their intention, student development theorists' framing of resilience as an individualistic construct has the unfortunate effect of pitting certain people who are "resilient" or "have grit" against those who do not. In relation to marginalized populations, those who are framed as "resilient" are posed as exceptional, while those who are "not resilient" are deemed lacking. This dualistic conceptualization not only creates intracommunity tensions but also poses serious challenges to possibilities for resilience-informed community building, which we discuss further throughout this chapter.

Recently, scholars have advanced critical and emerging perspectives on resilience. For example, several scholars have come to know resilience as a community-based practice, especially for racialized populations (Pérez II, 2017; Yosso, 2005). Yosso's (2005) notion of *community cultural wealth*, developed alongside Latina students, speaks to the ways in which Latina people cultivate resilience as a result of being in community with each other. Furthermore Green's (in press) work on Black cultural wealth connects genealogies of past, present, and future Black communities as a way of resisting the violent hegemony of anti-Black racism. Through these few examples, it becomes clear that the ways in which theorists have come to know resilience do not represent those marginalized college student populations. In addition, the ways in which notions of resilience connect communities across temporal and spatial locations signal an important turn student development theory has not yet recognized.

In this chapter, we explore what new possibilities may exist for understanding resilience as a construct of student development theory. We use our experiences as trans* people across racialized and disability identities to discuss resilience *as a community-based practice* when looked at through crip theory (McRuer, 2006), queer theory (Cohen, 1997; Johnson, 2001), and critical trans politics (Spade, 2015). As such, we use a duoethnographic approach to pick up on Butler's (2011) provocation to "work the weakness in the norm" (p. 181), particularly as it relates to previously held norms of resilience.

Duoethnography

Duoethnography is a research process by which two researchers come to understand self and society across differences (Norris & Sawyer, 2012). Working together to investigate a shared artifact (e.g., song lyrics), duoethnographic researchers focus on the individual meanings they make of that artifact, as well as how their understandings ripple out into broader societal meanings. Another critical component of duoethnography is its unabashed forwarding of social change as a result of the research process (Sawyer & Norris, 2013). Rather than seeing the exploration of self and society as a neutral practice, duoethnography implores researchers to think about how the research process can motivate change. In relation to the current chapter, the duoethnographic process is a way of recrafting, repurposing, and reimagining previously held assumptions about resilience. As a result of this repurposing, we use duoethnography to shift the discourse about resilience in a manner that resists deficient narratives of marginalized people as being at fault when we have difficulty navigating in hard, chilly, or downright hostile campus environments. In a sense, duoethnography as a methodology has the ability to become more than just a research process to investigate resilience. Instead, it is itself a *practice of resilience* (Nicolazzo, 2017) or a way to reimagine resilience as an ongoing process done in and across communities.

Positionality Statements

Because of the duoethnographic focus on coconstructed dialogue between two researchers across different identities and experiences, it is germane to discuss who we are as authors and how we have come to the topic of resilience. We also discuss how we have come into community with each other.

Z

As an early career scholar, I have focused much of my energy and attention on exploring how trans* students practice resilience, or the ways in which trans* students repeatedly attempt to find ways to navigate their negative campus climates. Being trans* myself, I have been personally and professionally consumed by the energy it takes to maintain a sense of resilience in hostile climates. Moreover, as a white trans* person who has invisible disabilities, I have become well attuned to how my identities converge to afford me differential levels of access to spaces. That is, I recognize how my whiteness, along with my educational privilege and socioeconomic status, reduces barriers and lessens my need to be resilient in various spaces. Furthermore, my disabilities often complicate my ability to practice resilience, as I often feel depleted and sometimes feel unable to control my mood, motivation, and capacity to produce in the ways I must for my job. As a result, I often feel like a resilience imposter, especially given my relationship to rethinking the notion through my scholarship. Moreover, when I feel like a resilience imposter is when I rely on my community to be resilient with and for me; in essence, when I feel like an imposter, I move closer toward community-based practices of resilience.

Riss

As an openly queer, trans*, Person of Color (QTPOC) college student on a predominantly white campus, I have often struggled to find spaces that truly encompass all of my multiple identities. I often feel as though I have to pick and choose which of my identities gets to be centered for that day, and I am frequently left feeling unheard and alone. Rather than understand this as a personal deficiency, I try to hold my university accountable for not creating spaces that nourish and support me as a whole person. In working to cultivate community, I try to involve myself in as many queer and trans* groups, actions, and programs on campus as I can, including working in queer places on campus. Although my involvement and work can be life affirming in many ways, it is also draining and sometimes leaves me thinking about how much work it takes for me to "be resilient" as a QTPOC person.

Coming Into Community

We began our relationship at Northern Illinois University (NIU) during the 2016–2017 academic year, when we began being in meeting and program spaces together. At the time, Riss was a sophomore on campus, and Z was in her second year as an assistant professor on campus. During our first connections, it became clear we held similar critical orientations toward how we viewed the approach and efficacy of gender-based work being done on campus. Because of the lack of trans* people at NIU, and our shared critical perspectives on gender-based work, we felt strongly about finding ways to cultivate our connection. Therefore, when the chance arose to write this book chapter, we decided to use it as a way to not only deepen our community but also explore the multiple—and potentially competing—ways we come to know notions of resilience.

Using Crip and Queer Theories to Understand Resilience

To anchor our exploration of resilience, Riss wrote a song on the topic (Figure 8.1), the lyrics for which follow. Taking this song as the artifact for our duoethnographic dialogue, we used it as a vehicle through which to explore our understandings of resilience. We do this through the analytical lenses of crip theory (McRuer, 2006), queer theory (Cohen, 1997; Johnson, 2001), and critical trans politics (Spade, 2015). Although educational scholars have used all three theoretical analyses (e.g., Denton, 2016; Miller, 2017; Nicolazzo, 2017), space precludes us from providing lengthy discussion of each here. Instead, we discuss central concepts of each through our duoethnographic dialogue, particularly the notions of ab/normality (crip theory), desire and destabilization of identities and experiences (queer theory), and cross-coalitional liberatory praxis (critical trans politics).

Figure 8.1.   Riss's song.

Note. Scan the QR code to view Riss's song, retrieved from https://www.youtube.com/watch?v=Wc4IdidcR84

Riss's Song

Re·sil·ience. Noun. The ability to recover from hardships. Synonyms: buoyancy,
adaptability, and the most popular: a word hated by Riss Carter.

> *Resiliency is a cop out phrase to me.*
> *A cop out, walking the streets, quickly tasing me.*
> *Looking disappointed to see my chest still rising up with ease.*
> *My shallow breaths heard in the distance.*
> *"Wow, Riss is so resilient!"*
> *A term used by the people*
> *That create these situations.*
> *That they never have to deal with.*
> *But I must learn to navigate them*
> *A participation trophy*
> *In a game I'm forced to play with*
> *The odds all stack against me*
> *I signed up with my existence.*
> *I didn't ask for this*
> *It's the build up*
> *Cut the tension with a knife*
> *Feel that build up*
> *And it's ruining my life*
> *Don't you dare scream, dare shout or fight*
> *Or you're checking off the box of your stereotype*
> *Pick up the pace now*
> *My people dying left and right*
> *I'm out of space now*
> *Constantly filled up with fright*
> *Light a candle for the loss*
> *But won't donate to the cause*
> *The system here is crooked but we ignore the flaws*
> *I'm tired of feeling*
> *I'm tired of being, please*
> *This resiliency*
> *Let go of the meaning*
> *The feeling that I must lead*
> *With resiliency*
> *These spaces I reside in aren't made for me to thrive in*

Holding all these identities within me I am hiding
Depending on the people around me I confide in
People like Z and Matthew Lonski steadily keep me from dying
Losing a piece of myself, every day that cause I can't center
The queer and Black and Latinx are all within this member
Of the human race, a waste of space,
My head is all over the place
However we'll dismiss it
Cause I'm so damn "resilient"
I'm tired of feeling
I'm tired of being, please
This resiliency
Let go of the meaning
The feeling that I must lead
With resiliency
I can't handle it, right now, not anymore
I can't handle it, right now, not anymore
I can't handle it, right now, not anymore
I can't handle it, handle it, handle it.
You don't know what's in store. Neither do I. Am I gonna die?

Duoethnographic Dialogue

Z: Riss, your song is so powerful—thanks for sharing! As I was reading your lyrics, I kept thinking about normalcy. In particular, I began thinking of "normal" conceptualizations of resilience and of how we as marginalized people must "be resilient" in order to project a sense of our being "normal" or "just like the rest of the world." My mind kept wandering back to a statement McRuer (2006) posed as central to understanding crip theory, which was, "A system of compulsory able-bodiedness repeatedly demands that people with disabilities embody for others an affirmative answer to the unspoken question, 'Yeah, but in the end, wouldn't you rather be more like me?'" (p. 9). In other words, the ways in which the world determines whose bodies and identities are "normal" means that we as marginalized people need to twist and conform to that notion, or else we will be marked as "sick," "deviant," or "wrong."

Riss: It's so interesting what we—as a society—view as normal and what's supposed to be the norm. Ultimately, everything is filtered through this white, cisgender, patriarchal lens, and when one deviates outside that norm, as I do, it starts affecting me as a queer Person of Color. My not fitting society's expectation of normal affects where I live, the money I get, the food I eat, and the basic things that I need to survive. But the thing is, I didn't choose this life, and I'm literally just trying to live my life. I'm not doing anything spectacular, but because my life deviates from other people's sense of normal, and because it's not what society deems acceptable, me living my life as a queer and trans* Person of Color is framed by others as me "being resilient." I can't stand that.

Z: Listening to you makes me think about an additional nuance to our discussion of normalcy, which is a notion I have discussed with several of my colleagues about what we refer to as the reality of living "betwixt-and-between" identities (Harris & Nicolazzo, in press; Ralston, Nicolazzo, & Harris, 2017). For example, when you talk about your racial identity, you mention being between monoracial categories as a multiracial person. The way in which you resist pronouns also furthers you from this "normal" understanding of a trans* person, right? Like, as trans* people, we are often thought of as using "different" pronouns, and even now, this difference has been absorbed as a new form of "normalcy."

Riss: Yeah, the pronoun thing is real, and it even comes up within the trans* community. Some trans* people actually ask me, "Wouldn't you rather use *they/them* as pronouns?" and I can't help but think they ask me this because we are all so stuck on normalized notions of what a trans* person is meant to be, including what pronouns we are meant to use. It's the same for transitioning, and this is hard because I identify as a gender nonconforming individual, and I am not transitioning to anything. I am not transitioning from something to something else. I am just trying to be the most authentic version of myself. And that's hard when I feel this pressure as a trans* person to change certain things about myself. Like, changing the name marker on my identification; I'm neither a man nor a woman, so I don't need to do that. When it comes to surgeries, how does one look nonbinary? You don't. I don't know how I'm meant to look nonbinary. But everyone expects when I say I'm trans* that there is a way a trans* person is meant to look, especially the way a Black trans* person is meant to look, which is important when we look at my multiple identities. I feel as though I don't ever really fit into any space, and it's become really difficult.

Z: Hearing your comments makes me think a lot about the notion of transnormativity (Jourian, Simmons, & Devaney, 2015), or the idea that there are normative ways a trans* person is meant to act, look, and be. And more than transnormativity being imposed by cisgender people, it's also imposed by other trans* people, which makes it feel all the more rough, right?

Riss: Yeah, it's definitely rough. I even find myself compromising in conversations, which sucks. Like, there is a larger community of trans* men on campus, and sometimes I will be hanging out with them, and they'll be talking about something like taking testosterone (T), and they'll ask me, "Oh, Riss, when are you gonna start T?" and I say, "Well, I dunno, I'm thinking about it," even though I know damn well I'm not gonna start T. But it's something that I feel the need to front, like I need to fit in within my own community. It's tough, and I haven't figured out how to deal with that yet.

Z: And then looping back to your song, you talk about these sorts of conversations and interactions being part of a "game you are forced to play." So because you don't have a community of nonbinary People of Color who reflect who you are, you are forced to play in white, trans*masculine spaces. Am I reading that right?

Riss: Yeah, totally.

Z: So, I want to shift gears a bit and talk about your song through the lens of queer theory. In particular, I was drawn to your use of the word *crooked*. If something is crooked, we can think of it as a metaphor for bent, or not straight, or deviant and abnormal. We can also think about Butler (2011) claim that we need to be "working the weakness in the norm" (p. 181), so perhaps a queer theoretical reading of your song opens up the possibility to think about how we as crooked people can expose the weakness of the norms we have been talking about, like transnormativity. And if we think about desire as a main tenet of queer theory (Abes & Kasch, 2007), then we may ask questions around how we can desire abnormality as a way of being in the world rather than trying to fit in or acculturate.

Riss: I like that perspective and would think about it as a both–and. You know, I think we should try to live as our true authentic selves and do it unapologetically. I also think, though, that at times, fitting in can be a type of survival. For example, I have to know when I need to fit in and go with the masses, so to speak. But at the same time, I do want to be as authentic and unapologetic as I can be. And so I think it is important to find spaces where we can be ourselves, even if it is just for us. For example, I do this with my music, and I do it in groups where I feel safe. Identifying which groups and spaces I need to live and thrive as Riss Carter is really important and helps me stay safe. And so, yeah, I definitely want to live my life as I want—as you talked about, desiring my abnormality and crookedness—but if something happens to me as a trans* Person of Color, I may be thrown in jail or worse. That's why I wrote the last line of my song: Am I gonna die?

Z: And the way I read your song, that death is both literal and figurative. So there's a lived materiality to this—am I going to cease from existing?—as well as am I going to cease to exist as a possibility as a nonbinary Person of Color?

Riss: You got it!

Z: You know, you've mentioned this word *authenticity* a couple of times, which has become a real buzzword in the field of student affairs and higher education. But again, taking a queer theoretical read of your song, it seems like authenticity may not be the same thing at all times (Jones, Kim, & Skendall, 2012).

Riss: I think about it as being authentic to all of my identities, because I have very different, overlapping identities. I also think about authenticity as centering all of my identities in a way that is best for me, and I think the best way educators can do this is let people name it for themselves rather than try to impose values or meaning on experiences for people (Jones et al., 2012). So when it comes to educators, folks should center what students need by asking the question, "How can I best assist you?" After asking this question, educators need to let students name what they need for themselves. I know for me, it's really hard to find places on campus to exist as my whole self as a queer, Black, and Latinx person. I still have yet to find a space where all of that is included and accepted at once.

Z: What you're talking about is queering, or destabilizing, notions of authenticity in order to forward your own resiliency as a practice (Nicolazzo, 2017). And when I talk about practices of resilience, what I'm picking up on is the ways in which we create and use and develop strategies to navigate these fucked-up spaces in which we live. Here, resiliency shifts from a thing either we have or we don't. Either we are able to bounce back or able to be buoyant, as you write about in your song, or it's our fault and not the fault of the system that we are unable to get through our days. And so what you are asking in your song is how can we queer authenticity so that it looks different at different times and places as a way to develop practices of resilience to navigate toxic campus climates?

Riss: Yeah, definitely.

Z: So sticking with this notion of queer theory in relation to your song, I am curious about your mentioning hiding identities. What is the world you desire in which you don't have to hide identities?

Riss: Recently, I had an experience where I didn't have to hide any of my identities. I went to a Transgender Day of Resilience reframing event. It was for Transgender Day of Remembrance, but instead of it being a sad day of remembrance for all of the trans* people who have been killed, we were able to come together, remember our dead, and then we turned it into a march, and we marched in the streets to show everyone we are here and aren't going anywhere. It was a trans* event that focused on People of Color and centered blackness within that. We focused so much on trans* People of Color, and even though it wasn't a space just for trans* People of Color, the event organizers were unapologetic in their focus, and it felt so good. I realize spaces like this can't happen all the time, but even if there were spaces where I didn't feel like I had to pick and choose what identities of mine get attention each day, I would take that. I feel like too often I have to tone down parts of myself depending on the spaces I am in, and as a result, I have to hide parts of myself. And I feel myself constantly doing that, especially in relation to my Latinx identity, which I feel like I hide every day.

Z: Yeah, so going back to the song, it's the concept of "losing a piece of myself every day."

Riss: Every day.

Z: And also you write, "My head is all over the place / However, we'll dismiss it," with the "we" being other people who are forcing you to pick and choose which identities you feel comfortable highlighting and sharing. And, in the end, they will dismiss the complexity of your experiences of these interactions by saying, "Oh my gosh, look at you, you're so resilient," which you also mention in your song.

Riss: Exactly.

Z: So this all makes me wonder, where and with whom do you feel most alive?

Riss: That's a really hard question to answer. I am in my first relationship with another trans* person, and definitely with my partner, I feel like I am the most alive, and I can talk about a lot of things. But then again, my partner is white, and sometimes I just need to be with People of Color. I think Creating Change [an annual conference for LGBTQ educators, artists, activists, and higher education professionals] is another one of those spaces. It's a week I get to spend with people who "get it" and identify similarly to me, which is really good. But the conference itself can be really draining for me, and I need to work to create those spaces even at the conference. And also Molly and Matt, who both work at the Gender and Sexuality Resource Center on campus, are great people.

Z: And yet it doesn't miss me that you do not name a single campus space that helps you feel alive, because even when you talk about the Gender and Sexuality Resource Center, you talk about two individual people, not about a space on campus, right?

Riss: Mhm . . . .

Z: So it seems to me there is a sense of partial and/or complete erasure whenever and wherever you are on campus. Is that right?

Riss: Yeah.

Z: And that this erasure, then—as you discuss in your song—and the stacking of these erasures, has a weight to it that is palpable and draining.

Riss: Definitely.

Z: So then there is this need to move off campus in order to feel whole and seen, which pushes against a lot of normative notions of student development (and there is that word *normal* again!). A bunch of older environmental research focuses on the need to cultivate spaces on campus where people feel recognized and seen and heard and understood, and that doing so increases one's sense of belonging. However, our environments aren't changing fast enough or well enough for some of our most marginalized students. And more than that, there are off-campus and virtual spaces we can leverage to extend notions of environmental and ecological student development theory (e.g., Jourian, 2017; Miller, 2017; Nicolazzo, Pitcher, Renn, and Woodford (2017).

Riss: Yeah, definitely there is no space on campus where I feel like who I am is centered. In fact, there are places on campus where people have gone out of their way to make sure I know I am not valued in my wholeness . . . unless they are in need of a diversity token. For example, some people want me around during recruitment events to showcase my diverse identities, but when I share my feelings of hurt and mistreatment, the very same people act like they don't have time to hear me or work with me to make my environment better. More than that, I am posed as being draining for other people when I ask for basic human decency, and it's so irritating [*laughs ironically*]. But I can't address it! God forbid I actually snap off at somebody, because then I'm just another "angry Black person" and just filling back into that stereotype. So I have learned to make do on campus. I think a lot of people think about resiliency as being strong and always fighting back, but sometimes my way of being resilient is just thinking, "You know what, whatever. I don't got time for that. I'm gonna go hang out with my partner off campus. I don't have time for you all [people on campus] right now."

Z: So it's almost like your practice of resilience as a student in college is to move away from college. Your practice of resilience to navigate campus is to move off campus.

Riss: Yeah, and then when I am on campus, it's just like my act of resilience is to not be resilient. I'm not going to sit there and be super tough and strong. Instead, I am just going to remove myself. I'm not havin' it.

Z: Right, because you are not the educator; you are not the savior; you are not going to basically give passes to people to let themselves think they are good people. So it's almost like you use these times and experiences with outside community to give you the strength and ability to cope with the shit you experience on campus. And then you pick and choose when you will push.

Riss: Exactly.

Z: And if we think about the entire campus as operating through a gender binary way of thinking (Nicolazzo, 2017), then we can even think about your move off campus as a manifestation of desiring abnormality. In a sense, this is similar to Kafer's (2013) work about desiring crip futures, in that we as queer people—as people who are "crooked," to go back to the queer theoretical reading of your song—are seeking something beyond the normalcy being thrust upon us. In that sense, then, we stretch beyond dominant white, cisgender, able-bodied visions of "normal" futures and strive to get closer to our own crooked realities.

Riss: Yeah, definitely.

Z: So I want to shift gears again to talk a bit about community and coalition-building for justice. Our previous conversation about transnormativity and how it affects you makes me think of this vital notion from critical trans politics around coalition-building (Spade, 2015). In essence, Spade (2015) discussed how we need to work across populations to center those who are most vulnerable, and by doing so, we can work toward access and rights that "trickle up" and benefit everyone. But doing this is hard, right? CeCe McDonald has talked poignantly about transnormativity, making the point that we need to stop treating our lives and transitions as a competition (BCRW Videos, 2014). And this seems to me to be the very crux of critical practice. We need to think about how we can build each other up and how we can reach across populations rather than saying, "Well, I'm better than you because I fit into this normalized understanding of a system."

Riss: Yes, definitely.

Z: Thinking further about coalition-building for justice, I'm really taken
        by this quote by Eli Clare (2002), who wrote

> I want us to cruise justice, flirt with it, take it home with us,
> nurture and feed it, even though sometimes it will be demanding
> and uncomfortable and ask us to change. Clearly I'm not talking
> about a simple one night stand but a commitment for the long
> haul. (para. 28)

        So I am wondering, what does it mean for you to cruise justice? Who
        do you want to cruise justice with? How do you think about taking
        justice home with you? And if we think about campus as a home—for
        example, a lot of administrators talk about creating campus environ-
        ments as a "home away from home"—how do you think about creat-
        ing a better home by moving toward justice?

Riss: I want to center people, and I want to cruise with the people who
        feel like me. Ways of trying to do that on the campus, and making
        this campus feel more like home for me, are continuing to do some
        of the work I have been doing on campus. For example, I have been
        invested in creating a QTPOC group where we, as queer and trans*
        People of Color, can get together and talk about what justice looks
        like. We can also talk about how we are going to fight together to
        get the things we need and how we are not going to take no for an
        answer . . . [*long pause*] . . . I like that quote a lot. It took me back
        [*laughs*].

Z: The thing I am resting with right now, too, is that it's hard to do this
        work with, as Clare (2002) wrote, people who aren't in it for the long
        haul. And it makes me wonder about notions of family, particularly
        queer notions of family. Because often, we fight alongside our family,
        or our kin.

Riss: I believe strongly in the notion of chosen family. I mean, family is a
        construct, and we get to choose who our family is. When we have peo-
        ple who choose every single day to love us and be with us, that bond is
        stronger than DNA. It's similar to how I think about my gender being
        more important than any biological designation or normative under-
        standings of my body, anatomy, or chromosomal makeup. My family
        are my friends and my partner. I have amazing people like you and
        Molly; I have people like Matthew and folks who I know I can turn to
        when I need.

Z: When you think about kinship and coalition-building, it sounds like
        it starts with queer and trans* people across racialized identities. How

else do you think about coalition-building, in particular across various different identities and experiences?

Riss: I think it's important to make sure that we are all standing in solidarity with each other. There are groups on this campus that I don't personally identify with—for example, undocumented students—but I still grow with that group, and I always support that group. And I also think it's important that when we ask for things on campus, we keep in mind other groups' needs. It's important that you build and grow with people who aren't just the same as you. I make family with everyone, if that makes sense.

Z: How do you think about resilience, then, as a community endeavor rather than an individual thing?

Riss: I love the way that's framed. I would much rather have it used in that way. My biggest problem with normative understandings of resilience is when it's being used as an individual construct. Like, I have to be resilient as one person who is bouncing back on my own, separated from my community.

Z: So this links back into critical trans politics, specifically the centrality of coalition-building to justice movements (Spade, 2015). I also think about Green's (in press) work around Black cultural wealth and community love. I also think about Yosso's (2005) work around community cultural wealth. And in thinking about this theoretical base, we can understand that justice asks of us to root our movement-building in and across marginalized populations. And this seems important not just because we experience similar things but because we have various identities. For example, we can't talk about gender without talking about race; we can't talk about race without talking about disability; we can't talk about disability without talking about nationality.

Riss: That also reminds me about how, when we think about making more accessible spaces on campus, we need to be doing that work with various populations in mind. For example, when we create gender-inclusive restrooms, we need to also lower tampon machines for people with disabilities. Because we grow together and shouldn't step on each other. So making sure we are including everyone together in our movements toward justice—that, to me, is resilience.

Z: And as you talk about in your song, we need to let go of older notions of resilience and understand resilience as community practice, as something we do together, and as cruising justice for the long haul.

Riss: Right.

Z: And still, while we are doing that, there is this last line of your song that has stayed with me. In essence, we can do all of this work and think about resilience as a community-based practice . . . but we still don't know what's in store for us. So even when we try to queer notions of resilience, even when we think of resilience as a community practice, even when we hold tightly to the ways we are abnormal or the ways we ruin normal conceptualizations of gender, there is still an unknown aspect of our future survival.

Riss: That's why I made sure to end the song on that note, because it is something that I carry with me every day. Like, what happens if I burn out? What happens if I die? I don't know if that's gonna happen, but at the same time, I don't feel like I can stop doing this work. I don't know who I can count on to do this work if I'm not doing it, so I would rather push myself to the last minute making sure I am doing the best I can to uplift myself, my community, and others with marginalized identities.

Z: And if we think about resilience as a community practice, then in some senses, our bodies, lives, and experiences are not ours alone; they are our community's. And so that both allows us to continue and is also a call for us to keep continuing.

Conclusion

Through our dialogue about Riss's song, we explored new understandings of resilience as a community-based practice. Furthermore, we elucidated resilience as a circuitous, messy, ongoing, and complex process and as a practice through which we can desire our own queer/crip futures. Our dialogue extends community-based conceptualizations of resilience, recognizing how the concept is *an ongoing practice we engage in, with, and alongside each other.* As a result, new possibilities emerge for how educational practitioners can understand and promote resilience as a developmental construct. For example, the unfolding process of desiring queer collective futures has the ability not only to disrupt normative present conditions but also to leverage marginalized populations' histories as a way to keep practicing resilience. Such a recognition of resilience not only unlocks new temporal understandings but also encourages educators to think deeper about spaces in which community can be built, including online and virtual platforms (Miller, 2017; Nicolazzo, 2017). It also promotes an understanding of the lives of marginalized people as being interconnected and a recognition of our interconnected lives as essential to forwarding liberatory student development praxis.

Discussion Questions

1. How has resilience as a community-based practice influenced your own development?
2. What salient identities do you have that mediate how you think about resilience as a practice?
3. How could you use duoethnographic dialogue alongside the students with whom you work to imagine new possibilities for resilience and student development?
4. What feels important about imagining new possibilities for resilience and student development?

References

Abes, E. S., & Kasch, D. (2007). Using queer theory to explore lesbian college students' multiple dimensions of identity. *Journal of College Student Development*, *48*(6), 619–636.

BCRW Videos. (2014, March 31). CeCe McDonald, Reina Gossett, and Dean Spade: Police + prisons don't keep us safe—we keep each other safe [Video file]. Retrieved from https://vimeo.com/90554286

Butler, J. (2011). *Bodies that matter*. New York, NY: Routledge.

Clare, E. (2002). Flirting with you. *Gendered bodies: Feminist perspectives*. Retrieved from http://www.disabilityhistory.org/dwa/queer/paper_clare.html

Cohen, C. J. (1997). Punks, bulldaggers, and welfare queens: The radical potential of queer politics? *GLQ: A Journal of Lesbian and Gay Studies*, *3*(4), 437–465.

Denton, J. M. (2016). Critical and poststructural perspectives on sexual identity formation. *New Directions for Student Services*, *2016*(154), 57–69.

Green, K. M. (Ed.). (in press). *Black trans love is Black wealth*. Washington, DC: Redbone Press.

Greene, R. R., Galambos, C., & Lee, Y. (2004). Resilience theory: Theoretical and professional conceptualizations. *Journal of Human Behavior in the Social Environment*, *8*(4), 75–91.

Harris, J. C., & Nicolazzo, Z. (in press). Navigating the academic borderlands as multiracial and trans* faculty members. *Critical Studies in Education*, Advanced online publication. DOI: 10.1080/17508487.2017.1356340.

Johnson, E. P. (2001). "Quare" studies, or (almost) everything I know about queer studies I learned from my grandmother. *Text and Performance Quarterly*, *21*(1), 1–25.

Jones, S. R., Kim, Y. C., & Skendall, K. C. (2012). Re-framing authenticity: Considering multiple social identities using autoethnographic and intersectional approaches. *The Journal of Higher Education, 83*(5), 698–724.

Jourian, T.J., Simmons, S.L., & Devaney, K.C. (2015). "We are not expected": Trans* educators (re)claiming space and voice in higher education and student affairs. *TSQ: Transgender Studies Quarterly, 2*(3), 431–446.

Jourian, T.J. (2017). Trans*forming college masculinities: Carving out trans*masculine pathways through the threshold of dominance. *International Journal of Qualitative Studies in Education, 30*(3), 245–265.

Kafer, A. (2013). *Feminist, queer, crip.* Bloomington, IN: Indiana University Press.

McRuer, R. (2006). *Crip theory: Cultural signs of queerness and disability.* New York, NY: New York University Press.

Miller, R. A. (2017). "My voice is definitely strongest in online communities": Students using social media for queer and disability identity-making. *Journal of College Student Development, 58*(4), 509–525.

Nicolazzo, Z. (2017). *Trans* in college: Transgender students' strategies for navigating campus life and the institutional politics of inclusion.* Sterling, VA: Stylus.

Nicolazzo, Z, Pitcher, E. N., Renn, K. A., & Woodford, M. (2017). An exploration of trans* kinship as a strategy for student success. *International Journal of Qualitative Studies in Education, 30*(3), 305–319.

Norris, J., & Sawyer, R. D. (2012). Toward a dialogic methodology. In J. Norris, R. D. Sawyer, & D. Lund (Eds.), *Duoethnography: Dialogic methods for social, health, and educational research* (pp. 9–39). Walnut Creek, CA: Left Coast Press.

Pérez, D., II. (2017). In pursuit of success: Latino male college students exercising academic determination and community cultural wealth. *Journal of College Student Development, 58*(2), 123–140.

Ralston, N. C., Nicolazzo, Z, & Harris, J. C. (2017). Betwixt-and-between: Counterstories from the borderlands of higher education. *About Campus, 22*(4), 20–27.

Sawyer, R. D., & Norris, J. (2013). *Duoethnography.* New York, NY: Oxford University Press.

Spade, D. (2015). *Normal life: Administrative violence, critical trans politics, and the limitations of law* (2nd ed.). Durham, NC: Duke University Press.

Yosso, T. J. (2005). Whose culture has capital? A critical race theory discussion of community cultural wealth. *Race Ethnicity and Education, 8*(1), 69–91.

9

DISSONANCE

Kari B. Taylor and Danyelle J. Reynolds

Although musicians can readily hear dissonance when chords clash to create an unharmonious cacophony, college educators do not have the luxury of using physical senses to appreciate the dissonance their students experience. Rather, they must look for nonverbal cues and subtle behaviors that indicate students are grappling with the internal feeling of inconsistency that dissonance creates. This internal feeling of inconsistency is thought to open the door for development to occur, yet it remains more theoretical than empirical in nature. Moreover, theories regarding dissonance originally stemmed from positions of unexamined privilege and thus are often inaccurate given that they do not account for students' lived experiences amid societal systems of privilege and oppression. This chapter reenvisions dissonance by using a Black feminist theoretical perspective (Collins, 1989; hooks, 2000; Smith, 1995). We begin with a narrative that illustrates Danyelle J. Reynolds's experience of dissonance during an international service-learning program in Ecuador.

The Collision of Colonialism and Racism in International Service

As another narrow curve approached, I squeezed my eyes shut and said another silent prayer. Despite my fear of heights, I stayed calm as our minibus continued to ascend the mountain toward the Indigenous Ecuadorian community where we would be engaging in a cultural exchange. I was reminded of the narrow roads that my dad would speed through with ease whenever we would visit family in Jamaica. These memories renewed my faith in our driver, and soon we arrived in front of the school in the Indigenous community. I considered the information our site liaison gave us the day prior about our interactions with the teachers and children. My expectations of teachers greeting us with smiles and waves and children jumping around with excitement were completely interrupted as I saw some of the children run to the white people in our group and the others stare in apparent shock and fear at the People of Color.

Still not processing what was happening, but eager to meet our community partners, I approached the children, who were at recess. Some of my fellow group members were immediately welcomed into games of chase and jump rope. I approached a group of girls, but they dispersed as soon as I came close. Their wide, shifting eyes communicated trepidation and fear, and it took only a quick scan across the school yard to see the other People of Color in our group had experienced something similar. We shared a look, and I walked to the teachers. I took my limited Spanish proficiency and joined a conversation with a teacher and our faculty member, all the while trying to understand why I felt lied to by our community partner.

When I learned about the opportunity to structure an international service-learning experience with graduate and undergraduate students, I was excited to put my skills into use in a new setting. We would be engaging in a cultural exchange and doing some English teaching with a school in rural Ecuador, home to an Indigenous community. As a graduate student who had never studied abroad, I was eager to add this experience to my personal and professional journey while learning more about service-learning, a field in which I knew I wanted to work more closely.

As our departure date approached, I found myself explaining my purpose in Ecuador to friends and family. As the daughter of two Jamaican immigrants, I knew that if I were to "do service," that experience would need to be different from that of the mostly white American *voluntourists* with whom some of my family members had possibly interacted. From my perspective, voluntourists represented people who provided short-term help by way of charity and without investment in the community's real needs and interests. I wanted to work *with* community members and learn from them another way of engaging with the world. Although my Jamaican heritage and dark skin have given me a different experience, I thought I would find a more immediate connection with the community members given a shared experience navigating the contemporary impact of colonialism and structural racism.

From my experiences and training, I understand the importance and value of hearing community voices to frame history and context of an area in service-learning experiences. In the semester prior to our cultural exchange in Ecuador, we spoke to our site liaison at length about how to effectively engage in the Indigenous community with whom we would be working. Our site liaison, an Ecuadorian woman with Indigenous roots, worked at a prominent university in Ecuador and had been facilitating conversations between U.S. campus partners and Ecuadorian community partners for several years. Her experience, along with regular Skype calls prior to departing for Ecuador, promoted a relationship of trust and respect.

Prior to our arrival at the school, our site liaison shared the importance of considering colonial history when developing rapport with community members. Specifically, we were encouraged to think about the presence of white men with light-colored eyes in an Indigenous community that did not interact with a lot of outsiders. I remember thinking, "Wow, I've never been in a situation in which white men had to be the most thoughtful on how they entered a space." I stole a glance at the three white men in our group; they appeared to be attentive and aware. So as we entered the community on the first day, I was aware of so much: the space we were entering, my other group members as they approached the school (would we perpetuate the "ugly American" idea we had read so much about?), and my own fears about not being able to connect with the children and teachers because of my limited Spanish proficiency.

Minutes later, however, I was most aware of one thing: These children had very clearly never interacted with a Black person before. The four Black women in our group, myself included, were met with wide, fearful eyes and students who ran away from us to their teachers and other, fairer skinned members in our group. Slowly, we tried to join games they were playing, and it was clear they did not want us to play with them. It took the better part of an hour to try to even talk to one of the children. The next day, it took less time, but the negative body language was still there. Their faces, reactions, and body language—this entire experience was traumatizing.

I wondered how I could engage in this partnership using best practices, demonstrating cultural humility, and balancing power dynamics if the children did not want to engage with me. More important, I wondered, "How did this happen without a warning from our site liaison?"

In the following days, conversations with the local teachers, my host family, and our site liaison would shed more light on the experience. First, I learned that this rural community had met only two groups of outside visitors, which consisted of white faculty members from universities, before our group entered their space. Second, through a follow-up conversation with our site liaison, I learned that while she was well aware of anti-Black racism in Ecuador, she was not proud of this history in her country and did not want to name it to our group. I had come to adore our site liaison and respected her greatly, but in that conversation I felt betrayed, angry, and confused. Why would she lie about something while still telling us it is important to learn about a community before engaging with it?

I carried this and other questions with me. Why would I pay money to leave the United States only to experience an anti-Black sentiment in a new, differently disturbing way? Would there ever be a space where race was not my most salient identity? What would the next few weeks look like for me in this community? These questions were never answered, though they were complicated. In the following days, I experienced racially charged street harassment that my host family dismissed as "flirting." I saw a primetime television show that featured a character in blackface. I smiled at an older couple on the street, only to hear them talk to each other in loud (enough) voices, "*Es muy negra, no?*" Years of training, my values, and any graciousness were not accessible. I had done everything I was supposed to do, and yet I was having such a hard time navigating this space so that I could fully appreciate and engage with the beauty of Ecuador and the communities with which we interacted. Meanwhile, other group members seemed to be having a great time interacting with strangers upon meeting them.

Again out of my comfort zone, I sought comfort in the reflective academic spaces that I had made my home as a graduate student. However, in processing our experiences with our group, one of my white male classmates and friends expressed he was "sick" of processing identity and wanted to disengage from the conversation. It seemed convenient for him to do so.

Eventually, I was able to make connections with more of the teachers and youth in the school, specifically with the toddlers in the classroom in which I was placed. There were more complications, slights, and observations that presented themselves, but I gained new insights about myself, like how I was able to effectively explain to my host family members some of my experiences in ways that helped them understand the harm I experienced. I was able to fully appreciate the history and culture of Ecuadorian communities. And while it would have been easy for me to internalize my negative experiences without seeking support, I was able to reflect and name my feelings with other Women of Color who provided community and support in ways that allowed me to have mostly good memories of my time in Ecuador and a desire to return.

The impact of this experience on my learning, identity development, and continued community engagement was long term. Even now, I cannot fully trust community partners to help me understand the entire context of a community. This seems counter to the work that I now do in community engagement and service-learning, in which I encourage students to trust community members as the experts of their experiences. I hold some discomfort about going abroad again, never wanting to experience the fear in people's eyes, the comments about my complexion, or possible new interactions that create similar trauma or harm. And while I experience marginalization in the midwestern region I now call home, I am always wary of the types of marginalization I might experience elsewhere.

Foundational Conceptualizations of Dissonance

Collegiate educators often point to *dissonance* as important to fostering student development (Hoover, 2014), but no clear definition or use of the term exists. Originally, the term stemmed from Festinger's (1957, 1962) cognitive dissonance theory. Festinger, a social psychologist, defined *cognitive dissonance* as the psychological discomfort that arises when individuals experience inconsistency in beliefs, expectations, and/or experiences. Other psychologists at the time, including Piaget and Sanford, also described the phenomenon of experiencing and navigating inconsistency but used different terms. Piaget (1950, 1965) discussed how individuals experience disequilibrium when they encounter new ideas that are more complex than their existing mental schemas. According to Piaget, disequilibrium represents an internal sense of conflict. Sanford (1966) explained that new ideas that lie beyond the ways in which individuals currently make meaning constitute challenge, which fosters development only when accompanied with sufficient support. Despite using different terminology to discuss dissonance, foundational scholars agreed that individuals strive toward psychological consistency and experience discomfort when they encounter inconsistency. Each foundational scholar also noted that development is but one possible outcome of navigating inconsistency.

Often, collegiate educators draw only loosely on these foundational scholars' work and tend to conflate dissonance with discomfort (Baker & Taylor, 2016, November). As a result, calls for ensuring that students experience discomfort during college—or, at least, do not remain too comfortable—abound. Popescu (2016) explained, "Isn't college by nature an uncomfortable experience? You leave your parents, your friends, your siblings, your neighborhood, even your dog . . . all of these experiences are discomforting but necessary for your development" (para. 9). Such discussions regarding the necessity of experiencing discomfort rest on dominant ideologies regarding college students and collegiate environments. Within dominant ideologies, college students appear as individuals who have never lived away from home, whose main source of discomfort arises from a physical relocation away from where they call home, and who ultimately need more challenge to develop. In turn, collegiate environments appear as places that push students to separate from family and friends and inherently foster development. These discussions overlook—if not altogether ignore—how systems of privilege and oppression affect experiences of discomfort.

Critical Conceptualizations of Dissonance

A Black feminist theoretical perspective represents a standpoint theory that emphasizes the examination of phenomena from the standpoint of individuals who stand at and experience the world through intersecting oppressive systems. Although it applies most directly to Black women, it helps to surface how systems of privilege and oppression influence student development as a whole. Thus, Black feminist theory is a useful lens by which to understand how marginalized communities experience dissonance. Also, it helps extend existing literature such as Belenky, Clinchy, Goldberger, and Tarule's (1986) *Women's Ways of Knowing: The Development of Self, Voice, and Mind* that used a feminist lens to theorize about student development.

Using a feminist perspective, Belenky et al. (1986) reframed dissonance from involving a sense of doubt and conflict to involving a sense of validation and connection. The authors explained,

> In the psychological literature concerning the factors promoting cognitive development, doubt has played a more prominent role than belief. People are said to be precipitated into states of cognitive conflict when, for example, some external event challenges their ideas. . . . On the whole, women found the experience of being doubted debilitating rather than energizing. (p. 227)

On the basis of interviews with more than 100 women with diverse social identities, Belenky et al. (1986) recommended that collegiate educators serve as midwives to help students "give birth to new ways of making meaning" (p. 227). Critical feminists further emphasized the importance of experiencing empowerment while encountering new ideas, especially in the face of the effects of systemic oppression. Speaking directly to readers, Anzaldúa (2002) explained,

> As you begin to know and accept the self uncovered by the trauma, you pull the blinders off, take in the new landscape in brief glances. Gradually you arouse the agent in this drama, begin to act, to dis-identify with the fear and the isolation. (p. 552)

Given that Women of Color often begin their collegiate journeys with doubt accrued from experiences with people invalidating their ability to know, the spark needed for development is not to begin doubting what they know but rather to begin believing that they can know.

From a Black feminist theoretical perspective, dissonance is an omnipresent phenomenon for Women of Color, whose position within intersecting oppressive systems involves a legacy of struggle and lack of agency (Anzaldúa, 2002; Collins, 2009). But as Smith (1995) noted, "An ability to cope under the worst conditions is not liberation" (p. 256). In the same way, an ability to navigate persistent dissonance is not development for marginalized communities. Rather, the experience of persistent dissonance represents the perpetuation of systemic oppression.

Development in this context and from this standpoint requires bringing the dissonance to light. As Collins (2009) explained, "Rather than raising consciousness, Black feminist thought affirms, rearticulates, and provides a vehicle for expressing in public a consciousness that quite often already exists" (p. 36). Such dialogue, which Anzaldúa (2002) suggested may begin as an internal process and which hooks (1994) advocated as an approach to teaching, serves to allow for new ways of knowing to emerge within community. A sense of community, in turn, helps displace fear and isolation, both of which present barriers to development. Providing a critical perspective on Sanford's (1966) theory regarding the balance of challenge and support, hooks (2000) distinguished between support and solidarity. According to hooks (2000), "Solidarity is not the same as support. . . . Support can be occasional. It can be given and just as easily withdrawn. Solidarity requires sustained, ongoing commitment" (p. 67). Because the dissonance Women of Color experience is persistent and pervasive, the form of validation required to balance it out must be equally persistent and pervasive. To effectively develop from the dissonance they experience, Women of Color must also experience solidarity—an unwavering commitment to shared beliefs, goals, and interests that unite Communities of Color (hooks, 2000).

Dissonance Reenvisioned Through Black Feminism

As a standpoint theoretical perspective, Black feminism emphasizes the importance of understanding the positionalities of both those experiencing dissonance and those interpreting such experiences. Positionality describes how scholars relate to the topics they are examining and is often influenced by scholars' social identities and formative experiences (Jones, Torres, & Arminio, 2014). Thus, we (Danyelle and Kari) begin the reenvisioning process by reflecting on the salient social identities and formative experiences we bring to this process.

Danyelle's Positionality

As I reflect on my time in Ecuador, translating my words into Spanish provided multiple opportunities to think about my social identities. Throughout the experience, my race, ethnicity, and gender (and their connections) were most salient. When asked where I was from, I had multiple options. Some days I would answer "*Los Estados Unidos*," a simple answer, but it did not feel right. Most days, I would provide a more complex response: "*Los Estados Unidos, pero mi familia es de Jamaica.*" Something about this response helped me feel that I was actually talking about where I was from, not just limiting myself to the geographic location of the house I live in. My Jamaican heritage provides a very different experience than that of African Americans, though our racial identities are often conflated. I assumed that with some similar histories of colonialism and imperialism, there would be some parallels between Jamaican and South American experiences. I also made an assumption that there would be less anti-Black racism in Ecuador because of what I had read and seen regarding Ecuador's history.

Given the history and context of gender in Ecuador, I expected to experience more overt acts of sexism as a cisgender woman. One day as we were walking to lunch, a street harasser yelled, "*Negrita, negrita!*" (little Black woman) at me as I passed by. Because most words in Spanish have gender woven through them, in this instance it was easier to see the intersection of race and gender. In words and actions, gender, race, and ethnicity shaped my perceptions and interactions during this experience.

Kari's Positionality

As I read Danyelle's narrative, I considered one of my most salient identities to be my race. As a white individual, I realized that I would have been someone who people in Ecuador would have readily welcomed and embraced. My connections to colonialists and imperialists would have been easily overlooked, if acknowledged at all, and my inability to speak Spanish would have been largely excused. Because of the privilege my racial identity affords me, I would have likely attributed any negative reactions primarily to my gender. Yet, given my socialization, which trained me to see gender differences as normal and natural, I may have internalized any such negative reactions and attributed them to my individual character flaws. Another salient aspect of my background I considered as I read Danyelle's narrative was my level of education. Through master's and doctoral coursework focused on college student development, I learned the importance of naming the existence and effects of systemic oppression. This lesson, which remains a work in progress, has become clearer to me only after years of wrestling with the anguish that comes from acknowledging how my own community, my own family, and, indeed, my own self perpetuate oppression. I simultaneously empathized with and cringed at the site liaison's choice to leave unspoken the anti-Black racism that exists in Ecuador.

Redefining Dissonance

From these respective positionalities, we each used a Black feminist theoretical perspective to examine collaboratively the phenomenon of dissonance within the context of Danyelle's narrative. "What is *dissonance*? How do we as educators define it?" I asked. Danyelle responded that dissonance occurs when you realize that what a societal system and its authorities have told you is a lie. Earlier in Danyelle's life, dissonance arose when she realized that the "hard work leads to success" message her pastor preached did not fit with her family's lived experiences. It arose again during college when a professor pointed out that feminism is rooted in respecting women, not hating men as the media had portrayed. And, in Ecuador, it arose when her experience at the school in the Indigenous community did not match the expectations she had established based on the site liaison's predeparture communication. In all cases, dissonance initially was a visceral experience. She felt it in her gut—a sudden, unexpected change similar to the drop in your stomach when you descend a steep hill quickly. First, shock. Then, anger and disappointment at not only the system that created and told the lies but also yourself for believing the lies in the first place. Danyelle noted that the anger at herself stems from questioning, "Why would you ever believe that this circumstance, space, or system was created for you or someone like you?" Such anger is not about not knowing. Indeed, Danyelle knows—and has known—how societal systems work. Rather, such anger is about being betrayed again by people she had trusted to see and tell the ugly but true realities of unequal societies.

The conceptualization of dissonance as the phenomenon of recognizing lies that societal systems and its authorities tell differs from foundational conceptualizations of dissonance in three key ways. First, it frames development as a process of unlearning ideas conveyed through socialization and understanding how systems of privilege and oppression distort reality. Although contemporary college student development theories describe dissonance as the spark needed to initiate the examination of prior knowledge learned from parents and other authority figures (e.g., Baxter Magolda & King, 2012), these theories take care not to label such prior knowledge as *lies*. Yet, the term *lies* is essential to a Black feminist theoretical perspective of dissonance because it connotes that much—if not most—of the knowledge gained during childhood and adolescence does not represent truth. To call it truth would be to accept the way it oppresses oneself and others. Also, the term *lies* indicates that development begins not just when one sees the need to gain different or deeper truths but also, and more important, when one senses the need to root out distortions, myths, and misperceptions. As Collins (1989) explained, "Black women cannot afford to be fools of any type, for their devalued status denies them the protections that white skin, maleness, and wealth confer" (p. 759). Black women do not have the luxury to search for new truths when their survival depends on recognizing lies within dominant ideologies.

Second, a Black feminist conceptualization of dissonance focuses attention on systems, not only on individuals. Several foundational theorists, including Festinger (1957, 1962), Piaget (1950, 1965), and Sanford (1966), recognized the importance of attending to interactions between individuals and their social environments but did not explicitly speak to how systems of privilege and oppression shaped social environments. Belenky et al. (1986) initiated discussion of systems of privilege and oppression by addressing how gender dynamics influenced women's development, though they left intersections among gender, race, and social class largely unaddressed. With the lens of Black feminism, intersections among interlocking systems of oppression are central to the interpretation of Women of Color's lived experiences. These intersections give Spanish terms such as *negrita* their power, and they raise the stakes for Women of Color to navigate dissonance so as not to be "fools of any type" (Collins, 1989, p. 759). For Women of Color, dissonance is a matter not of an individual authority figure sharing a lie but rather of a group of authority figures caught up in an oppressive system perpetuating lies. Yes, the site liaison made an individual choice not to discuss anti-Black racism that exists in Ecuador with U.S. students prior to the cultural exchange, but this individual choice represented a legitimate option because of the system in which the site liaison operated. Moreover, this individual choice generated dissonance for not only Danyelle but also all Black women in the context. When framed with a focus on individuals, the source of dissonance appears to be that Danyelle holds a different perspective about the social context of Ecuador than does the site liaison. But when framed with a focus on systems, the source of dissonance becomes broader—that is, more representative of the complexities of the situation: Dissonance arose because the site liaison, who identifies as a Woman of Color and is intimately familiar with the Ecuadorian cultural context, did not prepare students for the oppression they may experience in Ecuador because she herself was bound up in interlocking systems of oppression.

Third and finally, from a Black feminist theoretical perspective, dissonance inherently involves grappling with how power operates in society. The reenvisioned definition of *dissonance*—the phenomenon of recognizing lies that societal systems and its authorities tell—rests on the assumption that power legitimizes lies. Because oppressed groups lack control over socializing institutions such as schools and the media, they struggle to express and gain validation for their perspectives (Collins, 1989). As Smith (1995) explained, "Women of Color generally have the fewest choices about the circumstances of their lives" (p. 256). To resist such lack of control and choice, it is critical and primary that Women of Color recognize what restricts their control and choice and why. Resistance, rather than acceptance, of one's own oppression thus involves inquiring about authorities' reasons for lying and a system's ability to perpetuate lies, which leads at least to an implicit recognition of power. In Danyelle's experience in Ecuador, dissonance arose not just because what authorities believed was different from what she believed but also because authorities possessed more power than she did to shape what counts as true. For example, the site liaison was able to keep anti-Black racism invisible because the dominant culture ignored the existence of anti-Black racism. When Danyelle encountered dissonance, her response was not to resist or question the existence of anti-Black racism—a response educators might typically expect based on foundational conceptualizations of dissonance. Rather, her response was, "Why did I believe the site liaison?" This question points to examination of the ways in which power shapes knowledge. The knowledge was there but had to be freshly remembered given the specific cultural context at hand.

Distinguishing Dissonance From Trauma

"This entire experience was traumatizing," Danyelle recounted in her narrative as she reflected on initial interactions with community partners in Ecuador. This sentence jarred me. "Where is the line between creating dissonance and inflicting trauma during an educational experience?" I wondered. I searched the nooks of my bookshelf and the crevices of my mind for insights but found myself at a loss given that I had never considered the possibility that the two phenomena were so closely related. My own racial privilege had allowed me to consistently treat dissonance and trauma as different phenomena because the dissonance I myself experienced in educational settings was largely separate from my lived realities. Dissonance proved enlightening, not triggering, for me on most occasions. Gradually, as Danyelle and I discussed her narrative using a Black feminist theoretical perspective, we (re)articulated that dissonance is inextricably intertwined with power dynamics in society. Thus, dissonance always poses more risk to those who are oppressed than those who are in power. To prevent dissonance from crossing the line into trauma, educators must recognize this inequity in risk and question whether the risk is necessary for all involved.

Although dissonance is unavoidable for students from marginalized communities, trauma is by no means a necessary or acceptable outcome. By embracing a more inclusive conceptualization of dissonance, educators can validate Women of Color's legacy of struggle without perpetuating it.

Transforming the Use of Dissonance for Development

Having reenvisioned dissonance, Danyelle and I turned toward discussing how to use dissonance productively and inclusively to foster development among diverse students. I wondered, "Was it necessary for you to learn that Ecuador represents yet another example of an unjust system?" She explained, "If that is what I was supposed to learn, I would have rather done it in a classroom than experience it in the way I did." She continued, "The classroom, while it can be a hard space, is an easier space because there is a distance from it." As advocates of experiential learning and its ability to challenge students to step beyond their comfort zones, Danyelle and I both wrestled with the idea that the classroom would have provided a more developmentally effective space than a cultural exchange to learn that racial injustice exists as much in Ecuador as it does in the United States. Through our dialogue, we realized that Women of Color did not need to experience oppression in Ecuador firsthand because they could have translated their knowledge of oppression in the United States to Ecuador given appropriate contextual information. The experience of oppression was superfluous at best, traumatizing at worst.

From a Black feminist theoretical perspective, the productive and inclusive use of dissonance requires educators to distinguish between the need to experience and the need to name lived realities. For Women of Color whose lived realities are routinely unnoticed and invalidated (Collins, 2009; Smith, 1995), the key is to name what they have already experienced. Naming the anti-Black racism that exists in Ecuador would have helped show the pervasiveness of systems of oppression while validating Danyelle's lived realities as a Woman of Color. Moreover, naming this social inequity could have generated dissonance without betrayal and revealed lies a system and its authorities tell without perpetuating them. Perhaps most important, naming the anti-Black racism that exists in Ecuador could have granted control and choice to Danyelle to decide for herself whether she wanted to engage in a cultural exchange that would require navigating different forms of oppression. On a general level, producing dissonance through the act of naming requires educators to be willing and able to frame dominant ideologies as lies—or, perhaps more palatably, distortions that arise because of how power operates within society. This framing indicates the need to engage in the type of critical reflection for which Brookfield (2000) advocated. According to Brookfield (2000), critical reflection requires students to "engage in some sort of power analysis of the situation or context in which learning is happening" and to "identify assumptions they hold dear that are actually destroying their sense of well-being and serving the interests of others" (p. 126). The act of naming certainly does not replace firsthand experience, but it can better equip students to experience development as an outcome of firsthand experience. It also allows educators to recognize whether students need firsthand experience to broaden their perspective of themselves and the world around them.

Because dissonance is a given within Women of Color's daily lives, the challenge typically lies not in introducing dissonance that disrupts their current ways of making meaning but rather in helping them process the dissonance they encounter. From a Black feminist perspective, two resources are essential for processing dissonance: agency (see chapter 12) and dialogue. As Anzaldúa (2002) explained, agency allows students to take action and work through feelings of fear and isolation. Also, as Tatum (1992) noted, raising students' awareness of unjust social realities without giving them agency to create social change is "a prescription for despair" (p. 20) and an unethical educational practice. Exploring strategies to resist and change oppressive systems is particularly necessary to ensure that those who experience oppression gain empowerment, instead of experiencing further trauma, when they encounter dissonance. In Ecuador, Danyelle was able to find a sense of agency in interactions with her host family members as she helped them understand the harm she was experiencing. Yet, this sense of agency was only sporadically experienced. The goal for educators is to create spaces where critical reflection empowers all learners to work toward social change.

Dialogue represents a resource that allows for shared agency among a group and a collective pursuit toward broader understanding. As Collins (1989) explained, dialogue is central to Black feminist epistemology because Black women usually develop new knowledge claims with other members of a community. Pointing to call-and-response discourse as an example of the importance of dialogue within African American communities, Collins noted, "For ideas to be tested and validated, everyone in the group must participate" (p. 763). In Ecuador, this version of dialogue never fully materialized, because some U.S. students opted out of processing dissonance-inducing experiences. Also, the dialogue that occurred during reflection sessions in Ecuador never came to center on the questions that arose for Danyelle— questions such as, "Why would I pay money to leave the United States only to experience an anti-Black sentiment in a new, differently disturbing way? Would there ever be a space where my race wasn't my most salient identity? What would the next few weeks look like for me in this community?"

When dissonance arose, Danyelle had to seek out her own outlet for dialogue. Discomfort about going abroad again now lingers for Danyelle. Fear and isolation remain unresolved. From a Black feminist lens, dialogue represents a deeply communal activity—one that works toward collective uplift in which each person recognizes how their survival is tied to that of others. In this way, it differs from traditional forms of debate and argumentation within academic spaces (Collins, 1989). To help students, particularly those from marginalized communities, process dissonance, educators must shift the purpose of dialogue from one of intellectual performance to one of interdisciplinary problem-solving where no one person holds all the necessary knowledge. When everyone sees the need, and has the agency, to participate, dialogue as envisioned by a Black feminist theoretical perspective can occur.

Conclusion

As we conclude, we wish to remind readers that the reenvisioned definition of *dissonance* that we discuss is neither new nor novel. Instead, it represents an acknowledgment of the long-invisible, often-unnamed ways in which Women of Color and other marginalized communities experience psychological inconsistency within collegiate learning environments. By reenvisioning dissonance as the phenomenon of recognizing lies that societal systems and their authorities tell, we aim to help educators recognize that development for all students must involve seeing how power shapes knowledge. In turn, seeing how power shapes knowledge requires the courage to name oppression and create spaces that allow for truly equitable dialogue.

Discussion Questions

1. Considering the reenvisioned definition of *dissonance*, identify times when you have experienced dissonance. How have these situations required you to unlearn ideas conveyed through your socialization?
2. What lies (i.e., ideas that do not acknowledge systems of privilege and oppression) do you perpetuate, and how does your identity shape your ability to tell them and for others to accept them as truths?
3. How will the presentation of this reenvisioned definition of *dissonance* affect how you approach creating experiences that will help learners develop?
4. Identify an educational context where you are responsible for helping facilitate dialogue. To what extent does dialogue involve everyone in the

group working to test and validate ideas? What steps could you take to ensure more equitable participation?

References

Anzaldúa, G. E. (2002). Now let us shift. . . the path of *conocimiento*. . . inner work, public acts. In G. E. Anzaldúa & A. Keating (Eds.), *This bridge we call home: Radical visions for transformation* (pp. 540–578). New York, NY: Routledge.

Baker, A. R., & Taylor, K. B. (2016, November). *Examining the role of discomfort in collegiate learning and development.* Paper presented at the Association for the Study of Higher Education (ASHE) Annual Conference, Columbus, OH.

Baxter Magolda, M. B., & King, P. M. (2012). *Assessing meaning making and self-authorship: Theory, research, and application* (ASHE Higher Education Report, Vol. 38, No. 3). San Francisco, CA: Jossey-Bass.

Belenky, M., Clinchy, B. M., Goldberger, N., & Tarule, J. (1986). *Women's ways of knowing: The development of self, voice, and mind.* New York, NY: Basic Books.

Brookfield, S. D. (2000). Transformative learning as ideology critique. In J. Mezirow & Associates (Eds.), *Learning as transformation: Critical perspectives on a theory in progress* (pp. 125–148). San Francisco, CA: Jossey-Bass.

Collins, P. H. (1989). The social construction of Black feminist thought. *Signs: Journal of Women in Culture and Society, 14*(4), 745–773.

Collins, P. H. (2009). *Black feminist thought: Knowledge, consciousness, and the politics of empowerment* (2nd ed.). New York, NY: Routledge.

Festinger, L. (1957). *A theory of cognitive dissonance.* Stanford, CA: Stanford University Press.

Festinger, L. (1962). Cognitive dissonance. *Scientific American, 207*(4), 93–106.

hooks, b. (1994). *Teaching to transgress: Education as the practice of freedom.* New York, NY: Routledge.

hooks, b. (2000). *Feminist theory: From margin to center.* London, UK: Pluto Press.

Hoover, E. (2014). The comfortable kid: In educating students, colleges walk a fine line between empowerment and entitlement. *The Chronicle of Higher Education.* Retrieved from http://chronicle.com/article/The-Comfortable-Kid/147915

Jones, S. R., Torres, V., & Arminio, J. (2014). *Negotiating the complexities of qualitative research in higher education: Fundamental elements and issues* (2nd ed.). New York, NY: Routledge.

Piaget, J. (1950). *The psychology of intelligence* (M. Piercy & D. Berlyne, Trans.). London, UK: Routledge.

Piaget, J. (1965). *The moral judgment of the child* (M. Gabain, Trans.). New York, NY: Simon & Schuster.

Popescu, I. (2016). The educational power of discomfort. *The Chronicle of Higher Education.* Retrieved from http://chronicle.com/article/The-Educational-Power-of/236136

Sanford, N. (1966). *Self and society*. New York, NY: Atherton Press.

Smith, B. (1995). Some home truths on the contemporary Black feminist movement. In B. Guy-Sheftall (Ed.), *Words of fire: An anthology of African-American feminist thought* (pp. 254–267). New York, NY: New Press.

Tatum, B. (1992). Talking about race, learning about racism: The application of racial identity development theory in the classroom. *Harvard Educational Review*, *62*(1), 1–25.

10

SOCIAL CONSTRUCTION OF IDENTITIES

D-L Stewart and Shaunda Brown

In this chapter, we offer a reframing of the social construction of identities through critical theoretical frameworks as defined in the preface of this text. Before discussing our approach and how we enter into this discussion, we share how scholars have previously discussed and understood the social construction of identities. As noted by Jones and Stewart (2016), the focus on social identities in the second wave of student development theory's evolution "necessitated a view of identities as socially constructed because social identities are anchored in group memberships that are influenced and mutually constructed by larger societal contexts" (p. 20). Moreover, understanding identities as socially constructed means recognizing the role of systemic oppression in the formation of one's meaning-making (Jones & Abes, 2013; Jones & Stewart, 2016). In addition, as discussed in Patton, Renn, Guido, and Quaye (2016), citing Vignoles, Schwartz, and Luyckx (2011), societal and contextual definitions of what identities mean may change across time and location. This reflected a departure from first-wave theories of identity that portray social identities in a number of ways that are open to challenge from a critical theory paradigm: First, social identities are posited to be individual instead of contextual and communal in first-wave models. Second, in first-wave models, social identities are presumed to already exist; in other words, that there is such a thing as race and that blackness preexists the individual. One is seen as Black upon birth; one does not become Black. Third, first-wave theories of social identity are seen as static inasmuch as blackness (to continue with this illustration) is blackness for everyone and at any time. One matures and develops along a particular trajectory that is linear and has a particular endpoint.

(Re)Constructing a Construction

We also understand identity to be necessarily formed through engagement with social constructions. In other words, as discussed by Stewart (2009, 2015), perceptions and articulations of one's social identities are constructed through interaction with others, both those inside and outside one's social identity group. Through a critical lens, however, we note that social identities, and the meaning and import of those identities, are inherently shaped specifically by systems of power and historical contexts through which one moves. For example, as historians of race have argued (Campbell, Oakes, & Jordan, 1993; Davis, 1997; Fields, 1982; Holt, 1998), race was invented to maintain European colonial supremacy. Thus, whiteness became a socially constructed category that creates and recreates race (Fields, 1982). Through whiteness, race was mandated to be a significant social identity through classifying individuals according to race, systemically subjugating non-white racial groups and thus positioning people with minoritized racial identities as reactive agents needing to defend, restore, and make valid their humanity alongside whiteness (Hesse, 2007). Oppression informs identity; it does not just coexist with it.

To engage this multifaceted identity kaleidoscope, we approach this retelling of the social construction of identity through portraiture methodology (Lawrence-Lightfoot, 1983, 1995; Lawrence-Lightfoot & Hoffman Davis, 1997; Stewart, 2001). As a method, portraiture allows us to present a narrative unbroken by a narrator's interpretive commentary to frame and highlight the resonant refrains and repetitive themes in an individual narrative. In this reconstruction, Shaunda Brown, an early career student affairs professional, describes her journey toward crafting an authentic self in the midst of the social construction of her identities.

As a narrative form, portraiture also reflects meaning-making's temporality and its inherently coconstructed form. It is temporal because this portrait of Shaunda is a snapshot of her in a particular space in time, in her meaning-making capacity and articulation, and in the current societal development of the United States. In this way, Shaunda's portrait is as much crafted by as it is bound by the space in time she currently occupies. Furthermore, portraits are inherently coconstructed. As Lawrence-Lightfoot and Hoffman Davis (1997) illustrated, a portrait is an intimate conversation between artist and subject. Their relationship plays an essential role in how the portrait develops.

Coming Into and Positioning Relationship

D-L is a Black, queer, disabled, and trans* educator who uses masculine pronouns (*he, him, his*) and the singular *they* (*them, their*) as his proper gender pronouns of reference. D-L uses these pronouns interchangeably throughout the chapter. As a Black person, D-L's family and community tutored them to acknowledge, accept, and integrate a positive understanding of his Black racial identity. Over time, a critical race perspective formed through D-L's evolving meaning-making of their ancestral roots in the chattel slavery of Africans forcibly removed from their Indigenous lands on the African continent to labor in the United States. Disparaged by their religious community, D-L's acknowledgment, acceptance, and integration of a positive queer and trans* identity came much later in life. Despite D-L being a "late bloomer," his critical race lens and adoption of an intersectional perspective of systemic oppression helped him cultivate queer critical and poststructural lenses alongside racial theoretical criticism (Stewart, 2017).

Shaunda's positionality is extrapolated fully in her narrative immediately following, so it is not repeated here. Readers will see that she shares some identities with D-L: They are both Black and queer; each was assigned female at birth; each was diagnosed with mental illnesses; both are survivors of sexual violence; and both entered college as working-class, first-generation students. Shaunda met D-L during her first year at her undergraduate institution where D-L was a member of the faculty and serving as the adviser for the queer Student of Color organization on campus. Shaunda and D-L came to develop a close bond beyond faculty and student to mentor and protégé and (substitutionary) parent and child.

"Broke but Never Broken": Shaunda's Journey

As an 18-year-old, first-year student, I was sexually assaulted on campus. I begin this narrative here not because my identity development begins at this point but because this moment altered the context of my development. This intimate act of violence initiated my journey to learning, acknowledging, and challenging ideas of power, privilege, and place related to my social group identities. I am a Black, queer, cisgender, college-educated, disabled woman, and I am a survivor. This act of self-identification is vital for me as a political act of intentional visibility. The main anchors of my identity have been my racial, sexual, and gender identities. Although I foreground these three aspects, I interweave education, class, ability, and survivor status throughout.

I have had to assert a blackness within and against environments marked by the intersection of white supremacy, classism, and ableism. Access to higher education has had and continues to have large influences on my Black identity development. I am a first-generation, low-income student. I hold educational privilege as a person who has earned both a bachelor's degree and a master's degree in my chosen profession. My Detroit roots, steeped in blackness, feel like they are disintegrating as I attain this form of social privilege. My family and home community developed a construction of blackness in a social environment that lacked both educational access and any belief in their academic potential.

As a result, being Black made my academic experience different from that of my white peers, who had a legacy of educational privilege in their families; however, I have to acknowledge my own increasing social privilege. My own educational access has made me an outlier. Higher education has provided me with financial stability, a new language with which to name and evaluate my experiences, opportunities to expand my thinking beyond the confines of Detroit, and resources beyond my home community.

It has been a difficult and exhausting journey to become comfortable with my blackness, even before I started to explore my multiple social identities. Dominant society overlooks the unique challenges faced by Black women at the intersection of multiple minoritized groups. As a child in a Black household, I learned to internalize my feelings for the sake of those around me by observing maternal figures enduring emotionally traumatic situations, from financial and family crises to their own illnesses and intimate partner violence and domestic abuse. In college, I received a diagnosis of high-functioning generalized anxiety and major depression. Immediately, I felt broken. I was told to "just get some rest and stay strong," and so I neglected my mental health for years. This toxic notion of unassailable Black women's strength plagued, and continues to influence, generations of Black women in my family. Given my understanding of Black womanhood, I equated ignoring my depression with being strong. As a result, I glorified busyness, and this became an addictive habit. The final semester of my undergraduate career was my breaking point; I was anxious and mentally incapable of leaving my apartment. My mental breakdown required me to receive emergency mental health services and to begin using the campus counseling services. I could not ignore or hide what I was secretly battling. My mental illness was, and is, my reality.

Coming of age as a queer person in Detroit required me to make meaning of and negotiate my queerness more frequently than my blackness. The perception of queerness as "unnatural" or being "disappointing" pressured me into high-risk circumstances so that I would be perceived as heterosexual. I wanted and needed to be accepted. My community dictated the positive associations with (cisgender, heterosexual) blackness. Queerness, however, was deemed to be not-Black in a similar way as academia was. My queerness was the target of various forms of attack, including being kicked out of my house and having my queerness constantly challenged by my community.

Consequently, my most salient identity entering college was my queer identity.

Though I entered college "out" and comfortable with my sexuality, my leadership experiences in student organizations substantively contributed to my queer identity development. Specifically, my involvement and leadership in Honoring, Urging, and Empowering (HUE), a student organization specifically for students and community members who were queer and trans People of Color (QTPOC), was the first time I explored both my queerness and my Black identity concurrently. I vividly remember often feeling that I had to choose between my Black identity and my queer identity when wanting to get involved with student organizations as an undergraduate student. The primary Black student organization at the time was notably heterosexist and had no visible Black queer people in leadership. Meanwhile, the primary queer organization on campus was a notoriously racially hostile space and had no visible People of Color in leadership roles. As I began to understand the ways that the university overlooked the experiences of QTPOC students, I started challenging various student spaces and student affairs administrators to recognize the interaction of racial and ethnic cultural identity and queer identity for QTPOC students in hopes of preventing the continued structural marginalization of our existence.

At the same time, my journey to womanhood has been shaped by both personal and intellectual experiences. As a woman who has been sexually violated, I had to acknowledge and overcome everything that happened to me that evening in order to integrate womanhood into my identity development. Even as I write this narrative, I am aware that I cannot adequately make meaning of how being assaulted has affected my identity development as a woman. It is something that I tend not to think about.

My gender identity remained partially uninvestigated far into my college career. I was able to theoretically talk about gender beyond the binary and urge the administration toward more gender-expansive policies. However, I was not doing the intentional self-work essential for dismantling toxic notions of womanhood and femininity. It was not until my third year in college that a speaker at a conference indirectly challenged me to confront my cisgender privilege. I was urged to consider how and when I was unwilling to address violence against other Black women, specifically Black transwomen. I became more aware of the problematic way I was socialized to favor transwomen whose femininity followed normative gender scripts and how that made me feel seemingly comfortable in my womanhood. My personal journey to understand and redefine my womanhood in opposition to toxic femininity and cisgenderism has led to self-actualization, happiness, and love.

Through my relationships and academic classes, I have formed an identity as a cisgender woman who believes in actively fighting against structural and institutional racism and the problematic ideologies that erase blackness and transwomen from feminist spaces. These collegiate experiences prompted me to question and revise what it meant to live in a country that is hell-bent on blatantly ignoring the existence of the multiplicity of my identities. I am queer, Black, and a woman—identities that can never be separated.

Along the way, this path to integrating a complex, intersectional understanding of my blackness, queerness, and (cis)womanhood has not happened in isolation as an internal project. Environmental influences have mattered a great deal. As I have shared, my undergraduate years were formative and introduced several new elements to my identity development. Specific microclimates and environmental resources have also played a role in refining and maturing my identity meaning-making. Mentorships have been, and continue to be, essential in providing either significant challenge or significant support in my identity journey. Without the guidance and mentorship of various advisers and professors, I know I would not be as authentic or aware of my identities as I am now. As an undergraduate student, I needed to be called out on my problematic ideas, supported through trauma and self-doubt, and nurtured through endless book recommendations. None of these people told me what path to take; they provided guidance that helped me through the path I chose to take. Most important, mentorship provided unconditional love and the opportunity to be *seen*. The term *mentor* does not adequately describe the relationship between these individuals and me. Instead, I frequently refer to these folx (this spelling is commonly used among Black queer people) as my family. Because of my distant relationship with family, my mentors served as parents and confidants, as family on holidays or for special occasions and guidance through academia. This family provided me with support and challenge that influenced me to develop into my authentic self, free from fear and doubt. These were the first folx to show me I had something valuable to contribute to this world and to tell my mother that I was brilliant. They saw my potential and me, even when I did not know who I was or where I was going.

This should not be construed as an assertion that I was not also influenced by my home community. Black communities are having substantive conversations about their social conditions and intracommunity struggles, including the male gaze, the prison industrial complex, hypermasculinity, and gender performance. These conversations are had in the common language of streetwise people with a lifetime of intimate knowledge of the influence of systemic oppression on their lives. However, white supremacist educational systems have structurally shut out those who are streetwise from academic spaces and socialized them to believe that their blackness is an obstacle and an antithesis to the life of the mind. As such, the academic discourse that I have learned to use seems distant, unfamiliar, and subjectively not Black.

To disrupt this, I am making an effort to intentionally scrap academic jargon in order to have these conversations in a way that they can recognize as relevant and applicable to their daily lives. Even as I write this narrative, I am fighting to balance my roots, legacy, and hometown with the world of academia. I am writing this narrative *as a method of transformation and development* through acknowledging, critically analyzing, and transcending my journey. I am committed to sharing my story because it is an essential part of developing my authentic self and acknowledging resilience and resistance.

Re/Thinking With Theory: Paradigmatic Lenses

Shaunda deftly illustrates her awareness of societal oppression through in-group internalized oppression and out-group internalized dominance. This awareness became instructive for how she has come to understand how her minoritized and privileged identities operate on societal levels and within social groups as dynamic, fluid, and nonstatic.

> Redefining identity as fluid, dynamic, and co-constructed within and across communities operating within social systems mired in modernist encampments allows for recognition of the material effects of social group subjection without presuming that identities are solid, fixed, or stable. (Stewart, 2017, p. 288)

This redefinition reflects a different paradigmatic orientation than has previously been applied to considerations of the social construction of identity.

As noted in the introduction to this part of this book, scholars oriented in constructivist perspectives of the social construction of identities acknowledged the social context in which identity is formed, including the effect of oppressive systems, while also presenting identity construction as something crafted between and among individuals. As Young (2011) pointed out in her definition of social groups and how they are formed, we become who we are through mutual arrangement with the community (or communities) to which we belong. Young's discussion foregrounds a psychosocial approach to identity that occludes hegemonic systems of socialization as a factor in how identities are socially constructed. This *critical constructivist* perspective is reflected also in scholarship by Stewart (2015). Such an approach is inadequate for understanding Shaunda's narrative.

However, a *critical-poststructuralist* paradigm (Stewart, 2017) redefines identity and what social construction can mean. The messy and complex realities of life as a person with multiple minoritized identities defy simple analysis through one ontological or epistemic frame. Critical theories (e.g., critical race theory, critical feminist theory, and intersectionality) solidify social identities as rigid realities (Childers, 2014). In contrast, poststructural frameworks such as deconstructionism have a nihilistic view of identity that eschews identity-based activism (Burbules & Rice, 1991). In other words, this view claims that social identities are inherently unstable and therefore should not be used to inform resistance to power structures.

Neither theoretical perspective is sufficient to prioritizing doing justice through theoretical analysis. Blending the two allowed us to recognize individual and collective agency to "co-create, co-challenge, and co-resist existing power structures" (Stewart, 2017, p. 288). Following Childers (2014), Stewart (2017) referenced such use of multiple conceptual frameworks as "high-density theorizing" (p. 287).

Rethinking Social Construction of Identities Through High-Density Theorizing

Such high-density theorizing employs a critical-poststructural paradigm through multiple theoretical frameworks. In this way, we were able to engage both the pervasiveness of whiteness and white supremacy enunciated in Shaunda's narrative and the ways in which she engages with state apparatuses that attempt to shape how she constructs her social identities as Black, queer, disabled, educated, and a woman. This lens is also reflected through such postcritical and poststructural theoretical frameworks as QueerCrit and quare theories and posthumanism (Hesse, 2007; Johnson, 2001; Misawa, 2010, 2014, 2012; Weheliye, 2014). Posthumanism is a poststructural theoretical framework in the legacy of Indigenous and other preindustrial societies' long-standing recognition of the ways in which nonhumans exercise agency over humans and within human social groups. Specifically, posthumanism and its related frameworks, feminist materialism and postqualitative inquiry, reject modernist views of humanity as the sole agents of reality, knowing, and meaning. Please see Taylor (2017) for further discussion. Through these theoretical frameworks, we assert that Shaunda's narrative illustrates rejecting dehumanization and destabilizing identity.

Rejecting Dehumanization

Shaunda's queerness has been mutually constituted through her racial–gender identity as a Black woman. QueerCrit (Misawa, 2010, 2014, 2012) and quare theory (Johnson, 2001) both emphasize the intersectional relationship of racism and queer antagonism (the structures and systems that oppress queer people) with forming self and community understandings of what it means to be a queer Person of Color. When Shaunda talks about needing to define herself for herself between the queer antagonism of her community in Detroit and the white supremacy of predominantly white campus queer communities, she is negotiating a way to present and show up as a *Blackqueerwoman* in both spaces. Making meaning of her Black woman queerness required her learning to redefine what it meant to be Black, woman, and queer outside presumed heterosexuality and religio-cultural norms for (cis)gender relationships.

Through these frameworks, queerness is understood and interpreted through a racial lens that begins with recognizing that institutionalized systems of oppression always and already are re/producing the dehumanization and ostracism of one's body, worldview, and habits of being. Shaunda's community helped her recognize society's press to accept her racial dehumanization even as these elders and community institutions re/produced the dehumanization and ostracism of her queerness. Shaunda's home community was not wholly liberatory or repressive. Rather, Shaunda was able to perceive and recognize the processes of queer dehumanization and ostracism because her community had already taught her how to see those processes in relation to her race. That early community-based knowledge also facilitated her ability to insulate herself from the racism and white supremacy within the predominantly white queer community she found in college. Through QueerCrit and quare theories, Shaunda's narrative re/tells how identities are socially constructed by and against the both–and of racism and queer antagonism.

Destabilizing Identity

Through Shaunda's narrative, coming to terms with one's identity is presented as a destabilizing experience. Each moment of being confronted by a new aspect of her identity—sexual assault survivor, queer woman, disabled, increasing educational and class privilege, professional socialization—was personally destabilizing. These repeated downturns in her mental health as her emotional, psychological, and physical stress was heightened reflect what Hesse (2007) and Sharpe (2016) discussed as the effects of engagement with hegemonic systems and structures, particularly enslavement and racial terrorism. Furthermore, Hesse (2007) argued that what has been termed as *racial identity development*, for example, reflects a process of learning to live with and under white supremacy. Constructivist models of racial identity development (e.g., Cross & Fhagen-Smith, 2001; Cross, 1971) are reflective not of the development of a critical liberatory consciousness but rather of the development of a consciousness that accepts white supremacy as a natural feature of social life that one becomes increasingly better at managing. The consequences of this are racial stress and fatigue that have material effects on mental and physical health. Understanding Shaunda's social identity development only within a constructivist framework that acknowledges but does not criticize such oppression fails to engage criticalism's liberatory goal for minoritized individuals and communities.

Her journey has also been one of destabilizing supposedly fixed notions of certain social identities. For example, integrating educational privilege and multiple other minoritized identities has disrupted the fixity and norms associated with Black racial identity that she was tutored in by her family and Detroit community. The acceptance and integration of her disability and queer identities, as well as her educational privilege, have brought Shaunda to a place where blackness has been expanded and become multifaceted, more like a kaleidoscope than a one-dimensional surface. She now rejects the fixity, stability, and consistency of a Black racial identity formed merely in opposition to whiteness. Shaunda also rejects what Kendi (2016) described as *uplift suasion*, the idea that proving moral equivalency and even superiority to white people will grant Black people humanity in the eyes of white people. Instead, Shaunda deliberately claims those aspects of her social identities (e.g., disabled and queer) that are constructed as dishonorable according to Black racial narratives that extol strength and morality according to cishetpatriarchal norms. Those identities constructed as anathema are now central to and mutually constitutive (not singular or separate from each other) in her construction of self.

Furthermore, through a posthumanist lens on identity, Weheliye (2014) theorized that social identities inherently defy fixity, stability, and consistency. Individuals, especially those with racially minoritized identities, must sift through multiple competing ideologies about their identities from social institutions and within their own identity communities. The process of engaging with institutionally conveyed societal messages and multiple, varying, and conflicting interpersonal communities influences self and community understandings of what it means to hold a particular identity. Meaning-making and articulations of identity are therefore subject to (d)evolution and should be expected to (d)evolve across time and space. Identifying in one way and making meaning of an identity in the same way over time are made impossible through the destabilizing effects of these varied and conflicting messages.

For Shaunda, recognition, acceptance, and integration of multiple minoritized identities means having to dismantle and rebuild what she previously understood the other aspects of her identity to be. Through such critical-poststructuralist perspectives, social identities are subjected to dynamic and evolving reframings beyond second-wave theorists' assumptions of a progression in integrating and articulating social identity within oppressive contexts.

Facilitating Social (Re)Construction of Identity

Student development theories, including social identity models, have not merely described the developmental process but also proposed factors that facilitate such development (Patton et al., 2016). We eschew development—the presumption of increasing complexity—as an effective descriptor for Shaunda's identity meaning-making and construction; her constructions were already complex. Yet, we do recognize the need to consider contributing factors to her meaning-making process. Two of these contributing factors are evident in Shaunda's narrative: mentoring and community engagement.

Mentoring as Other-Mothering

In her narrative, Shaunda shares the key role that mentoring has played in her ability to craft a positive self-concept and understanding of the construction of her social identities. The parental role that she attributes to these mentors reflects the "other-mothering" that James (1993) and Griffin (2013) theorized. Posited both as a tool for social transformation (James, 1993) and as a form of social exchange (Griffin, 2013), other-mothering challenges constructivist and binarist views of the role of external authority figures in the development of self-authorship (Baxter Magolda, 2001, 2004) and mature identity development (Chickering & Reisser, 1993). Despite attempts to position external authority figures as capable of promoting maturity and development, these models still require young adults to first "push away from the dock" as Parks (2000, p. 100) described. Adults are replaced by peers as the primary influences in young adulthood.

In direct contrast to this, Shaunda credits her mentors—these other-mothers (though not all women-identified)—in her life with helping her develop the confidence to construct internal formulas that would begin to guide her identity meaning-making, decision-making, and how she is sharing her story. Shaunda never pushed away from these mentors but rather drew closer to them as possibility models for how she could live her own life with authenticity and confidence. In Shaunda's story, other-mothering—through relationships with adults, not apart from them—is a facilitator of redefining her identity despite the press of external, social constructions of what her identities should mean.

Community-Engaged Praxis

A final important element in Shaunda's narrative is the way she describes her community engagement, through activism and advocacy, as having a role in shaping her professional and personal commitments to herself and in community with others. Shaunda's identity meaning-making was shaped in no small part through her engagement in various communities, such as feminist and queer Students of Color organizations. Engaging with these communities was a demonstration of the unifying of ideology and action—a praxis. The enactment of her values through a praxis of community engagement leads to greater identity integration and more complex understandings and articulations of her identities.

Shaunda's commitment to a transinclusive feminism and the conflict she felt in transantagonist, white feminist spaces led her to recognize and accept her privilege as a cisgender woman. As a result, she is integrating a more complex understanding of what it means for her to be a Black queer cisgender disabled woman who has survived sexual violence. Her activism both clarified her values and her understanding of how a cissexist society socially constructed womanhood and affords her social privilege. This community engagement was both facilitator and outcome as she mobilized her social identities to transform the spaces that she occupied.

Activism has been framed in early second-wave psychosocial identity models as the endpoint of social identity development as the identity becomes more salient in an individual's life (e.g., Bilodeau, 2005; Cross, 1971; D'Augelli, 1994). Oppression serves as the context in which identity is formed and at which it is later directed. Although later second-wave theorists moved away from this perspective (e.g., Cross & Fhagen-Smith, 2001; Feldman & Gallegos, 2001), the role of activism in the process of identity meaning-making was not discussed.

Through a critical-poststructural paradigm, community-engaged praxis—including activism—is an essential aspect of doing the work of justice, seeking to transform thinking. Doing justice is not an outgrowth of increasing complexity in a developmental process. Rather, critical-poststructuralism understands doing justice is an enactment of rejecting dehumanization and destabilizing fixed notions of identity. It is the outcome of rejecting societal constructions of what one's identities should mean.

Conclusion

Redefining social constructions of identity through a critical-poststructural paradigm has multiple implications for both theory and practice. First, for future research and theory development, it is necessary to recognize the intimate role that oppression plays in *forming* identities, not just as the context within which identities are formed. Second, the interplay of privilege and oppression within minoritized communities (e.g., the cisheteronormativity and ableism that may exist within racially minoritized groups) especially deserves further attention regarding how it may shape and dictate meaning-making about one's identities. Third, we challenge researchers to develop a more complex and nuanced perspective of the role that adults can play in young adult identity development. Young people may need to push away from some adults—especially those who are toxic and hostile to core aspects of their identity. However, these parental roles may be filled by other adults whose roles are not to direct the young adult's becoming but rather to affirm, support, and enable that becoming.

Implications for practice follow from these theoretical recommendations. First, it is important to challenge student groups to study and analyze their within-group diversity as an essential element in the group's self-definition. This disrupts the tendency to draw hard boundaries around identity groupings that ultimately exclude or force developmentally regressive choices in order to find one's people. Second, mental health resources need to include professionals who recognize and can support the mental health effects that accompany the labor required to acknowledge, accept, and integrate a positive self-concept for an identity subjected to social constructions of stigma and minoritization. Third, we recommend that mentoring models in college recognize the positive effects that faculty and staff can have on identity development, not just academic and career development (see also Tillapaugh, 2012). Alongside this, we note that the burden of this emotional labor falls unevenly and more heavily on minoritized faculty and staff. As a result, faculty and staff evaluation and reward structures need to tangibly acknowledge this as an element of the workload of those who engage in other-mothering with undergraduate and graduate students. Finally, as Shaunda notes at the end of her narrative, telling one's story is a developmental exercise in itself. We challenge educators to intentionally provide opportunities for students to tell the stories of their own lives.

> Telling my story is a method of transformation and development. Through this, I am acknowledging and critically analyzing my journey, while transcending it to reach new aspects and depths of being. —Shaunda

Discussion Questions

1. How might you use portraiture to learn about the social construction of identities among young adults? What other critical methodologies can work to center students' self-perceptions and meaning-making?
2. How can you apply the implications to practice we offer here to working with college students? What structural challenges exist that may impede these options?
3. How does reading Shaunda's narrative and our retelling of the social construction of identities change how you might approach teaching this aspect of student development theory? In what ways can you prompt students to offer their own self-portraits of the factors that have influenced their social identity meaning-making?

References

Barbules, N., & Rice, S. (1991). Dialogue across differences: Continuing the conversations. *Harvard Educational Review, 61*(4), 393–417.

Baxter Magolda, M. B. (2001). *Making their own way: Narratives for transforming higher education to promote self-development.* Sterling, VA: Stylus.

Baxter Magolda, M. B. (2004). Evolution of a constructivist conceptualization of epistemological reflection. *Educational Psychologist, 39*(1), 31–42.

Bilodeau, B. L. (2005). Beyond the gender binary: A case study of two transgender students at a midwestern university. *Journal of Gay and Lesbian Issues in Education, 3*(1), 29–46.

Campbell, J., Oakes, J., & Jordan, W. (1993). The invention of race: Rereading *White Over Black* [Review]. *Reviews in American History, 21*(1), 172–183.

Chickering, A. W., & Reisser, L. (1993). *Education and identity* (2nd ed.). San Francisco, CA: Jossey-Bass.

Childers, S. (2014). Promiscuous analysis in qualitative research. *Qualitative Inquiry, 20*(6), 819–826.

Cross, W. E., Jr. (1971). Toward a psychology of Black liberation: The Negro-to-Black conversion experience. *Black World, 20*(9), 13–27.

Cross, W. E., Jr., & Fhagen-Smith, P. (2001). Patterns in African American identity development: A life span perspective. In C. L. Wijeyesinghe & B. W. Jackson III (Eds.), *New perspectives on racial identity development: A theoretical and practical anthology* (pp. 243–270). New York, NY: New York University Press.

Davis, D. B. (1997). Constructing race: A reflection. *The William and Mary Quarterly, 54*(1), 7–18.

D'Augelli, A. R. (1994). Identity development and sexual orientation: Toward a model of lesbian, gay, and bisexual identity development. In E. J. Trickett, R. J.

Watts, & D. Birman (Eds.), *Human diversity: Perspectives on people in context* (pp. 312–333). San Francisco, CA: Jossey-Bass.

Feldman, B. M., & Gallegos, P. I. (2001). Racial identity development and Latinos in the United States. In C. L. Wijeyesinghe & B. W. Jackson,III (Eds.), *New perspectives on racial identity development: A theoretical and practical anthology* (pp. 32–66). New York, NY: New York University Press.

Fields, B. J. (1982). Ideology and race in American history. In J. M. Kousser & J. M. McPherson (Eds.), *Region, race, and reconstruction: Essays in honor of C. Vann Woodward* (pp. 143–177). New York, NY: Oxford University Press.

Griffin, K. A. (2013). Voices of the "othermothers": Reconsidering Black professors' relationships with Black students as a form of social exchange. *The Journal of Negro Education, 82*(2), 169–183.

Hesse, B. (2007). Racialized modernity: An analytics of white mythologies. *Ethnic and Racial Studies, 30*(4), 643–663.

Holt, T. C. (1998). Explaining racism in American history. In A. Molho & G. S. Wood (Eds.), *Imagined histories: American historians interpret the past* (pp. 107–119). Princeton, NJ: Princeton University Press.

James, S. M. (1993). Mothering: A possible Black feminist link to social transformation? In S. M. James & A. P. A. Busia (Eds.), *Theorizing Black feminisms: The visionary pragmatism of Black women* (pp. 44–54). New York, NY: Routledge.

Johnson, E. P. (2001). "Quare" studies, or (almost) everything I know about queer studies I learned from my grandmother. *Text and Performance Quarterly, 21*(1), 1–25.

Jones, S. R., & Abes, E. S. (2013). *Identity development of college students: Advancing frameworks for multiple dimensions of identity.* San Francisco, CA: Wiley.

Jones, S. R., & Stewart, D-L. (2016). Evolution of student development theory. In E. S. Abes (Ed.), *Critical perspectives on student development theory* (New Directions for Student Services, No.154, pp. 17–28). San Francisco, CA: Jossey-Bass.

Kendi, I. X. (2016). *Stamped from the beginning: The definitive history of racist ideas in America.* New York, NY: Nation Books.

Lawrence-Lightfoot, S. (1983). *The good high school: Portraits of character and culture.* New York, NY: Basic Books.

Lawrence-Lightfoot, S. (1995). *I've known rivers: Lives of loss and liberation.* New York, NY: Penguin Books.

Lawrence-Lightfoot, S., & Hoffman Davis, J. (1997). *The art and science of portraiture.* San Francisco, CA: Jossey-Bass.

Misawa, M. (2010). Musing on controversial intersections of positionality: A queer crit perspective in adult and continuing education. In V. Sheared, J. Johnson-Bailey, S. A. Collin III, E. Peterson, & S. D. Brookfield (Eds.), *The handbook of race and adult education: A resource for dialogue on racism* (pp. 187–199). San Francisco, CA: Jossey-Bass.

Misawa, M. (2012). *Social justice narrative inquiry: A queer crit perspective.* Paper presented at the Adult Education Research Conference, Saratoga Springs, NY. Retrieved from http://newprairiepress.org/aerc/2012/papers/34

Misawa, M. (2014). *Professional identity development: An Asian queer crit perspective in adult and higher education.* Paper presented at the Adult Education Research Conference, St. Louis, MO. Retrieved from http://newprairiepress.org/cgi/viewcontent.cgi?article=3633&context=aerc

Parks, S. D. (2000). *Big questions, worthy dreams: Mentoring young adults in their search for meaning, purpose, and faith.* San Francisco, CA: Wiley.

Patton, L. D., Renn, K. A., Guido, F., & Quaye, S. J. (2016). *Student development in college: Theory, research, and practice* (3rd ed.). San Francisco, CA: Jossey Bass.

Sharpe, C. (2016). *In the wake: On Blackness and being.* Durham, NC: Duke University Press.

Stewart, D-L. (2001). *Awareness and integration of multiple sociocultural identities among Black students at a predominantly white institution* (Doctoral dissertation). Retrieved from http://rave.ohiolink.edu/etdc/view?acc_num=osu1407344347

Stewart, D-L. (2009). Perceptions of multiple identities among Black college students. *Journal of College Student Development, 50*(3), 253–270.

Stewart, D-L. (2015). Know your role: Black college students, racial identity, and performance. *International Journal of Qualitative Studies in Education, 28*(2), 238–258.

Stewart, D-L. (2017). Trans*versing the DMZ: A non-binary autoethnographic exploration of gender and masculinity. *International Journal of Qualitative Studies in Education, 30*(3), 285–304.

Taylor, C. A. (2017). Rethinking the empirical in higher education: Post-qualitative inquiry as a less comfortable social science. *International Journal of Research and Method in Education, 40*(3), 311–324.

Tillapaugh, D. W. (2012). *Toward an integrated self: Making meaning of the multiple identities of gay men in college* (Doctoral dissertation). University of San Diego, CA.

Vignoles, V. L., Schwartz, S. J., & Luyckx, K. (2011). Introduction: Toward an integrative view of identity. In S. J. Schwartz, K. Lyuckx, & V. L. Vignoles (Eds.), *Handbook of identity theory and research* (pp. 1–27). New York, NY: Springer-Verlag.

Weheliye, A. G. (2014). *Habeas viscus: Racializing assemblages, biopolitics, and Black feminist theories of the human.* Durham, NC: Duke University Press.

Young, I. M. (2011). *Justice and the politics of difference.* Princeton, NJ: Princeton University Press. (Original work published 1990).

11

COMPLEXITIES
OF AUTHENTICITY

*V. Leilani Kupo (Kānaka Maoli/Native Hawaiian) and
Symphony Oxendine (Cherokee/Choctaw)*

A uthenticity has been used as a means to encourage individuals to better understand and conceptualize the ways in which they understand who they are. The concept of *authenticity* has been defined in many ways but "involves features such as being genuine, becoming more self-aware, being defined by one's self rather than by others' expectations . . . and critically reflecting on self, others, relationships in context" (Kreber, Klampfleitner, McCune, Bayne, & Knottenbelt, 2007, pp. 40–41). Authenticity involves actively attending to and managing external perceptions and expectations while navigating one's own identity (Jones, 2016; Jones, Kim, & Skendall, 2012). To be clear, authenticity is complex, multifaceted, and ever changing. Within the area of college student development, Baxter Magolda's (2001, 2008) work centering self-authorship creates a foundation or framework to explore concepts of authenticity. Authenticity can be used as a means to encourage self-reflection, exploration of self, and personal development (Jones et al., 2012). However, authenticity is also shaped by external factors, including community and societal expectations, environment, oppression, and socialization. Learning what is considered authentic and what is not can add additional complexities to understanding one's authentic self, particularly for those who are asked (and at times required) to define and justify who they are and their concept of self. Navigating these hidden and explicit rules and expectations can affect the ways in which individuals make meaning of their authentic selves.

Reflections and findings focusing on "what it means to live an authentic life or to express an authentic sense of self is omnipresent in the identity literature" (Jones et al., 2012, p. 708). However, authenticity is viewed as an end goal; it is presumed to be present and achievable. It is also treated as static. A key component of identity development includes the development of core identity, the foundation of one's identity, and an authentic sense of self (Baxter Magolda, 2001, 2008; Chickering & Reisser, 1993; Erikson, 1968). Delving into the notion of authentic self and the ways in which authenticity is conceptualized, Jones et al. (2012) posed two intriguing questions: (a) "Is authenticity also contextual?" and (b) "If one is constantly negotiating identities and managing the perceptions of others, is that an authentic way to live?" (p. 708). These two questions challenge the notion that authenticity is static or a single state which one must strive to achieve. The questions provide opportunities to explore how one's authenticity can change because of external forces and the importance of managing and understanding not only one's perception of authentic self but also others' perceptions. These questions encourage explorations into how external judgments confirm legitimacy or invalidate one's authentic self. For many Native and Indigenous community members, authenticity is constantly being negotiated, fluid, and often influenced by perceptions of others' understanding of what it means to be a "real" or "true" Native or Indigenous person. As we interrogate notions of authenticity, we situate ourselves as Indigenous women scholars who have specific lived experiences. We want to clearly highlight and name that Indigenous worldviews are not monolithic. We emphasize the fact that Tribal and Native Hawaiian community politics are complex, contextual, historical, and ever changing. We acknowledge this will serve as a brief overview and will not address all complexities.

We begin by posing the question, "Is it possible to decolonize authenticity?" Significant complexity and tension exist within the standards of how authenticity is judged for Indigenous and Native peoples. Many Native and Indigenous peoples conceptualize and legitimize their authentic selves through genealogy, relationship to land, and community. Complicating this process, authenticity has also been confirmed and legitimized with performance of identity, phenotype, and biology (Kauanui, 2008; Trask, 1999). Also, standards established by the government, tribes, community, nation, and individuals influence and shape concepts of authenticity. Simply stated, Indigenous identity politics are ever changing and multifaceted as identity depends on not only community expectations but also governmental and societal standards. It is an illustration of how authenticity is dependent on one's own self and the factors listed previously as well as a description of how community judges its own and evaluates authenticity and belonging.

For Native and Indigenous communities colonized by the United States, specifically Native Americans, American Indians, Native Alaskans, Native Hawaiians, and Pacific Islanders, questions of authenticity have not only applied to the concept of self but also included justification of nativeness based on definitions and policies created by the U.S. government. Regarding Native American tribes or "Indians," beginning in the mid-1800s the U.S. government, under the Jackson administration, sought to implement policies to assimilate individual tribal nations to create "large, easily manipulated political-social units" (Satz, 1975, p. 136). Thus, "developing the concept of monolithic tribes was the government's way of simplifying treaty negotiations and making it easier for agents to administer federal Indian policy and control Indian society" (Satz, 1975, p. 136). Consequently, the implementation of these federal policies included the government defining who was legitimately classified as an "Indian" in order to receive entitled benefits. Eventually, because of pressure from the government, tribes started engaging and adopting the government's identity policies to align and comply.

Disturbingly, this has also resulted in legalized genocide for Indigenous communities as requirements are based on proving blood quantum (degree of ancestry) and genetic descent (Kauanui, 2008) through the establishment of blood quantum thresholds. These governmental requirements differ from Indigenous community definitions of identity, which are grounded in genealogy, community, cultural knowledge, and connection to land (Kauanui, 2008; Trask, 1999). The differences set up tensions within communities regarding who belongs, who qualifies as real, and who should be able to claim the identity or label of "authentic" Native.

Native and Indigenous communities have, in some ways, adopted this monolithic sense of "Native/Indigenous" authenticity. Communities value criteria such as tribal enrollment and blood quantum because, by necessity, they have adopted governmental standards for determining authenticity. However, these criteria may not have necessarily eliminated the community's inherent judgments of authenticity. Community standards also include the ways in which you engage in your culture, language, geography, and location. Standards also include an examination of direct and indirect ties to land and foodways. Consequently, the concept of "Indian country" is a form of groupthink. It is exemplified in the creation of a system where some people will fit into the system of identity, and some people will not. Policies described originally applied to Native Americans on the continental United States. However, as Indigenous territories and peoples have been, and continue to be, colonized by the U.S. government (e.g., Native Alaskans, Native

Hawaiians, Chamorro, Carolinian), the concept of "Native" authenticity continues to grow more complex.

Why does this matter? As conversations about authenticity continue, it is critical to acknowledge authenticity is fluid and contextual. For some, the conception of self is informed by external forces, including historical events, the government, eugenics, and assimilation (Brayboy, 2005; Kauanui, 2008; Trask, 1999). These factors, along with others, influence how one can understand authenticity. Although one's concept of self may feel authentic to them (Baxter Magolda, 2008; Jones et al., 2012), issues including proving one's legitimacy and meeting external expectations and standards to demonstrate authenticity continue to complicate what it means to be and live one's authentic self. We continue to trouble concepts of authenticity and return to the question, "Is it possible to decolonize authenticity?"

Language

For the purpose of this chapter, we will be using the language of Native and Indigenous communities as a means to discuss and describe experiences and histories of Native Americans, American Indians, Native Hawaiians, Native Alaskans, and Pacific Islanders. For context, we will be focusing on communities colonized by the U.S. government. We acknowledge that these labels encompass many different nations and that the communities represented are unique and not monolithic.

Frameworks

To interrogate the ways in which one can embody authenticity and live authentic lives, we believe it is important to identify context and worldviews. Both authors of this chapter identify as descendants of Indigenous peoples who were colonized by the United States. We live our lives navigating messages grounded in assimilation and colonization. Laenui (2006) argued that colonization requires Indigenous people to go through a process in which the colonizer's denial of the validity of Indigenous culture is accompanied by Indigenous people denying and withdrawing from their own culture. Although the process of colonization, according to Laenui (2006), proceeds through "stages of eradication and denigration, the final stages involved a co-optation of Indigenous culture into the epistemological framework of dominant society and an exploitation of Indigenous cultural practice for commercial, artistic or political value" (pp. 1–2). To address this assimilation and colonization, we use the frameworks of decolonization, tribal critical race theory (TribalCrit) and Indigenous

Knowledge Systems to make meaning and understand the world around us. By understanding and making meaning of the world around us, we then better understand our authentic selves.

Decolonization

To recover, one must experience the process of decolonization. According to Laenui (2006), five stages of decolonization exist: (a) rediscovery and recovery, (b) mourning, (c) dreaming, (d) commitment, and (e) action. For Indigenous peoples, "being colonized was—is—a violent process" (Marshall, 2011, p. 1).

> Being colonized meant that the very possibility of Hawaiian existence—the possibility of specifically Kānaka Maoli ways of being and knowing—was deliberately erased. Being colonized means foreign penetration deep into the psyches, souls, and cells of indigenous Hawaiians. (Marshall, 2011, p. 2)

At its core, decolonization is about overcoming the shame of being colonized. It requires the process of remembering traditions of ancestors and reinterpreting and rewriting histories that have been told only from a colonial point of view. Decolonizing is about challenging Western interpretations of Native and Indigenous culture and history and reinterpreting from a Native and Indigenous point of view to meet the needs of Indigenous peoples in the twenty-first century.

TribalCrit

Lumbee scholar Brayboy (2005) introduced TribalCrit to explore and interrogate the issues of Indigenous people in relationship to the U.S. government, specifically its laws and policies. Though racism is identified as a significant component, colonization serves as a primary tenet within TribalCrit, as it is endemic in nature to processes in society. TribalCrit functions to "expose the inconsistencies in structural systems and institutions . . . [to] make the situation better for Indigenous students" (Brayboy, 2005, p. 441). Similar to critical race theory, TribalCrit is a mechanism for truth telling, for testimony—"to speak back to colonization and oppression" (Writer, 2008, p. 3).

Indigenous Knowledge Systems

Indigenous people have their own ways of experiencing, navigating, and relating to the world, the universe, and each other (Ascher, 2002; Barnhardt,

2005; Eglash, 2002). Traditional education processes centered observing nature and natural processes, adapting and revisioning methods of survival, gathering sustenance from the plant and animal world, and using natural materials to make tools and implements. Demonstration and observation accompanied by thoughtful stories in which the lessons were embedded made this education understandable (Cajete, 2000; Kawagley, 1995). As noted by Houseman (2015), "Cultural practices in the area of genealogy, history, religion, traditional stories, farming, fishing, canoe making, navigation, sports, martial arts, hula, lei-making, food preparation, and medicine are still vital parts of everyday living" (p. 55). Traditional knowledge holds essential keys that are critical to understanding the Native worldview (see chapter 5 and chapter 13).

We engage decolonization, TribalCrit, and Indigenous Knowledge Systems, as current Western and traditional student development theories do not attend to the unique lived experiences of Native and Indigenous peoples. Decolonization, TribalCrit, and Indigenous Knowledge Systems trouble the ways in which Western forms of knowledge are conceived. These frameworks decenter the individual, center community, and acknowledge how the U.S. government defines who can claim Native or Native identity. When coupled with TribalCrit, decolonization and Indigenous Knowledge Systems work as a powerful trio and push issues of historical trauma, oppression, settler colonialism, and the government's role in defining authenticity and belonging to the forefront. The frames enhance each other and allow conversations regarding identity and authenticity to broaden and deepen. These frames provide a platform to trouble traditional college student identity theories and explore how authenticity is reimagined and redefined. Decolonization, TribalCrit, and Indigenous Knowledge Systems encourage deeper explorations regarding the ways in which authenticity can be decolonized.

Student Development Theory: Erasure and Reclamation

There are currently no theories that focus on the development of Native or Indigenous students within the U.S. collegiate setting. Horse (2005) developed a framework of influences on identity for Native American peoples based on shared aspects or "collective consciousness" of this diverse population. Horse's model is not an identity development model. Rather, it is a framework designed to serve as a means to understand collective consciousness. In their Native American college students' guide to success, Pavel and Inglebret (2007) identified the need for Native students to maintain their roots within the individual, family, community, and tribe. These four standards serve as a foundation to better understand Native American and

Native Alaskan identity and, by extension, Native and Indigenous identity. Collective consciousness and the four standards create starting points that can be used to explore Native and Indigenous student identity development, while acknowledging there is no one development theory available for practitioners and scholars to inform their work.

As practitioners who work with Native and Indigenous students, we have witnessed how concepts of authentic identity emerge and become normalized on our campuses. On an individual-by-individual basis, these students define their sense of Indigenous identity based on their unique family, community, and tribal definitions (Horse, 2005) and how they live as Indigenous people (e.g., matrilineal–patrilineal, reservation–urban, language). There is also a governmental policy paradigm that judges identity based on blood quantum (Kauanui, 2008; Trask, 1999), tribal enrollment, living on or off reservation or trust land, and governmental recognition or lack thereof. For professionals in higher education, whether Indigenous or not, it is critical to ensure understanding of the ways that the standards of individual, family, community, government, and campus culture affect concepts of authenticity. It is essential to examine our own biases to disrupt the perpetuation of intertribal, -nation, and -community violence and the delegitimization of one's conception of self.

Who We Are

In congruence with traditions stemming from each of our communities, we will share who we are and how we understand our concepts of self.

Leilani

Aloha *mai e kākou.* I come to this work as a descendant of the ancient navigators of the Pacific. Those whose *kuleana* (responsibility) was to *mālama 'aina* (care for the land) of Maui. Those who *mālama 'aina* of Ukumehame. A descendant of Pilahi Paki. A descendant of Lāhapa. A descendant of Leonard Achong Kupo Sr. A descendant of Grace Leilani Girardi Aki Kupo. The daughter of Leonard Achong Kupo Jr. The daughter of Karen Sue DeMyer Kupo. I am named after my grandmother and my great aunt. I am *Kānaka Maoli* (Native Hawaiian). A mixed-raced Native Hawaiian *wahine* (woman). I was raised away from my ancestral home of Ukumehame, Maui, on the North American continent. I learned about my ancestors from afar. I am descended from brilliant warriors who harvested from the *moana* (ocean) to care for community, served as healers, and kept culture alive through their skills as musicians and dancers. I am descended from royalists, those who support the Hawaiian monarchy. My grandfather believed the way to overthrow the colonizer was to learn their ways, to infiltrate from within, and to protect the sacred. My grandmother was a great gardener and a woman of deep faith. She would often tell me

> Leilani, your *kūleana* (responsibility) is to *mālama 'aina* (care for land/that which feeds). When you *mālama 'aina* (care for land/that which feeds), *'aina* (land/that which feeds) will care for community. Community will care for *'ohana* (family). *'Ohana* (family) will care for you. It is the cycle of life. Hold this in your heart. In your mind.

As an adult, it is how I understand who I am. It helps me navigate the state of being both *too Hawaiian* and *not Hawaiian enough*. It was through our time in the garden that I learned about what it meant to be *Kānaka Maoli* (Native Hawaiian), about the *koko* (blood) that runs through my veins, and the legacy gifted to me. I learned lessons from plants; medicine of the land. The learning that can be done by doing and observing. My responsibility as an adult is to care for community. I am reminded daily that my responsibility is to be a better ancestor. And for that I am grateful.

Symphony

Osiyo. I am a Cherokee/Choctaw Biracial woman from Creek County in Tulsa, Oklahoma. My lived experience is one of colonization. I spent my school years in Iowa, Nebraska, and New Mexico while my single mother pursued her education. Though we lived outside of our home community, my mother invested substantial time and resources instilling in me the values and traditions from her Cherokee family, while also coming to terms with the fact that there was no connection to our Choctaw family because my grandmother was adopted outside of her tribe. The importance of family and community was my mother's primary focus; she would tell me stories of spending summers with her patrilineal grandparents in Muldrow and Arkoma, Oklahoma, and we would make 12- to 18-hour trips back home to Oklahoma as often as once a month to be with family. The value of reciprocity to, and importance of, family, home, and community has been and continues to be the most significant driving force of my life. She ensured that I valued a larger sense of community and identity in all of the different places we lived by connecting with Native communities in the area. This created relationships with many diverse Native peoples, and I experienced other tribal cultures and traditions.

My identity as a Cherokee/Choctaw woman has occasionally been a source of tension in my interpersonal relationships. Having lived away from my tribal community for a majority of my life, I wasn't immersed daily within Cherokee and Choctaw tribal communities to be able to learn and experience my tribes' cultures intimately. I chose to attend college at Oklahoma State University (OSU), and the return to daily life in Oklahoma combined with the tension of being a Biracial woman and being light-skinned continually caused insecurity in my identity. During my collegiate years, I struggled with feeling I had to prove my nativeness to other Natives while also explaining that I do not identify as white, as I was not raised in or around my white family. I remember at one point during college I introduced my mother to my Native friends saying, "See, I really am Native," because my mother is "visibly" Native. Even though I have never questioned my own identity in my mind, I constantly felt defensive when identifying myself to everyone else. In college, I was fortunate to have mentorship from Native faculty and staff at OSU that helped me overcome my identity "crisis." I also connected more with my extended family and friends to learn what I hadn't been able to growing up.

Authenticity: A Dialogue

As Indigenous scholars, we chose to engage this work in ways that align with our cultural traditions. Storytelling serves a critical role in the transmission of knowledge as it provides context and often holds hidden and/or deeper meanings. When we introduce ourselves through ancestry, land, and culture, we engage in formal acts of resistance that align with decolonization, TribalCrit, and Indigenous Knowledge Systems. Our introductions are congruent with our cultural practices (Brayboy, 2005; Laenui, 2006; Marshall, 2011; Trask, 1999) and serve as a reflection of our authentic selves. Aligning with decolonization, TribalCrit, and Indigenous Knowledge Systems, our introductions and narratives demonstrate how theory is lived and informed by storytelling. As noted by Brayboy (2005), "Locating theory as something absent from stories and practices is problematic in many Indigenous communities" (p. 426). Indigenous stories are valid data, legitimate, and powerful. As illustrated in the following narratives, decolonization, TribalCrit, and Indigenous Knowledge Systems ground and frame our experiences as Indigenous women.

Leilani: To be honest, the concept of authenticity is difficult for me. When I think about who I am, I think about my ancestors. The lessons they taught me. The *'aina* (land). It is those who came before me. It is all those who are with me. It is all those who come after me. However, it is difficult to articulate this in English. English is too limiting.

My grandfather taught me many lessons. I remember early one quiet morning, watching a *honu* (sea turtle) swim by. He looked at me and said, "That is an ancient one who is free. He knows the ways of the ocean. Knows how to navigate the dangers. He survives and thrives." I knew there was a lesson in his words. However, I did not understand. He taught me lessons through storytelling and allowed me to learn the lessons on my own. The lesson has taught me how to navigate higher education.

I navigate a world of assimilation and rules. At times, I feel like a chameleon. At my very core, I do understand who I am as a *Kānaka Maoli wahine* (Native Hawaiian woman). However, I also have to understand the rules of engagement and the unwritten rules associated with the politics of legitimacy both in the academy and in community. I navigate the world of being too Hawaiian and not Hawaiian enough. I have found that I cannot be "too much" *Kānaka Maoli* in the academy or I am perceived to be not smart enough. Yet, I have to demonstrate my *Kānaka Maoli*–ness to fit in academy, community, and governmental standards. It is exhausting. I learn strategy from the *honu* and the lesson my grandfather taught me that morning long ago.

Symphony: Authenticity has been a concept that I have had tension with in my life. It has taken consistent reflection, guidance from elders and mentors, and a holistic acceptance that I developed the ability to be my authentic self. However, I still struggle at times to not revert to a defensive stance of feeling a need to prove my identity. For instance, writing this chapter has resurfaced issues surrounding my identity. Talking with my mother throughout this writing process, we have shared stories about our family, our history, our home place. She shared the guilt she feels about moving away from Oklahoma and her sorrow about how it contributed to my identity struggles. I have challenged myself to reframe issues around my identity by thinking about what is unique to me and how those show up as strengths. One of those strengths is since I was raised around many diverse Indigenous communities, my values of reciprocity and advocacy are deeply rooted in my identity.

Leilani: As a scholar-practitioner, I have found it important to honor my ancestors and center their teachings. This can be difficult and is counter to training I have received. It has been pivotal to who I am as a *Kānaka Maoli* professional and scholar. I have learned the importance of safety: emotional, intellectual, psychological, and physical. I am strategic in what I reveal and with whom I engage. I am thoughtful and cautious about the ways in which I utilize scholarship. I understand the language of the colonizer and intentionally follow and break the rules of the colonizer. I navigate the rules strategically so that I can embody the values of my ancestors, advocate for community, and gain access to spaces I would not normally have because I can "pass." My grandfather was right. I have learned the rules of the colonizer and learned how to subvert and disrupt them. Ironically, I have learned more about my authentic self by learning how to assimilate. Within those assimilatory and violent constructs, I find ways to engage my authentic self and stay true to who I am as a *Kānaka Maoli wahine* (Native Hawaiian woman). I reaffirm my cultural values and embody them. As my grandmother taught me to do, I hold culture, my *'ohana* (family) close to my heart. At times, I feel that my identity is hypervisible and objectified. I have to prove my right to claim my Hawaiian-ness because I do not "fit" into the other's conception of Hawaiian-ness. My sense of authenticity is challenged by external forces, and I often have to defend and define who I am. As I think about who I am, I have to question, "Why?"

Symphony: There is a constant awareness that as a Native person in academia, I don't fit. During my student affairs graduate program, I was frustrated with the blatant invisibility and erasure of Indigenous people. The theories, policies, and practices that I learned were framed in colonization/settler colonialism. My socialization into the student affairs profession went against all of my "raisings." In my work, I interrogated and attempted to dismantle the ways that higher education continued to maintain settler colonialism through policies, structures, practices, and privileging Western norms. The decision to pursue my doctorate was so that I could contribute to the research of Native students in higher education. During my doctoral program, I taught my first master's-level graduate preparation course. I encountered current and future student affairs professionals who had "never met" someone Native and didn't know anything other than how the media has portrayed Natives. Eventually, I realized that combating the socialization could be accomplished by an awareness of Indigenous people, knowledge systems, and research during graduate school while students were forming their professional knowledge and identity. This experience led me to become faculty and to use my experiences as a practitioner to provide a perspective in the classroom that future student affairs professionals and higher education professionals had most likely never encountered before. My authenticity comes at a price, and I am challenged in my research and teaching. The messages I receive from the academy are that I research Native people in higher education because it is "easy," that I can't be "objective" because I am Native, or that quantitative research on Native people isn't "robust" enough because of our small number. The feedback in my teaching is that I am too "outside the box," I focus too much on race and diversity, and I am too critical of the higher education system. What keeps me motivated, regardless of the challenges, is the hope that if even one small change can come from this work, then the experiences of future generations of Indigenous people in higher education will be a little bit better.

Leilani and Symphony:
As discussed previously, we have grappled with concepts of authenticity and continue to work to navigate the ever-changing ways in which we understand and conceptualize our authentic selves. Authenticity is determined not only by self but also by a community, knowledge of culture, connection to ancestors, how one does or does not align with definitions put forth by the government determining one's ability to qualify as Native, and connection to land (Trask, 1999). Our lived experiences as Indigenous women have included direct and indirect impact of colonization and loss of culture. We have learned that failing to assimilate and adopt the ways of the colonizer resulted in violence, isolation, and death. The stakes were, and still are, too high.

We argue authenticity *is* contextual. For many Indigenous and Native people, colonizers' concepts of good and bad are grounded in notions of settler colonialism and have been used as a frame to define who is "authentically" Indigenous or Native. In contemporary society, these definitions still exist, continue to be used to perpetuate intercommunity trauma, and are fueled by racism, phenotype, and eugenics. Understanding that our authentic selves are deeply influenced and shaped by colonization, we continue to ask the question, "Is it possible to decolonize notions of authenticity?"

Why This Matters: Reconceptualizing Authenticity

Western schooling has been used as a tool of assimilation for Native and Indigenous children. Western schools have been sources of trauma, violence, and harm for many Native people (Trask, 1999). Native and Indigenous histories have been erased and/or misrepresented within curricula in K–20 education. The overall message has been, and continues to be, that it is bad to be Native or Indigenous. In fact, the only way Native and Indigenous people survived was to assimilate and adopt Western ways of being. Unfortunately, vestiges of these forms of violence still exist in contemporary education. The university, for many Native and Indigenous people, is experienced as a location of assimilation and trauma. Native and Indigenous students are asked to reflect on and identify who they are and to find their authentic selves. However, they are also taught their nativeness is not acceptable. To clarify: The very location we ask Native and Indigenous students to find their authentic selves is also the place where they are forced to deny their culture and assimilate.

The university setting creates the perfect storm for individuals confronting the questions of authenticity in an Indigenous person's identity. As Indigenous scholars in higher education, we recognize the difficult work of decolonizing the academy and showing up as our authentic selves. This is in part due to negative messages we received about our authentic selves, about being too Native and not Native enough. Yet, there is an opportunity to offer alternative understandings to notions of authenticity. We ask our non-Indigenous colleagues to understand that authenticity is not only fluid and contextual but also grounded in history, community, geopolitical context, storytelling, and, at times, blood. We ask our non-Indigenous university professionals to examine how we understand and conceptualize authenticity. When we ask students to reflect on the question "Who am I?" let us also consider the questions "Who am I related to?" "Who are my ancestors?" "What location does my family come from?" "Where do I come from?" and "Does my environment and/or location inform and influence the ways in which I answer the question?"

Final Thoughts

Is it possible to center authenticity as a scholar and a practitioner in higher education? Is it possible to decolonize authenticity? We argue yes. We both understand and value student development theory and acknowledge how theory can be used to inform scholarship and practice, as well as provide context. However, current student development theory does not attend to the identities and lived experiences of Native American, American Indian, Native Alaskan, Native Hawaiian, and Pacific Islander college students. As such, a multipronged approach must be used to address issues of authenticity and identity, particularly because of a dearth of available research and the incongruence between Western and Indigenous worldviews.

Concepts of self-definition and authenticity need to be broadened and troubled to allow for greater fluidity and attend to the ways in which external forces frame and influence self-concept (e.g., government definition, community definition) and the impact colonization and assimilation have on concepts of authenticity. At this moment, it is difficult to use student development theory as a means to examine the experiences of Native and Indigenous students. Though authenticity is complex, contextual, and ever changing, it provides an opportunity for individuals to gain a deeper understanding of how external forces, including government and environment, affect how we understand who we are and interact with others. Though not perfect, authenticity allows for opportunities to be one's true self, as it allows for fluidity, context, change. Future work and scholarship must include a reframing of authenticity in a way that troubles notions of authenticity and begins to decolonize this concept.

Discussion Questions

We must rethink how we ask students and, in the case of research, participants, to engage in reflection about how they understand their authentic selves. The following are some questions to ponder:

1. How do we respond to the ways that students make meaning of their authentic selves?
2. Are students and participants forced to continue to legitimize and define who they are and why they identify as they do?
3. Are students and participants forced to provide access to their personal lives in order to gain legitimacy as a Native and Indigenous person?
4. Are students' and participants' values diminished if they do not provide enough evidence of their authentic selves? Are they increased if they do? What impact does this have?
5. How might external forces influence the ways in which students make meaning of their authentic selves?

References

Ascher, M. (2002). *Mathematics elsewhere: An exploration of ideas across cultures.* Princeton, NJ: Princeton University Press.

Barnhardt, R. (2005). Indigenous knowledge systems and Alaska Native ways of knowing. *Anthropology and Education Quarterly, 36*(1), 8–23.

Baxter Magolda, M. B. (2001). *Making their own way: Narratives for transforming higher education to promote self-development.* Sterling, VA: Stylus.

Baxter Magolda, M. B. (2008). Three elements of self-authorship. *Journal of College Student Development, 49,* 269–284.

Brayboy, B. M. J. (2005). Toward a tribal critical race theory in education. *The Urban Review, 37*(5), 425–446.

Cajete, G. (2000). *Native science: Natural laws of interdependence.* Santa Fe, NM: Clear Light Publishers.

Chickering, A. W., & Reisser, L. (1993). *Education and identity* (2nd ed.). San Francisco, CA: Jossey-Bass.

Eglash, R. (2002). Computation, complexity and coding in Native American Knowledge Systems. In J. E. Hankes & G. R. Fast (Eds.), *Changing the faces of mathematics: Perspectives on Indigenous People of North America* (pp. 251–262). Reston, VA: National Council of Teachers of Mathematics.

Erikson, E. H. (1968). *Identity: Youth and crisis.* New York, NY: Norton.

Horse, P. G. (2005). Native American identity. In M. J. Tippeconnic Fox, S. C. Lowe, & G. S. McClellan (Eds.), *Serving Native American students* (New Directions for Student Services, No. 109, pp. 61–68). San Francisco, CA: Jossey-Bass.

Houseman, A. (2015). Guiding principles of Indigenous leadership from a Hawaiian perspective. In D. Aguilera-Black Bear & J. W. Tippeconnic III (Eds.), *Voices of resistance and renewal: Indigenous leadership in education* (pp. 49–75). Norman, OK: University of Oklahoma Press.

Jones, S. R. (2016). Authenticity in leadership: Intersectionality of identities. In K. Guthrie, T. Bertrand Jones, & L. Osteen (Eds.), *Developing culturally relevant leadership learning* (New Directions for Student Services, No. 152, pp. 23–34). San Francisco, CA: Wiley.

Jones, S. R., Kim, Y. C., & Skendall, K. C. (2012). (Re-) framing authenticity: Considering multiple social identities using autoethnographic and intersectional approaches. *Journal of Higher Education, 83*(5), 698–724.

Kauanui, J. K. (2008). *Hawaiian blood: Colonialism and the politics of sovereignty and indigeneity.* Raleigh, NC: Duke University Press.

Kawagley, A. O. (1995). *A Yupiaq worldview: A pathway to ecology and spirit.* Prospect Heights, IL: Waveland Press.

Kreber, C., Klampfleitner, M., McCune, V., Bayne, S., & Knottenbelt, M. (2007). What do you mean by "authentic"? A comparative review of the literature on conceptions of authenticity in teaching. *Adult Education Quarterly, 58*(1), 22–43.

Laenui, P. (2006). *Process of decolonization.* Wai'anae, HI: Institute for the Advancement of Hawaiian Affairs. Retrieved from http://www.sjsu.edu/people/marcos.pizarro/maestros/Laenui.pdf

Marshall, W. E. (2011). *Potent mana: Lessons in power and healing.* Albany, NY: State University of New York Press.

Pavel, D. M., & Inglebret, E. (2007). *The American Indian and Alaska Native student's guide to college success.* Westport, CT: Greenwood.

Satz, R. N. (1975). *American Indian policy in the Jacksonian era.* Norman, OK: University of Oklahoma Press.

Trask, H. K. (1999). *From a Native daughter: Colonialism and sovereignty in Hawai'i.* Honolulu, HI: University of Hawai'i Press.

Writer, J. H. (2008). Unmasking, exposing, and confronting: Critical race theory, tribal critical race theory, and multicultural education. *International Journal of Multicultural Education, 10*(2), 1–15.

12

A BLACK FEMINIST
RECONSTRUCTION
OF AGENCY

Wilson Kwamogi Okello and Kiaya Demere White

T he opening lyrics of "Freedom," a track on Beyoncé's album *Lemonade* (Knowles-Carter, 2016), mobilize the sentiments of many Black women in contemporary culture and, too, lay the groundwork for a public critique of agency. Beyoncé beckons the listener to bear witness to a tense struggle with a complicated term, *freedom*. These lyrics call into question the project of freedom, understood in this chapter as agency or the ability to move and act upon the world. Traditional framings of agency lean on rational and patriarchal interpretations of the construct. Recognizing the inherent farce in aligning with these traditional ideas, Lorde (1984) stated, "There are a wide range of 'pretended' choices and rewards for identifying with patriarchal power and tools" (p. 117). This trepidation necessitates the need for this chapter and its desire to "document and explain Black women's diverse reactions to being objectified as the Other" (Collins, 1990, p. 83) and advance alternative possibilities for agency that surface by centering Black feminisms. Specifically, we take up James's (1999) metaphor of limbos to articulate how Black women manufacture creative pathways out of irreconcilable positions; that is, how they reconstitute agency.

Black feminisms possess resuscitating and life-giving instruction. A student of their teachings, in my art and scholarship, I (Wilson Kwamogi Okello) endeavor to articulate and model their possibilities. I pursue this knowing that Black, cisgender, heterosexual men occupy a precarious and rightfully contested position in relationship to Black feminist thinking and tools of analysis. As an author of this chapter, I recognize the historical evidence and present-day suspicion attached to my interest and desires to work and write with a Black feminist perspective. I own and take up the responsibility to bear witness to its teachings in my laboring with the work, to amplify the voices that guide my thinking and analysis, and to persist in interrogating my own life as an example of what I have gleaned. Alongside Kiaya Demere White (coauthor), we weave the autobiographical throughout this chapter to explicate a critical conceptualization of agency. According to Saidiya Hartman, "the autobiographical example is not a story that folds onto itself . . . it's really about trying to look at historical and social process and one's own formation as a window onto social and historical processes, as an example of them" (as cited in Sharpe, 2016, p. 8). In doing so, we question the legitimacy of current agentic frames and offer a probable alternative that centers the minoritized body in a Western, U.S. context.

As such, we begin this analysis with a reflection from Kiaya that captures the essence of our critique. We believe, like hooks (1989), that "oppressed people resist by identifying themselves as subjects by defining their reality, shaping their new identity, naming their history, telling their story" (p. 43). Kiaya *talks back* (hooks, 1989). From there, we offer a review of agency and parallel notions in student development theory as an entry point into the thrust of this chapter, which will explicate our use of Black feminisms as interventions in the construct of agency.

Education Is the Key to Freedom: Kiaya Part I

Ever since the colonizers stole my ancestors from their homes and brought them here, Black children have been told by their families and communities that education is the only way to obtain a better life. It is followed up with "education is your key to freedom." I remember the first time this message was told to me; it was my first day of kindergarten. My grandmother looked at me from her rearview mirror and said, "Baby, this is the first day of your journey of education." My mother followed up by saying, "Kiaya, your education is the most important thing you can have." Various family members, some of the Black and Brown educators I have encountered, and various societal messages from Black films and television shows delivered this same message. My Black friends always seem to relate to this generational message, while my white friends are told that education is something you just do.

The "education equates to freedom" motto lingered in my brain as I pushed through my four years at Miami University. This was the same message I told my students when I worked as a college and career counselor at an underserved public school. This was the same narrative I told myself as I applied to the student affairs in higher education program at Miami University. I found out that this idea that education equates to freedom is false. Black folks can never achieve the freedom that is designed by the colonizers. We were never going to gain freedom when Black bodies were kidnapped and brought to America. Our chains were never removed from our ankles when slavery was abolished; they just looked different. Our chains now looked like biased laws, inequitable education, and racially motivated killings of Black bodies by the police. Education doesn't rid us of our chains; it only hyperexposes us to them and the limitations we have in this country.

Navigating Miami University was how I learned what it felt like to be an outsider. I came from an inner-city high school where the majority of the students were on free or reduced lunch, all but 1 or 2 of my classmates looked like me, and a Black woman taught me honors physics. I was very unfamiliar with this new world of Miami University. I was in a lecture hall of 150 students, and only 4 of us were Black. Out of the 4 years I was at Miami, I had a single Black instructor. My first year, I had to leave my residence hall to engage with other Black students who weren't my roommate. I learned not only what it felt like to be an outsider but also how people treated outsiders. I was constantly telling white folks, "No, you can't touch my hair." I prepared myself for rejection when it was time to work in groups and none of my peers wanted to work with me. I could feel the stares and glares as I walked around campus with my kinky curly 'fro or my colorful head wraps. For survival, I began to normalize these experiences. I trained myself to not pay so much attention to what was happening around me. Truly unaware, I began to make myself palatable to white folks. I didn't laugh or talk as loud in public spaces. I advocated for more gender issues than race because that seemed more acceptable to my peers. I laughed at the racist undertone jokes made by former friends because it wasn't worth the energy to explain why I wasn't.

When I graduated with my bachelor's degree, I started to become aware that my degree didn't protect me from the inequalities of the world. I encountered racially insensitive and culturally unaware supervisors and coworkers. When I landed my first job after graduation, I was the only Black person; I held the highest degree next to higher level management, and I was the youngest employee. My work was always challenged even though it was always correct. I was the first to enter the office and the last to leave. I trained everyone in the office, including the owner, on our technology and office material. And for some reason, I was the first to be let go when the company hit financial hardships. I believe I was let go first because of the identities that I hold. The other full-time jobs that followed weren't any better. I had to combat the Angry Black Woman stereotype by making sure my directness was paired with a lower and gentler tone of voice. I had to make sure that my niceness and willingness to help wasn't taken advantage of and I wasn't becoming the office's Black Mammy. I began to become aware that my body and presence were perceived as a general threat to whiteness.

When I would take my lunch breaks, drive to and from work, and spend limitless amount time on social media, I would ask myself the same question: "Where was the freedom that I was promised with this education?" When I talk about freedom, I'm not talking about the release of adult responsibilities; rather, I am asking, where was the peace? Where was this peace that I can strive for excellence in my job and white folks would leave me alone and not question my every move? Where was this peace that I can walk into a department store and browse and shop without all the sales associates stalking me? Where was the freedom that I can not only exist but also thrive in my Black Woman body without any interruptions?

I would stalk my former classmates; those who identified as white seemed to have this peace. It seemed as if they found this freedom. But where was mine? Why couldn't I find it? Did I do something wrong while in undergrad? It felt like there was a piece of information that everyone knew that helped them obtain this freedom, and I just didn't know it. After two years of searching for this freedom, I replayed the line "Education is your key to freedom," and I decided to go back to obtain my master's degree.

Review of Agency and Parallel Notions in Student Development Theory

Fanon (1967) suggested, "As soon as I *desire* I am asking to be considered. I am not merely here-and-now, sealed into thingness. I am for somewhere else and for something else" (p. 170). Desire summons the capacities of individuals to, by their own actions, influence their existence in the world and the course that their lives take. It is this power of desire—the creative, charismatic, and persistent longing that takes place at the very limits of one's authority—that may be understood as agency, or the belief that one plays an integral part in shaping their life (Bandura, 1997; Fanon, 1967). Agency as a concept supposes that one is capable of being a curator and an arbiter of cultural production offering a rebuttal to determinism, which says that every decision and action are the inevitable and necessary consequences of preceding events (Bandura, 1997). Human agency, as outlined by Bandura (1997), comprises four distinct yet interlocking components: intentionality, forethought, self-reactiveness, and self-reflectiveness. Intentionality describes functions where the individual formulates outcomes and plots a strategy to achieve them. Centrally, it asks, how do I bring about the desired ends that I seek? The second component of agency is recognized as forethought. This notion suggests that there is a cautious overview of prospective actions and careful attention to how those actions may influence intended outcomes. In a sense, visualized futures are brought into the present as guiding logics to steer behaviors. The third component, self-reactiveness, speaks to actors' capacity to self-regulate. Agency, thus, is the ability to not only make choices and identify plans but also work in the gap, self-correct, and adjust between those choices and desired ends. The fourth agentic function is self-reflectiveness. Through functional self-awareness, actors consider their thoughts and actions and the meaning behind their pursuits.

If agency is the manifestation of desire, then efficacy is the mechanism that makes agency possible. Self-efficacy denotes an actor's beliefs in personal causative capabilities. Self-efficacy is the belief held about one's ability to control a specific situation or set of circumstances, or, simply, it says "I can produce desired effects by my actions" (Bandura, 1997). In human development terms, this notion of the individual functioning from an internal system to make decisions in an external world is compatible with understandings of self-authorship (Baxter Magolda, 1992, 2001, 2008; Kegan, 1982, 1994). The construct of self-authorship articulates that individuals are equipped with the capacity to take ownership of their internal authority and foundations and establish their own sets of values and ideologies (Baxter Magolda, 1992; Kegan, 1994). Self-authorship attributes meaning-making complexity to subject–object reflection (Kegan, 1994, 1982). Discussing the subject–object relationship, Kegan (1994) stated that *object* represents "those elements of our knowing or organizing that we can reflect on, handle, look at, be responsible for, relate to each other, take control of, internalize, assimilate, or otherwise operate on" (p. 32). This articulation suggests that *what we know* is not the same as *what we can do with what we know. Subject* refers to "those elements of our knowing or organizing that we are identified with, tied to, fused with, or embedded in" (p. 32). Kegan (1994), and proponents of self-authorship, posited that the *transformation* that takes place between these dichotomous positions liberates us from "that in which we are embedded, making what was subject into object so that we can 'have it' rather than 'be had' by it" (p. 32). Kegan continued by pointing to the achievement of the object position as the possession of *consciousness*. In this way, conceptualizations of agency, or one's ability to be a producer of their life and not merely produced by it (intentionality, forethought, self-regulation, and self-reflectiveness), appear to mirror the theoretical grounding of self-authorship, which affords the individual the ability to coordinate, integrate, act upon, or invent values, beliefs, convictions, generalizations, ideals, abstractions, interpersonal loyalties, and intrapersonal states.

Previous student development theories have positioned agency as the primary indicator of complexity in a subject–object relationship (Baxter Magolda, 1992; Kegan, 1994, 1982; King & Kitchener, 1994; Perry, 1970). This emphasis reflects how steeped these models are in rational and scientific approaches to knowledge. Such approaches are limited in their capacity to explain how students with minoritized bodies cultivate meaning given the indomitably irrational presses they must endure. In the opening narrative, Kiaya concluded that the notion of freedom is false and unattainable. Her desire or, as Fanon (1967) might suggest, her *desire to be seen* is evident. Her cognitive processing appears to mirror that of the agentic individual. What is it, then, about her existence that delimits possibilities of authority in society? Here, we want to suggest that the linear logic that fixes our understandings of agency and authorship ought to be complicated by considering the broader existential questions surrounding Kiaya and her ability to wield these presupposed powers.

Cultivating Agency in the Wake

Existentialism deals with "the systematic formulation by an individual or group of an ongoing consciousness of its existence that is first, concretely, realized in everyday intersections and practices" (Henry, 1997, p. 15). Gordon (1997) seemingly agreed with this statement when he commented, "Any theory that fails to address the existential phenomenological dimension . . . suffers from a failure to address the situational dimension" (p. 70). A consciousness of existence, thereby, is determined by the constraints and possibilities experienced in one's life/existential situation. Agency in its current rendering tightropes on the brink of idealism; agency is unwilling, it seems, to grapple with the realism that undergirds oppressive realities. Taking our cue from critical theorist Derrick Bell, our theorizing about agency ought to move judiciously:

> I would urge that we begin . . . with a statement that many will wish to deny, but none can refute. It is this: Black people will never gain full equality in this country. Even those herculean efforts we hail as successful will produce no more than temporary "peaks of progress," short lived victories that slide into irrelevance as racial patterns adapt in ways that maintain white dominance. This is a hard-to-accept fact that all history verifies. We must acknowledge it and move on. . . . That acknowledgement enables us to avoid despair and frees us to imagine and implement racial strategies that can bring fulfillment and even triumph. (Bell, 1992, p. 373)

Unwavering in his analysis, Bell forced a reckoning with readers' optimism and poststructural sensibilities. Fundamental to critical race theory, yet often understated, is the axiomatic claim that racism is permanent. This is not a comforting proposition for most, the manifestation of which shows up in theorizing about the potential and possibilities of minoritized students. Namely, the assumption has been that these students possess similar authorities to act upon the world in a manner that they desire; that their bodies and very ambitions are unencumbered. Echoing this point, Kiaya contended,

> For Black women, we have to constantly fight for our ability to live the lives we want to live because of the limitations placed on us by various systems of oppression. Before I came into my graduate program, I would've argued that I had the same agency as everyone else, but that was an illusion placed upon me by society when in fact my control is limited and is a constant struggle to attain.

The irrefutable evidence of permanence tells the story of racism and its enduring effects but also points to those who avoided despair, specifically Women of Color, who imagined new realities within the fiery furnace in which they were engulfed.

Historically, Women of Color have had to forge identities for themselves, having always recognized themselves as dialectically oppressed and in possession of human agency (Anzaldúa, 1987; Collins, 1990; Dillard, 2000; Hurtado, 2003). They do not experience themselves as "floating signifiers," "dark others," or "incoherent subjects" (Hurtado, 2003, p. 221). Daring to see themselves as more than *other*, Women of Color advance a way of knowing and being that can be articulated and self-defined, constituted as *theory in the flesh*. Moraga and Anzaldúa (1981) discussed that this frame is an attempt to bridge contradictions through naming, telling stories, and giving language to their experience. They noted, "A theory in the flesh means one where the physical realities of our lives—our skin color, the land or concrete we grew up on, our sexual longings—all fuse to create a politic born out of necessity" (p. 23). Theories in the flesh will inevitably lead us toward *endarkened epistemologies* (Dillard, 2000) that challenge physically and psychologically a dependency on white, Eurocentric preferences for reason and rationality (i.e., a colonial complex) and provoke a rich tradition of *theorizing in the wake of crisis* (Sharpe, 2016), calling for a refashioning of agency to treat these realities.

At this juncture, several questions arise for us: If these are but a few of the realities of minoritized people in a Western, U.S. context, how are they to manage forces impinging on their body, behaviors, and desires? Relatedly, how might analyzing the relationship between human desires (pursuit of things that give us meaning) and demands (wake of crisis, forces, possibilities of terror) expand and deepen conceptualizations of agency? Consideration of these motives and their interplay, we argue, will provide educators with a richer and more complete rendering of how minoritized students function in, and make meaning of, the world(s) they find themselves in. Entry into these shifting and composite positions can be facilitated by theorizing with Black feminisms.

Black Feminist Conceptualization of Agency

By naming the multiple sites wherein power lies (e.g., material, ideological, emotional, psychological), Black feminisms illustrate the complex interrelatedness of Black bodies and argues for the inherent philosophical and political relevance of theorizing from lived experience. As an affront to Western forms of knowing, learning, and theorizing, we will articulate in the section that follows how Black feminisms' embodied and reflexive character can serve as an intervention in conceptualizing agency (Boylorn, 2013).

Spillers (2000) discussed labels on bodies as "markers so loaded with mythical prepossession" (p. 65) that there is no simple manner in which those pressed upon may be able to loosen themselves from its weight. Related to the labor one must take up, she continued, "In order for me to speak a truer word concerning myself, I must strip down through layers of attenuated meanings, made an excess in time, over time, assigned by a particular historical order" (p. 65). Seeking to reclaim and reveal a Black subjectivity that has been erased, misread, and misunderstood, we turn to Black feminist Joy James's (1999) notion of limbos to articulate the complex choreography at play as minoritized bodies enact agency.

Limbos are known to entail "vulnerable backbreaking postures as well as isolated states" (James, 1999, p. 41). In these limbos, Black feminisms cultivated models and strategies for resistance that rejected injunctions of the status quo. According to James (1999), limbo, in its primary usage, references liminal spaces, "oblivion and neglect, or suspension between states" (p. 42). In its secondary, and more playful, usage, it is characterized by "play, struggle and pleasure—the black/Caribbean performance where dancers lean backward, with knees bent to pass below a bar that blocks their path. It represents determined progress despite the vulnerability of the position" (p. 42). As choreographers of agency, Black feminisms' conservative or liberal ideologies conduct varying limbos as they negotiate the plurality of its meanings. They advance emancipation projects while simultaneously being distanced from the center of issues of oppression and yet continuously extract agency from these margins. This fluidity allows them to interpret, dissect, improvise, describe, and agitate,

displaying an agility and imaginative power to deconstruct and reconstruct. James (1999) conveyed the work of such limbos as that which syn-
thesizes emancipation theories. Nonlinear in essence, limbos capture an
important feature of Black feminisms in their exposure of one-dimensional
liberation theory. They assist in illustrating and analyzing intersections
and multidimensionality of oppression and freedom. In addition, limbos
are ideal spaces for *witnessing*, giving language to experiences that might
otherwise remain muted. Finally, in their progressive movement forward,
limbos "often bend backward toward historical exemplars to retrieve the
sidelines of conventional memory important [to] ancestral leaders for current considerations and political struggles" (James, 1999, p. 43).

Limbos model a necessarily complex rendering of agency for minoritized
persons that bridges the tenets of intentionality, forethought, self-regulation,
and self-reflectiveness with an awareness of one's histories and vulnerabilities
and the notion of self-preservation. This analysis is consistent with Black
feminisms (Collins, 1990) and research that suggests that the pursuit of self-
actualization is a subordinate goal to which human behavior aspires (Carver
& Scheier, 1981; Steele, 1988). Instead much of human behavior is rooted in
the need for protection from epistemic and material violence, or what Lorde
(1982, 1984) called *self-preservation*. A more robust rendering of agency, thus,
should be understood as a dialectical dance between defensive motives and
self-actualization motives. If power and hegemony are ever-present impositions (Foucault, 1980), then it stands to reason that a great deal of energy
must be devoted to maintaining our meaning-making constructs, such as
one's faith or cultural worldviews (Lorde, 1982, 1984). Sustaining a durable
self-esteem and self-appraisal by meeting defensive maintenance needs, however, does not foreclose enrichment capacities to create, explore, and pursue
curiosity. This is to say that Kiaya's statement on *freedom*, detailed earlier, was
intentional, not a casual statement. The ideal, agentic, self-authored person,
free from the defensiveness instigated by external formulas (object), autono-
mous in their striving for actualization (subject), is not possible. Realizable,
and perhaps the most optimal condition, is a melding of subject–object poles
into an embodied position. In this integrated space defensiveness generally
precedes the expansive creativities, tending to the needs of actors in an environment (Maslow, 1955), but we submit that the two work in tandem, similar to that of a contracting and expanding coiled spring. Imagine that the
coils of a spring are given their shape because of historical and present-day
systems of oppression—the wake. Actors, as springs, are predisposed to a
defensive posture, anticipating and thus equipped to buffer the weights of
anxiety, distress, and terror. When pressed upon, the coils compress down-
ward, at first overwhelmed by external forces. This defensiveness, trained by

historical memory, is able to absorb or make meaning of the force(s). From there, creative sensibilities take over, as the coils, having made sense of the opposing motives, reclaim and repurpose the momentum that was originally designed to dominate them into an upward proclamation that we would call agency. The result is an expanding spring that is much more tested, conscious, and resolved. In this limbo, instructed by critical race realism and Black feminisms, there are no promises of escape from meaning-making tasks mediated by the wake. To think otherwise is to presume that systems of oppression are static. The agency we propose is altogether futuristic and historical, deeply hopeful, and determinedly realistic. The intent here is not to reproduce romanticized versions of uplift with great persistence, effort, and faith or versions that are girded up by positive psychological trends of grit. Rather, as Black feminisms call for, we demand a deliberate reckoning with the social, historical, and political oppressions engendered by *living* in a minoritized body (Wingfield, 2015), as such requiring interpretations of agency to do the same. Agency, from a Black feminist standpoint, sees the body as fluent and intelligible.

Movement forward (limbo metaphor) or upward (spring metaphor) appears to happen with attentiveness to the intersecting variables mentioned and a recognition of the creative affordances and possibilities available within a particular context. We offer a revised conceptualization of agency from the themes and narratives discussed previously in concert with reflection on the ways Black and minoritized bodies have engaged in resistance, rupture, and disruption aesthetically and materially over time. The themes that emerged, for what we term *embodied agency*, are inclusive of one's existential situation, an appraisal of competing forces against the individual, one's historical memory in concert with their current meaning-making capacities, and the implementation of creative capacities. The following narrative and analysis will lead educators in interpreting agency, anew, through this critical agentic function.

"Won't Let My Freedom Rot in Hell!": Kiaya Part II

I spent so much time with this bottled-up frustration and anger with this lack of agency I felt in graduate school, and I had no ways of releasing it. I had thoughts of withdrawing from my program and pursuing another career path. I realized I couldn't run from the systems of racism and sexism. They were always going to be here; they were always there. I prayed every day for God to send me a release. The stress of the world and my graduate program was spiritually killing me, and I needed to let go of the toxic energy. One night, as I was saying my daily prayer, the Lord placed on my heart Black and Bold, a T-shirt line created to empower Black folks to live their lives unapologetically. Societal messages communicate to Black folks that there is something wrong with us when it comes to our blackness. That narrative is wrong! Blackness is beautiful and brilliant and deserves to be celebrated, and that is the driving purpose of what Black and Bold is. I focused all of my anger and sadness into this T-shirt line. Each time something problematic was said in class or during a work meeting, I channeled it to Black and Bold.

On top of creating Black and Bold, I began to incorporate Black women scholars into my class assignments. Every assignment that was required for class, I used Black women scholars in my work: Kimberlé Crenshaw, bell hooks, Assata Shakur, Patricia Hill Collins, and Audre Lorde. I used their voices to combat the European masculine toxic messages that were often presented in the literature given in class. I incorporate Patricia Hill Collins's (1990) *Black Feminist Thought* in almost every paper I write for graduate school. *Black Feminist Thought* puts Black women in the center and show-cases how Black women are agents of knowledge and our knowledge is valu-able and credible to the world, especially in politics and academia. The voices of Black women scholars speak to me more than anything I am required to read for class.

I am forced to create a second curriculum in order to survive graduate school. This process is highly frustrating, and I feel both anger and joy. I am angry that my professors don't value the experiences and voices of Black women enough to put their work in the course material. I am angry that I have to do more than the required reading, which means longer hours and more work overall. In the midst of my anger, there is a joy. I feel affirmed when I read the works of bell hooks or Angela Davis. My emotions of anger, sadness, and loneliness become validated, and I become whole again. I no longer feel invisible; I feel powerful and energized to move forward.

Embodied Agency: A Black Feminist Reimagination

"Where was the freedom that I can not only exist but also thrive in my Black Woman body without any interruptions?" Kiaya's lamentation is a direct challenge to rational constructs of agency. The failing of current definitions appears to rest in the dependence on cognitive procedures to speak on behalf of material realities. Theories in the flesh allow us to envision the body as a dynamic entity, interlaced in a mental, emotional, spiritual, and spatial construct (Hill, 2014), and therefore begin from a place that centers the body in culture, vis-à-vis *limbo*. Consistent with this theorizing, we propose that reconstituting the body, mind, spirit, and voice is central to the achieve-ment of an *embodied agency*. With regard to the agentic themes introduced

earlier, embodied agency circumstantially choreographs an existential situation, competing forces, historical memory, meaning-making capacities, and
creativity. In doing so, Kiaya yields a Black feminist reimagination of agency
that is both stable and enduring. The claim here is not that an antidote exists
for how to move, with authority, through the world. Alternatively, the variables alert us to the many facets of a reality that should be considered in
discussions of agency.

Kiaya acknowledged the impertinent nature of oppression, her existential situation, when she stated, "I realized I couldn't run from the systems of racism and sexism. They were always going to be here; they were
always there" (p. 151, this volume). This acknowledgment is not resignation but perhaps a more honest rendering of how one is positioned in the
world and what that means for their existence. In this instance, Kiaya is
not bound to an empty hopefulness or chained to the sympathies of an
unpredictable democracy to self-correct in favor of her personal senses
of dignity and/or authority. In other words, Kiaya maintains a healthy
distrust that resists floundering in the wake of troubled waters, enabling
her to anticipate competing forces. Importantly, this awareness does not
release one from the effects of competing forces. The spring metaphor
shows us that competing forces are designed to distract, dehumanize, and
cause distress, felt and experienced by the compression of coils down-
ward. We believe something is occurring, however, in this compression. Instinctively, the individual resorts to their historical memory and
meaning-making capacities. Kiaya attends to daily trials by reaching back
to consider how she has responded before and how others like her have
made sense of similar lots. This approach manifests in nightly prayers: "I
prayed every day for God to send me a release. The stress of the world
and my graduate program was spiritually killing me, and I needed to let
go of the toxic energy" (p. 151, this volume). This passage illuminates the
importance of examining the body in culture, as Kiaya calls attention to
the affective, physiological, and spiritual in her use of the words *stress*,
spiritually, and *energy*. Distinct from cognitive processing, she articulates
and desires a release from the holistic entanglement of oppression, not
just the mental barriers. Historical memory and one's meaning-making
capacities absorb the weight of competing forces and make sense of them
in unique ways, giving way to creativity.

The genius of embodied agency is in this creative impulse. Creativity
surfaces after the implemented meaning-making structure is unable to coordinate a new competing force (Okello & Quaye, 2018). Creative improvisa-
tions continuously work to invent new forms of being that operate within,
and are partly constituted by, a particular context. In this way, agency is

part relational. At times, minimal amounts of creativity will be necessary to achieve *freedom*; that is, the authority to move and act upon the world uninterrupted. In other situations, extensive amounts of creativity will be required to resolve movement forward. Kiaya multiplies a highly creative response onto an agentic conundrum that had canceled itself out—exercised all available meaning-making resources—thereby motivating her movement upward and forward:

> Blackness is beautiful and brilliant and deserves to be celebrated, and that is the driving purpose of what Black and Bold is. I focused all of my anger and sadness into this T-shirt line. Each time something problematic was said in class or during a work meeting, I channeled it to Black and Bold. (p. 152, this volume)

We also witness creativity on display in Kiaya's commitment to a second curriculum. Importantly, creativity, despite its fashionable regard, is replete with labor, though experiences of joy may flow from it. According to Okello and Quaye (2018), imagination, or the achievement of ideas and images not yet present for the purpose of establishing new forms of being, is instigated as a result of need, as Kiaya wrote:

> I feel affirmed when I read the works of bell hooks or Angela Davis. My emotions of anger, sadness, and loneliness become validated, and I become whole again. I no longer feel invisible; I feel powerful and energized to move forward. (p. 152, this volume)

The notion of power in Kiaya's reflection should be understood as embodied agency, an existential practice and process.

"'Cause I Need Freedom Too!": Concluding Thoughts and Questions

Freedom is not distributed equitably, but all students ought to be able to experience their conception of it. To support our students in this endeavor, we encourage educators to consider the following:

1. How have I been schooled about agency?
2. Reflecting back on my time as an educator, where have I seen minoritized students take up embodied agency? What was my response?
3. What can I do to support, and encourage, embodied agency as a response to competing forces?

4. After reading this chapter, what additional knowledge do I need to cultivate to be able to support minoritized students' revisions of agency? How
willing am I to engage with the literatures of Black women and Black
feminists to acquaint myself with the theoretical knowledge base?

Kiaya and the many others not named deserve appreciation for how, by
living in their bodies, they modeled complex versions of agency. Embodied
agency is an existential practice, a series of decisions in and against the very
things contending for one's esteem and personhood that reconstitute the
voice, body, mind, and spirit in ways that allow the individual or group to act
upon the world and give meaning to it. This chapter, itself a textual embodiment of limbo, pushes back on traditional framings of agency as it moves us
forward toward a reconstituted framing. Educators ought to be mindful of
the manner in which they forward proverbial ideas that hold loose, if any, relevance to the lives and flesh of their students. Alternatively, they should assist
them in understanding their existential situation and normalize competing
forces without pessimism. Educators do not benefit minoritized students
with the absence of this discussion. From there, educators ought to remind
students of their meaning-making capacities and the importance of historical
memory. This process will go a long way in helping students see that they are
capable individuals of both past responses and creative future activity.

References

Anzaldúa, G. (1987). *Borderlands/La Frontera: The new mestiza*. San Francisco, CA:
Spinsters/Aunt Lane.
Bandura, A. (1997). *Self-efficacy: The exercise of control*. New York, NY: Macmillan.
Baxter Magolda, M. B. (1992). *Knowing and reasoning in college: Gender-related pat-
terns in students' intellectual development*. San Francisco, CA: Jossey-Bass.
Baxter Magolda, M. B. (2001). *Making their way: Narratives for transforming higher
education to promote self-development*. Sterling, VA: Stylus.
Baxter Magolda, M. B. (2008). Three elements of self-authorship. *Journal of College
Student Development, 49*(4), 269–284.
Bell, D. A. (1992). Racial realism. *Connecticut Law Review, 24*(2), 363–379.
Boylorn, R. M. (2013). *Sweetwater: Black women and narratives of resilience*. New
York, NY: Peter Lang.
Carver, C. S., & Scheier, M. F. (1981). *Attention and self-regulation*. New York, NY:
Springer-Verlag.
Collins, P. H. (1990). *Black Feminist Thought: Knowledge, consciousness, and the poli-
tics of empowerment*. New York, NY: Unwin Hyman.

Dillard, C. B. (2000). The substance of things hoped for, the evidence of things not seen: Examining an endarkened feminist epistemology in educational research and leadership. *International Journal of Qualitative Studies in Education, 13*(6), 661–681.

Fanon, F. (1967). *Black skin, white masks.* New York, NY: Grove Press.

Foucault, M. (1980). *An introduction: The history of sexuality* (Vol. 1) (Robert Hurely, Trans.). New York, NY: Vintage.

Gordon, L. R. (Ed.). (1997). *Existence in Black: An anthology of Black existential philosophy.* New York, NY: Routledge.

Henry, P. (1997). African and Afro-Caribbean existential philosophies. In L. R. Gordon (Ed.), *Existence in Black: An anthology of Black existential philosophy* (pp. 11–36). New York, NY: Routledge.

Hill, D. (2014). *TRANSGRESSNGROOVE: An exploration of Black girlhood, the body, and education* (Doctoral dissertation). University of Illinois at Urbana–Champaign, Urbana and Champaign, IL.

hooks, b. (1989). *Talking back: Thinking feminist, thinking Black.* Boston, MA: South End Press.

Hurtado, A. (2003). Theory in the flesh: Toward an endarkened epistemology. *International Journal of Qualitative Studies in Education, 16*(2), 215–225.

James, J. (1999). *Shadowboxing: Representations of Black feminist politics.* New York, NY: St. Martin's Press.

Kegan, R. K. (1982). *The evolving self: Problem and process in human development.* Cambridge, MA: Harvard University Press.

Kegan, R. (1994). *In over our heads: The mental demands of modern life.* Cambridge, MA: Harvard University Press.

King, P. M., & Kitchener, K. S. (1994). *Developing reflective judgment: Understanding and promoting intellectual growth and critical thinking in adolescents and adults.* San Francisco, CA: Jossey-Bass.

Knowles-Carter, B. G. (2016). *Freedom. On Lemonade* [CD/DVD]. New York, NY: Parkwood Entertainment & Columbia Records.

Lorde, A. (1982). *Zami: A new spelling of my name.* Trumansberg, NY: Crossing Press.

Lorde, A. (1984). *Sister outsider.* Trumansberg, NY: Crossing Press.

Maslow, A. (1955). Deficiency motivation and growth motivation. In M. R. Jones (Ed.), *Nebraska symposium on motivation.* Lincoln, NE: University of Nebraska Press.

Moraga, C., & Anzaldúa, G. (1981). *This bridge called my back: Writings by radical Women of Color.* Watertown, MA: Persephone Press.

Okello, W. K., & Quaye, S. J. (2018). Advancing creativity for pedagogy and practice. *Journal of Curriculum and Pedagogy, 15*(1), 43–57. Retrieved from https://doi.org/10.1080/15505170.2018.1437577

Perry, W. G., Jr. (1970). *Forms of intellectual and ethical development in the College years: A scheme.* New York, NY: Holt, Rhinehart & Winston. (Original work published 1968).

Sharpe, C. (2016). *In the wake: On blackness and being.* Durham, NC: Duke University Press.

Spillers, H. J. (2000). *American literary theory: A reader.* New York, NY: New York University Press.

Steele, C. M. (1988). The psychology of self-affirmation: Sustaining the integrity of the self. In L. Berkowitz (Ed.), *Advances in experimental social psychology* (pp. 261–302). San Diego, CA: Elsevier.

Wingfield, T. T. (2015). (Her)story: The evolution of a dual identity as an emerging Black female scholar. In V. E. Evans-Winters & B. L. Love (Eds.), *Black feminism in education: Black women speak back, up, and out* (pp. 81–92). New York, NY: Peter Lang.

13

IT'S MORE THAN US

Knowledge and Knowing

*Stephanie J. Waterman (Onondaga Turtle Clan) and
Cori Bazemore-James (Seneca, Turtle Clan)*

R eferencing the Three Sisters agricultural practices of many Indigenous people, Robin Kimmerer (2013) stated,

> For millennia, from Mexico to Montana, women have mounded up the earth and laid these three seeds [corn, beans, and squash] in the ground, all in the same square foot of soil. When the colonists on the Massachusetts shore first saw indigenous gardens, they inferred that the savages did not know how to farm. In their minds, a garden meant straight rows of single species, not a three-dimensional sprawl of abundance. (p. 129)

Three Sisters agriculture was unrecognized as a solid scientific practice until relatively recently. Despite the lack of Western recognition, the practice has continued like other traditions that maintain our ways of being. In this chapter, we discuss the Indigenous Knowledge Systems (IKS) that shaped and continue to shape us, grounding our ways of being that are in contrast to student development theories, which are typically based on the individual, locating knowledge with power. *Meet the students where they are* is a common student development/ student affairs philosophy. We discuss how IKS exemplifies that philosophy. The frameworks we discuss help the reader reenvision ways of knowing.

Story, as theory and its role in relationship and reciprocity (Archibald, 2008; Brayboy, 2005), is foundational to this chapter. Mohawk (1992, 2010) emphasized that our way is a thinking tradition. Through story we reflect, we think, we converse; we are instructed to use our minds to resolve differences. Stories are repeated on a regular basis to reinforce teachings and acknowledge that life experience and the way a story is told influences our understanding of the story. Porter (1992) and Shenandoah (1992) emphasized relationship and balance that include all of Creation, not only humans. This axiology supports relationships and requires time. Settler colonial concepts of time require us to think quickly, speak quickly, and move through higher education at a predetermined pace. Shahjahan (2015) argued that we "must interrogate the epistemological foundations of knowledge that privilege linear notions of time" (p. 496). Reflection to understand, to build relationship, and to engage deeply requires time. Today's neoliberal higher education environment relies on outcomes and on papers and topics covered within limited time frames (e.g., a 12-week semester, a 15-minute time slot at a conference). Settler colonial notions of time work in partnership with higher education structures to suppress; there is less time to listen, less time to explore ways of knowing and being. Time limits affect classroom content, activity, discussion, and relationship building. The settler colonial concept of time is just one example of colonization's current impact on higher education. Tribal critical race theory (TribalCrit) (Brayboy, 2005) extends critical race theory (CRT) (Delgado & Stefancic, 2012) to incorporate Indigenous peoples' liminal experience "as both racial and legal/political groups and individuals" (Brayboy, 2005, p. 427) within their homelands in what is called North America. The tenets of TribalCrit provide a framework for critiquing the ongoing impact of colonization and forced assimilation, thus "expos[ing] the inconsistencies in structural systems and institutions—like colleges and universities—[to] make the situation better for indigenous students" (Brayboy, 2005, p. 441). This is done by centering Indigenous ways of knowing in the research process and practice, particularly by recognizing stories and personal narratives as real and legitimate sources of data and theory (Brayboy, 2005).

IKS

"Native scholar Greg Cajete has written that in an indigenous way of knowing, we understand a thing only when we understand it with all four aspects of our being: mind, body, emotion, and spirit" (Kimmerer, 2013, p. 47).

The diversity of Indigenous people, relationality, reciprocity, and responsibility to community is covered in chapter 5 of this book. We share common experiences of colonization, similarities in our worldview, and thus common epistemologies. An *epistemology* is how one views knowledge and how it is gained (Johnson & Christensen, 2013). Epistemology involves the study of knowledge itself—its nature, how we come to know it, and how we evaluate it. Epistemology informs how we relate to the world around us and thus how we come to know what we know. Most Native educators and researchers ascribe to IKS as their epistemological stance (e.g., Brayboy & Maughan, 2009; Cajete, 2005; Minthorn, 2014; Waterman & Harrison, 2017; Weber-Pillwax, 2004). The four essential elements of IKS are community, lived experience, relationships, and place (Brayboy, Fann, Castagno, & Solyom, 2012). These are described further later in this chapter.

As educators and researchers we have a responsibility to use antideficit models (Harper, 2012) and to understand that research data belong to the community from which they originate (Weber-Pillwax, 2004). Knowledge is rooted in lived experience (Brayboy et al., 2012; Cajete, 2005; Wilson, 2008) and is situated in a community's cultures, philosophies, values, histories, and spiritual and educational practices (Brayboy & Maughan, 2009; Minthorn, 2014). IKS is an oral tradition, and therefore our stories of lived experience make up our theories (Brayboy, 2005). Finally, Indigenous people have a special relationship with the specific lands of their tribal creation stories (Cajete, 2005) and the lands of their ancestors (Weber-Pillwax, 2004). As all institutions of higher education occupy Indigenous land, we believe it is an institutional responsibility to acknowledge this and find relationally accountable ways to support Indigenous students, employees, and local communities.

Unfortunately, many institutions and student development theories do not take such Indigenous epistemologies into account (e.g., Morgan, 2003; Patton, McEwen, Rendón, & Howard-Hamilton, 2007; Smith, Trinidad, & Larkin, 2017; Sonn, Bishop, & Humphries, 2000). Although there has been some improvement toward appreciating Indigenous culture and epistemologies, barriers still exist (Morgan, 2003). We are not seeking special treatment in the academy; we just want our institutions and theories to incorporate the four *R*s of respect, relevance, reciprocity, and responsibility (Kirkness & Barnhardt, 1991). We want to offer "an education that respects them [our students] for who they are, that is relevant to their view of the world, that offers reciprocity in their relationships with others, and that helps them exercise responsibility over their own lives" (Kirkness & Barhnhardt, 19991, p. 10).

Letters

Indigenous cultures value humility and indirectness. Therefore, we often use indirect storytelling to communicate our thoughts to the intended audience (Wilson, 2008). This puts the responsibility of learning on the receivers of knowledge and allows them to develop their own insights and interpretations. In this section, we exercise the Indigenous practice of indirect communication by sharing our stories to the reader through correspondence with one another, in which we discuss our lived experiences and relate them to IKS.

Cori to Stephanie

Nya:weh. Hello, I am glad you are well. We met briefly at the ACPA convention in Montreal. As you are an elder Haudenosaunee woman and veteran in the field, I wanted to reach out to you for some support. I am in my third year of doctoral study in college student affairs administration and am having some struggles in the student affairs world. I wonder if I can really make it as an Indigenous person in this field.

Growing up in South Dakota, I was a member of a Native community in a college town and was very involved in social gatherings and ceremonies. In undergrad, I was always either a mentor in a Native peer mentoring program, working in the Native American cultural center, or the president of the Native student club. Even though I was at a non-Native college or university (NNCU) (Shotton, Lowe, & Waterman, 2013), I always had a Native community in which I felt that I belonged.

After graduation, I worked in a few student affairs roles with Native students at my alma mater. I loved this work, and it developed my passion for supporting Native students in NNCUs. However, I was frustrated, as upper administration was making top-down decisions for my work that were not congruent for the Native student community. No matter how much I tried, I could not get a seat at real decision-making tables and neither could any other Native faculty or staff. The closest I ever got was when I was invited to meetings with some upper administrators in which the goal was to make me "let go" of the Native mentoring program I was coordinating. I strongly resisted for a few intense meetings until I was finally told, "We just can't give anything more to the Native students or we'll piss off the Black students." My jaw hit the floor, and my mentoring program was over. Beyond blatantly pitting Native and Black people against each other, the administrators were not listening to things I was continuously trying to convey to them based on my experience. The decisions these administrators made, such as getting rid of the mentoring program, removed a means of creating a Native community.

I think that they didn't listen to my suggestions because it was based on experience, not data. What they failed to understand was that for us, our experience *is* our data (Brayboy, 2005)! They did not understand that cultural knowledge is just as important as empirical knowledge (Wilson, 2008). When they refused to hear me, they disregarded my cultural, intuitive knowledge (Kovach, 2009; Wilson, 2008); my voice; and my ability to advocate for my younger cousins (my students). I felt myself becoming "the angry Indian" on campus. Have you ever had this experience?

Anyway, I decided that the best way to access those decision-making tables was to go to graduate school to attain higher credentials. When I first got here, I was shocked at how people spoke to each other. It felt like people were very aggressive in that they spoke loudly, constantly interrupting each other. Students even interrupted professors! I wondered how I would ever get a word in. In my community, space for silence is allowed so that everyone may have a chance to speak, especially elders. I am quiet in the classroom because I am respecting the wisdom and knowledge of my professors. I do not attempt to challenge others' knowledge in order to respect *their relationship* to the knowledge and allow room for multiple truths (Wilson, 2008). This has been an ongoing struggle for me here. When I try to adopt this more assertive style of speaking, I feel embarrassed for being so rude, and then I shut down. Yet, when I don't, I get called out for being too quiet, too passive, or just plain checked out. It is hard to get people to understand our ways of being and knowing.

I have also had some difficulty in learning about student development theories and research practices. What was most blatantly obvious in my theories courses was that there is such a Black–white binary (Brayboy, 2005; Delgado & Stefancic, 2012) in most student development theories and articles. I often found it difficult to continue reading while thinking, "Yeah, okay, but what about *us*?" There is a lot of focus on *individual* needs and development, but we do not operate in such individuality. I was raised to operate as a *community member* (Brayboy & Castagno, 2011) and to think about the needs of the community over my own. What has made it worse is that I am the only Native person in my program and often the only non-Black Student of Color in my classes. So I have often felt the pressure to educate my peers and professors about our ways of knowing and being. This can also feel inappropriate to claim to be an *expert* on something because I was taught that only elders should be held in such regard.

I especially struggled with this when we were assigned to read research articles about Native students by non-Native authors who used deficit models and clearly missed important nuances from Native participants' perspectives (Brayboy & Deyhle, 2000). I found that it has been up to me to make clarifications about the inaccuracies in these readings when my professors and peers would otherwise take them as fact. It has also been painful to be in research classes that devalue our existence altogether. In quantitative courses, I learned that Native students are too small a population to include in data sets, that we need to control for *outliers*, and that individual differences are *bad.* In qualitative courses I learned that, depending on your epistemology, it can be okay to *penetrate* so-called primitive cultures and that it is bad practice to supposedly "go Native" by becoming too close with participants. In Indigenous ways of knowing, none of these things makes sense. Our individual stories and various relationships with knowledge are all valid and important (Brayboy, 2005; Wilson, 2008). To be in a research relationship with participants is to tell *their* stories, so we must form a trusting, reciprocal, and ongoing relationship to gain their permission to write their stories (Kovach, 2009; Weber-Pillwax, 2001, 2004; Wilson, 2008).

My whole existence and purpose in life is to support the next generation of Native students, but I feel like I am failing them as a role model. I just want to feel like I have a place in student affairs where I can do what I love. I feel like my way of knowing and being is looked down upon, like the field sees it as primitive and so I need to assimilate to another way. But my way of knowing and being is integrally connected to who I am as an Indigenous person. Am I wrong for feeling obligated to uphold my Native identity, or do I have to change who I am to make it in this field?

Nya:weh s:geno,
Cori Bazemore-James

Stephanie to Cori

I am honored and humbled that you reached out to me. I, too, feel it is my purpose to support Indigenous students and to conduct myself as a role model. I want to educate higher education and student affairs personnel so they can support our students and Native faculty and staff to create a welcoming environment. We have much in common in addition to being Turtle Clan relatives. I, too, saw inequities in higher education. While I was at meetings with decision-makers, I came to understand that my voice was not valued, that I would continue to be consulted, but not for my input—as window dressing. My dissertation topic is a direct result of having to work on National Center for Education Statistics (NCES) and the Integrated Postsecondary Education Data System (IPEDS) reports that, because of the federally defined cohort, erased the majority of Native students on campus. The literature we used at the time was deficit based, blaming language and culture for Native nonparticipation and graduation.

I understand the important role for supporting our students and ourselves in community. I attended Syracuse University for my doctorate, and although I had no Native classmates or instructors, I was home. The Onondaga Nation was my support, the medicine for being in a hostile environment. I, too, was horrified by the rudeness I experienced and what I considered overfamiliarity non-Indigenous students had with faculty. Our way of being was likely interpreted as being quiet or shy or disengaged and not our IKS.

IKS operates as a foundation; it is complex and sometimes not recognized by dominant systems of cognition and power and can be misinterpreted. This is similar to how the root and leaf system and complementary nature of the Three Sisters was first misinterpreted as a lack of agricultural knowledge. Rather, the cornstalk provides the beans a place to climb, the prickly vines of the squash discourage insects, and the bean produces nitrogen that benefits all three plants (Kimmerer, 2013). Together the plants produce more than if planted separately. One could admire the Three Sisters for their beauty alone, but the magic happens beneath the surface. The settlers who arrived in Massachusetts could not see the magic because their lens was fixed on a different notion of garden.

Dominant ideologies silence and devalue the experiences of marginalized peoples. Taylor (2016) discussed the dominant definitions of *cognition* that directly contrast IKS. She argued that the dominant ideologies can suppress cognitive development. As we've both experienced, our communication style and our desire to form community and kinship have been discouraged. We are rarely given time to reflect in higher education. Dominant ideologies move at a fast pace, a result of neoliberal forces such as accountability as well as to keep us from having the time to look below the surface and examine a system that is rooted in stolen land, slave ownership, strict understandings of gender, and a curriculum that erases non-Western knowledges.

Cajete (2005) identified mind, body, emotion, and spirit as IKS components. Brayboy et al. (2012) listed the following four elements of IKS: community, lived experience, relationships, and place. Embracing these elements with the four *R*s of respect, relevance, reciprocity, and responsibility (Kirkness & Barnhardt, 1991) holistically supports Indigenous students.

Meeting students where they are, a common student affairs developmental mantra, encourages practitioners to use developmental theories to challenge and support students to facilitate more complex thinking (Sanford, 1962). Yet, in our experiences as graduate students, you and I were challenged but not supported. I was also either silenced in the classroom, asked to speak for all Indigenous people, cast as angry if I offered correction, or excused as "she's going through a lot." These are ways the system silences and invalidates emotion as part of students' embodiment. We were not respected as whole persons (Kirkness & Barnhardt, 1991). Higher education is shaped by a particular dominant norm and status quo based on settler colonialism that seeks to erase or silence us—our history, norms, and context—to maintain powers of dominance.

And yet, our IKS, through story and relationship, exemplifies this philosophy of meeting students where they are. Our stories, told throughout our lifetimes by different Speakers, build community and encourage the use of the mind, emotion, and spirituality.[1] In *Indigenous Storywork*, Archibald (2008) wrote that a basket maker will interpret a story differently than a hunter. Life experience builds on prior life experience, influencing the meaning we make of stories at different times in our lives. Stories, and the dialogue that follows, encourage relationships and can challenge previously held beliefs or understandings, which supports the development of complex thinking. The stories shared by our elders are concrete examples of how to be; it is our job to interpret over our lifetimes. Like Brayboy et al. (2012) wrote, student growth is rooted in relationships and community.

The dominant relationship to knowledge is power, as in knowledge as power. In contrast, Haudenosaunee medicine societies share ceremonial knowledge with their members instead of knowledge resting with a single individual or limited individuals in a community. Once a ceremony is performed for an individual, they become a member of that medicine society for life and is then responsible for learning the ceremony and engaging in such ceremonies when other community members need the ceremony. In this way Indigenous knowledge is shared, maintained, relational, and spiritual. It is *for* the community. It is also an example of the relational responsibility within the community rather than the rugged individualism and meritocratic ideology of settler colonial North America.

Cori, you ask if you can make it in higher education. You can. You have a community that needs you to, I need you to, and you have an Indigenous higher education community to support you. When I'm stressed, I think of my community, the hills, our garden, my grandchildren, and the support expressed by my community, and I know this is more than me. It's about all of us.

Oneh,
Stephanie Waterman

How We Reenvision Student Development Theory to Include IKS

We prefer to communicate our thoughts in an indirect manner, thus allowing readers to develop their own insights from our stories (Wilson, 2008).

However, in the Western world of academia, we must conform in some ways for our work to be deemed "legitimate" and to be certain that the knowledge we share is clear. So in this section we write directly to you, the reader, to convey our own thoughts and interpretations from our lived experiences.

To Our Colleagues

Development theories discuss how individuals become "authors of their own truths" (Love & Guthrie, 1999, p. 80) in different ways, but ultimately students become more complex thinkers, are better able to identify and judge evidence, and become less influenced by external forces. The majority of these theories are based on Western worldviews of individuality, meritocracy, and men. Institutions fail to acknowledge their role in suppressing IKS and other worldviews while sustaining a system that maintains a status quo that supports the settler colonialism upon which they were founded.

In a relational, reciprocal, and responsible way of being, *development* may not look like the examples in our theory texts. An Indigenous relationship to [A]uthority is complicated by the relationship and responsibility to the community and one's understanding of the issues at hand. Sharing, as opposed to independent competitive behavior, could appear as being less confident in one's intellectual or emotional competency rather than behavior consistent with Indigenous ways of being. The complexity to cope with competing expected non-Indigenous behaviors and internal values should be recognized, including the stress this can cause. Student development moral theories involve how individuals process the meaning-making of ill-defined dilemmas (Patton, Renn, Guido, & Quaye, 2016). The dilemmas used to inform these theories have been criticized for their disconnections to actual situations individuals face. Moreover, these theories fail to consider the complex moral dilemmas that result from individuals' accountability to their community, their family, future generations, and the land, including nonhumans.

Indigenous students have been characterized as being present oriented, leaving school to take care of family or to work without thinking of the long-term educational consequences (Sanders, 1987). With an orientation that requires us to think of consequences to the seventh generation, the challenge to present orientation needs rethinking. Having our families disrupted, and our ways of being disrupted intentionally by the boarding school and schooling (Adams, 1995), taking care of family and community in the present, now, is nation building; it is sustaining our ways into the future. How can we support this unrecognized complex thinking when an Indigenous student leaves for a ceremony or to take care of siblings?

We ask you to interrogate the assumptions and locations of power in the theories that we use in student affairs. Consider the multiple intersections Indigenous people experience. In addition to impositions of colonial and patriarchal systems, we have (or are reclaiming) gender identities, racial identities, culture, and language and are subject to long-standing stereotypes that are sometimes reinforced by our very own institution. Horse's (2001) paradigm reflects a consciousness of identity acknowledging the complex role of community, recognition, and the diverse definitions of Indigeneity and is a good place to start your understanding. Do not discount historical events as being only in the past; we are still confronted with issues of settler colonialism and the violence of the residential school system.

Conclusion

Native people need a voice in decision-making about Native people (Shotton et al., 2013). Community is of utmost importance for helping Native students thrive, so having community-building programs is imperative to Native student retention (Bazemore-James, 2017) and to support the whole student. Native people are relational, including with regard to knowledge (Wilson, 2008). We each have our "own relationship with ideas" (Wilson, 2008, p. 94). We look for and create familial relationships when we enter an institution so that we can situate ourselves within it. We rely on those relations to guide us and advocate on our behalf (Bazemore-James, 2017). In this chapter we discussed how the complex relationality and responsibility of Indigenous ways of knowing have influenced our experiences in higher education, discussed our challenges within the field and understanding of student development theories, and posed suggestions to the profession.

We propose the following guiding questions for readers to conclude our chapter:

1. Is it possible to change student development theories to include collectivistic ways of knowing like IKS, or do we need to create entirely new theories? How would we go about creating new theories when the field developed in positivistic, structural, and settler colonial paradigms?
2. Discuss ways we could use *story* and *lived experiences* to support Indigenous student development.
3. What biases in your education, personal experience, and practice might hamper your understanding and awareness of Indigenous ways of knowing? Discuss ways you can help others increase their awareness.

4. How might we incorporate cultural values of *respectful silence* and *indirect communication* in understanding Indigenous student development?

Note

1. A person described as Speaker in our way is one who knows valuable traditional knowledge and can speak our ceremonies and stories in our language. Speakers are respected for carrying the responsibility associated with this knowledge that is to be shared with others.

References

Adams, D. W. (1995). Education for extinction: American Indians and the boarding school experience, 1875–1928. Lawrence, KS: University Press of Kansas.

Archibald, J.-A. (2008). *Indigenous storywork: Educating the heart, mind, body, and spirit*. Vancouver, Canada: University of British Columbia Press.

Bazemore-James, C. (2017). *Creating Ganë:gwe:göh: The roles and experiences of Native American directors of Native student support services*. Unpublished manuscript, University of Georgia: Athens, GA.

Brayboy, B. M. J. (2005). Toward a tribal critical race theory in education. *The Urban Review, 37*(5), 425–446.

Brayboy, B. M. J., & Castagno, A. E. (2011). Indigenous millennial students in higher education. In F. A. Bonner II, A. F. Marbley, & M. F. Howard-Hamilton (Eds.), *Diverse millennial students in college* (pp. 137–155). Sterling, VA: Stylus.

Brayboy, B. M. J., & Deyhle, D. (2000). Insider-outsider: Researchers in American Indian communities. *Theory Into Practice, 39*(3), 163–169.

Brayboy, B. M. J., Fann, A. J., Castagno, A. E., & Solyom, J. A. (2012). *Postsecondary education for American Indian and Alaska Natives: Higher education for nation building and self-determination* (ASHE Higher Education Report, Vol. 37, No. 5). San Francisco, CA: John Wiley & Sons.

Brayboy, B. M. J., & Maughan, E. (2009). Indigenous knowledges and the story of the bean. *Harvard Educational Review, 79*(1), 1–21.

Cajete, G. A. (2005). American Indian epistemologies. In M. J. Tippeconic Fox, S. C. Lowe, & G. S. McClellan (Eds.), *Serving Native American students* (New Directions for Student Services, No. 109, pp. 69–78). San Francisco, CA: Jossey-Bass.

Delgado, R., & Stefancic, J. (2012). *Critical race theory: An introduction* (2nd ed.). New York, NY: New York University Press.

Harper, S. R. (2012). Race without racism: How higher education researchers minimize racist institutional norms. *The Review of Higher Education, 36*(1), 9–29.

Horse, P. (2001). Reflections on American Indian identity. In C. L. Wijeyesinghe & B. W. Jackson III (Eds.), *New perspectives on racial identity development: A theoretical and practical anthology* (pp. 91–107). New York, NY: New York University Press.

Johnson, B., & Christensen, L. (2013). *Educational research: Quantitative, qualitative, and mixed approaches* (5th ed.). Thousand Oaks, CA: Sage.

Kimmerer, R. (2013). *Braiding sweetgrass: Indigenous wisdom, scientific knowledge, and the teachings of plants.* Minneapolis, MN: Milkweed Editions.

Kirkness, V., & Barnhardt, R. (1991). First Nations and higher education: The four Rs—respect, relevance, reciprocity, responsibility. *Journal of American Indian Education, 30*(3), 1–15.

Kovach, M. (2009). *Indigenous methodologies: Characteristics, conversations, and contexts.* Toronto, Canada: University of Toronto Press.

Love, P. G., & Guthrie, V. L. (1999). *Understanding and applying cognitive development theory* (New Directions for Student Services, No. 88). San Francisco, CA: Jossey-Bass.

Minthorn, R. S. (2014). Perspectives and values of leadership for Native American college students in non-Native colleges and universities. *Journal of Leadership Education, 13*(2), 67–95.

Mohawk, J. C. (1992). The Indian way is a thinking tradition. In J. Barreiro (Ed.), *Indian roots of American democracy* (pp. 20–29). Ithaca, NY: Akwe:kon Press.

Mohawk, J. C. (2010). Thoughts of peace. In J. Barreiro (Ed.), *Thinking in Indian: A John Mohawk reader* (pp. 240–248). Golden, CO: Fulcrum Press.

Morgan, D. (2003). Appropriation, appreciation, accommodation: Indigenous wisdoms and knowledges in higher education. *International Review of Education, 49*(1–2), 35–49.

Patton, L. D., McEwen, M., Rendón, L., & Howard-Hamilton, M. F. (2007). Critical race perspectives on theory in student affairs. In S. R. Harper & L. D. Patton (Eds.), *Responding to the realities of race on campus* (New Directions for Student Services, No.120, pp 39–53). San Francisco, CA: Jossey-Bass, pp.

Patton, L. D., Renn, K. A., Guido, F. M., & Quaye, S. J. (2016). *Student development in college: Theory, research, and practice* (3rd ed.). San Francisco, CA: Jossey-Bass.

Porter, T. (1992). Men who are of the good mind. In J. Barreiro (Ed.), *Indian roots of American democracy* (pp. 12–19). Ithaca, NY: Akwe:kon Press.

Sanders, D. (1987). Culture conflicts: An important factor in the academic failures of American Indian students. *Journal of Multicultural Counseling and Development, 15*(2), 81–90.

Sanford, N. (1962). *The American college.* New York, NY: Wiley.

Shahjahan, R. A. (2015). Being "lazy" and slowing down: Toward decolonizing time, our body, and pedagogy. *Educational Philosophy and Theory, 47*(5), 488–501.

Shenandoah, A. (1992). Everything has to be in balance. In pp. J. Barreiro (Ed.), *Indian roots of American democracy* (pp. 36–42). Ithaca, NY: Akwe:kon Press.

Shotton, H., Lowe, S. C., & Waterman, S. J. (Eds.). (2013). *Beyond the asterisk: Understanding Native students in higher education.* Sterling, VA: Stylus.

Smith, J. A., Trinidad, S., & Larkin, S. (2017). Understanding the nexus between equity and Indigenous higher education policy agendas in Australia. In J. Frawley,

S. Larkin, & J. A. Smith (Eds.), *Indigenous pathways, transitions and participation in higher education* (pp. 15–30). Singapore: Springer.

Sonn, C., Bishop, B., & Humphries, R. (2007). Encounters with the dominant culture: Voices of Indigenous students in mainstream higher education. *Australian Psychologist, 35*(2), 128–135.

Taylor, K. B. (2016). Diverse and critical perspectives on cognitive development theory. In E. S. Abes (Ed.), *Critical perspectives on student development theory* (New Directions for Student Services, No. 154, pp. 29–41). San Francisco, CA: Jossey-Bass.

Waterman, S. J., & Harrison, I. D. (2017). Indigenous Peoples Knowledge Community (IPKC): Self-determination in higher education. *Journal of Student Affairs Research and Practice, 54*(3), 316–328.

Weber-Pillwax, C. (2001). Coming to an understanding: A panel presentation: What is Indigenous research? *Canadian Journal of Native Education, 25*(2), 166–174.

Weber-Pillwax, C. (2004). Indigenous researchers and Indigenous research methods: Cultural influences or cultural determinants of research methods. *Pimatisiwin: A Journal of Aboriginal and Indigenous Community Health, 2*(1), 77–90.

Wilson, S. (2008). *Research is ceremony: Indigenous research methods*. Black Point, Canada: Fernwood.

14

CONTEXT AND CONTEXTUALIZING STUDENT DEVELOPMENT USING CRITICAL THEORY

Antonio Duran and Susan R. Jones

*C*ontext is a term that is integral to the lexicon of student development, because the process of development always takes place in a larger context. However, although context is presumed to be central to student development, the term is often used interchangeably with others such as *climate, culture, systems,* and the *social* in *psychosocial.* This definitional slippage is taken up in the introduction to this part of the book, but it is important to note again, because the ways in which *context* is defined and put to use in the scholarship on student development affect how it is understood. In this chapter, we examine context when critical theory (Kincheloe & McLaren, 2011) is applied. What this means is that in much scholarship on student development, the individual is the primary unit of analysis, and researchers depend on individuals to make meaning of context. When critical theory is used, scholars must not only address context but also, more important, presume it as a significant influence on development, regardless of whether the individual sees it as such. Furthermore, context, when applying critical theory, is always tied to larger structures of inequality and an analysis of power. In this critical framing of context, we draw on the work of Collins and Bilge (2016), who wrote about the importance of *contextualizing* as the "impetus to think about social inequality, relationality, and power relations in a social context," and that this means "being aware that particular historical, intellectual, and political contexts shape what we think and do" (p. 28). This conceptualization of context then suggests the importance of contextualizing student development by employing structural analyses.

To investigate critical perspectives on context, we first situate ourselves in this work by providing an autobiographical rendering (Jones, Torres, & Arminio, 2014) to the prompt "where I am from" as a basis for understanding our perspectives that follow; in this rendering, we also make it a point to acknowledge the spaces where we are today ("where we are now"). We then present Antonio Duran's contextual narrative as a way into our dialogic engagement with the questions and considerations that emerge when examining context in student development. In the end, we hope to provide new insights on the influence of *context* and the importance of *contextualizing* to understandings of student development. After all, as poignantly suggested by Collins and Bilge (2016), "Once people are changed on the individual level, they are likely to remain so. Focusing on self, on its wholeness, provides a major impetus for individual and collective empowerment" (p. 135). We extend their claim to think about how transformative potential is activated by recognizing the relationship between individuals and the larger structural, cultural, political, and historical contexts in which they move.

"Where I Am From" and "Where I Am Now": Reflections on Our Positionality

Drawing on the concept of *context*, we found it important to begin this chapter by contextualizing our own positionality and introducing how we have come to be in community with one another. We, Antonio Duran and Susan R. Jones, first connected as Antonio was selecting a program for his doctoral studies. We both recall exactly where we were when Antonio was finalizing his decision: Antonio was calling Susan while he was at a NASPA Annual Conference, and Susan was in the parking lot at the veterinarian's office. As we are two scholars who are passionate about the study of student development, specifically in relation to marginalized populations, our relationship continues to develop as we both value and benefit from the perspective that each other offers. To further highlight the unique standpoints that we bring to this scholarly exploration, the following section showcases the experiences that have led us to our current places in life. We indicate these journeys through "where I am from" statements, those that indicate past formative events, before then describing our current contexts and identities, "where I am now."

Antonio Duran

Where I am from: I am from hot Phoenix days where your skin sizzled once you met the sun's rays. I am from neighborhoods of government housing, surrounded by Black and Brown bodies that welcomed us. I am from early Sunday mornings waking up to loud Spanish music, knowing this was my mom's cue that it was time for us to clean. I am from parties with relatives— *tias, tios, primos, familia*—that lasted until the early mornings, followed by the *recalentado* the next day. I am from summers in Juarez, Chihuahua, crossing border walls and being able to return simply by saying "American citizen."

I am from the messages that others told me when I was younger: "Boys aren't supposed to move their hips like that," "You should be playing sports with your cousins," and "You will be the one to take us out of poverty." I am from the books that I escaped into to forget about my difference. I am from *Little Women, Lord of the Flies,* and *Harry Potter.* I am from a family that told me that education was a means of survival despite being known as the nerd of the familia.

Where I am now: I am a friend, a brother, a partner, and a student. I am someone who struggles labeling himself as a scholar, yet I have entered the academy to show students that they matter. I am critical of the structures of power and domination in society and in our schools. I am an individual who approaches his work with love and care, seeing research and teaching as an emotional and spiritual experience. I am appreciative for the mentors, friends, and familia who have gotten me to where I am today. I would not be here without them.

Susan Robb Jones

Where I am from: I am from New Jersey, Chicago, and Cleveland—nice houses in the suburbs where most everyone in my neighborhood looked like me. I am from great schools and dinner table conversations about presidents, leaders, and taking a stand. I am from tractor rides at the farm and kick the can at the lake; places where I got to spend time with my grandparents and learn the story of my family. I am from rules: Don't chew with your mouth full; do unto others; *hey* is for horses; respect your elders; some things we just don't talk about; honesty is always the best policy; and secrets about sexuality, substance abuse, and illness. I am from feeling different.

I am from JFK, RFK, MLK Jr., the Vietnam War, where have all the flowers gone, we shall overcome, and hell no we won't go. I am from the books and music I buried myself in and that nurtured my sense of self and stirrings of social justice. I am from Peter, Paul, and Mary; Crosby, Stills,

Nash, and Young; the Beatles; Simon and Garfunkel; Judy Collins. I am from *A Separate Peace, Catcher in the Rye, To Kill a Mockingbird, Black Like Me.*

Where I am now: I try to do justice, love kindness, and walk humbly. I am a spouse, sister, daughter, and aunt and grateful for the communities to which I belong. I educate because education can make the world a better place. I am committed to using what I know, and realizing when I don't know, to understand the vexing issues facing higher education and college students. I am delving deeply into how I am implicated and what I can do about it. I am generative and support the theorizing of new scholars who stand a chance to advance equity and inclusion. I am with bell hooks (2007) that the "practice of love is the most powerful antidote to the politics of domination" (p. 40), that education is a practice of freedom, and learning is a place where paradise can be created.

Journeys Through Different Spaces: Antonio's Narrative

> Like many other individuals, I often say that college helped shape who I am. As someone who now studies collegiate environments, I have started to figure out why. The spaces that I have occupied have molded me into the person I am today. (A. Duran)

Precollege Experiences

To truly understand the crucial role that higher education played in my development, I find it important to begin by highlighting my experiences prior to my arrival at my undergraduate institution. Growing up in Phoenix, Arizona, I often interacted with people who were like me. I lived in a neighborhood that housed predominantly Latinx and Black families. Most of these families emigrated from countries near and far, hoping to provide a better life for their children or family members back home. My own parents emigrated from Mexico about seven years before my birth. They quickly settled into this new space, this new normal.

My first experiences in an educational system were shared with people who were racial and ethnic minorities and from lower class backgrounds, like those in my neighborhood. The district of my primary and elementary school was and continues to be considered one of the most at-risk districts in the state of Arizona. However, my young mind did not think about the label of "at-risk district" when I was in these schools. I was simply happy to be there, absorbing every bit of knowledge that I could. As my mom would always state, I was much more content reading a book than playing sports like the rest of my family. My primary and elementary schools cultivated this educational thirst. I was in the gifted and talented program, participated in our National Junior Honor Society and student council, and even showed off my school spirit in my brief stint as our mascot, the Wilson Wildcat. Beyond my involvement, people knew me as an individual who was always jovial, beaming a large smile wherever I went.

When the time came to transition into a high school environment, I had my eyes set on Brophy College Preparatory, a prestigious Jesuit private institution in Phoenix. As a result of a partnership between Brophy and my elementary school, students whom they accepted into this high school automatically received a full-tuition scholarship. I was thus excited when I passed the necessary entrance exam for admission and soon enrolled in this institution. Still, I never anticipated the amount of dissonance I would encounter at Brophy.

For the first time in my life, I found myself surrounded by individuals who came from a different world. Gone were the diverse languages that I had been used to hearing in my previous schooling. The student demographic at Brophy was dramatically different. The majority of individuals with whom I shared a classroom space were white, and as a result of the high cost of tuition, they were also mostly wealthy. My first year at Brophy represented a pivotal time in my life when I recognized that I was different. This realization was solidified by moments like the instance when a classmate of mine told me, "You know you're in the bad part of town when all of the signs are in Spanish," after visiting my house. I never brought anyone home after that.

When I found myself surrounded by a largely homogenous student body, I retreated in many ways. I came to hate my own background, constantly rejecting the great sacrifices that my parents made on a daily basis. I ran to my mom's truck in the hopes that no one would see the *Arizona Republic* newspapers in the back and discover that my mom was a newspaper deliverer. I tried to hide the fact that I bought the polos I wore, and that were required for our dress code, from our neighborhood Goodwill store. I also stopped speaking Spanish, fearing that this would alienate me from my peers even more. On top of coming to hate my racial and class background, my general affect also transformed. I became angry and introverted.

These precollege experiences proved to be an important foundation for understanding my development in higher education. I acknowledge that attending Brophy College Preparatory accomplished the goal declared in its name—it got me to my next step despite the emotional and personal turmoil that I underwent. When the time came to apply for college, I was subconsciously searching for something extremely unlike what I had encountered in high school. For that reason, it is unsurprising that I chose a school and city drastically different from those of my high school years. In May 2010, I sent my acceptance and deposit to New York University (NYU), located in the heart of Greenwich Village in Manhattan.

College Experiences

NYU was what I wanted, and, more important, it was exactly what I needed. Lacking the financial means to visit schools, I accepted NYU's admission offer without even seeing the campus. I still remember the first time I rode in a taxi on my way to orientation and sat in the front seat, a move that most likely showed my taxi driver that I was clearly not from New York City. Still, when I arrived to the orientation residence hall, I recall looking up at the buildings on the corner of 12th Street and 4th Avenue. At that moment, I knew that I was where I was meant to be.

As I walked the busy streets, I could look around and feel like I was back in my childhood neighborhood, hearing various languages being spoken. It was also at NYU that I started to reconcile various tensions that arose at Brophy. For example, during my first year, I received an invitation to a first-year workshop known as Intersections, a diversity program for first-year students. In addition to completing various dialogue-based activities, we also saw *Avenue Q*. This program challenged me to reflect on my identities, discovering the power that each of them held. I underwent this personal journey alongside students who were from across the university, country, and world. The weekend I spent with these individuals also represented one of the first times that I came out as queer to my peers.

I began to discover my sexuality when I was also coming to recognize the origins of my anger in high school. As I took courses with people from places such as North Carolina or Abu Dhabi, I learned that every one of us had a unique story. The classrooms were not as homogenous as the ones that I had come to know and to reject. Moreover, the experiences I had outside of the classroom challenged me to reconcile the feelings of embarrassment I once held. I had the opportunity to attend NYU thanks to a full-tuition scholarship awarded to three to four first-generation college students every year. As time progressed and a mentor of mine encouraged me to think about my passions, I increasingly felt the positive influence that this scholars program had on my development. We were superseding the expectations of our families and our communities. And we were doing so in one of the best cities in the world.

My time at NYU was formative for a number of different reasons. First of all, it taught me that it was important to be around people who hold similar identities as I do. I loved the city environment because I could learn more about my own culture while also exploring others. I came to know my sexuality by visiting historic landmarks such as Stonewall or stopping by NYU's LGBTQ Center. Second, I learned how to use my voice in order to center the experiences of the marginalized. Going to college in New York City was like nothing that I had ever experienced before. I regained the jovial nature that I once had, having lost it in high school after succumbing to feelings of inadequacy in a predominantly white space. I was happy again.

Postcollege Experiences

After graduating from NYU, I decided to pursue a career in higher education. It was my dream that I could help other students come to understand their identities. Now, as an aspiring faculty member in the academy, I have to stop myself from retreating into the sentiments of not being good enough. Part of my driving force involves knowing that my presence in higher education can be important in changing the environment and culture. By striving for a position in the academy, I hope to create pathways for future scholars and practitioners.

Use of Critical Theory

This chapter uses the tradition of critical theory to provide a new perspective on context as it relates to student development. Throughout this chapter, we mention frameworks that fall under the umbrella of critical theory, including critical race theory and intersectionality, which advance power-based definitions of *context*. As explored in the preface, critical theory challenges educators to consider how society is structured around historical and contemporary legacies of inequality (Kincheloe & McLaren, 2011). Specifically, the task of the critical researcher involves identifying the ways that systems of power simultaneously privilege certain groups and oppress others. Finally, critical theory strives not only to increase understanding of these structures of domination but also to contribute to their dismantling through social action.

Critical Questions About Context

Using Antonio's narrative as a guide, this next section explores how the concept of context differs with critical theory in mind. To bring a critical lens to this construct, we engaged in a dialogic conversation, challenging one another to move beyond constructivist understandings of context and its influences on student development theory. We thus chose to structure this portion of our chapter around four orienting questions that emerged from our dialogue, each challenging individuals to foreground systems of power when analyzing context. To follow Jackson and Mazzei's (2012) notion of thinking with theory, we include excerpts from our dialogue in the following section to highlight how our thinking varied and coalesced when understanding the construct of context. Importantly, we also include thoughts for scholars and practitioners who hope to employ this construct from a critical perspective.

Who Gets Privileged in Current Assumptions of Context?

> I think in my first forays into student development theory, something that I increasingly struggled with is the notion of the collegiate context feeling like a container . . . whereas critical theories would conceptualize what it is that the student is encountering not only within these kinds of college gates but within society. (A. Duran)

In this quote, Antonio articulates the belief that theory and higher education research frequently fails to consider how experiences that occur outside of colleges and universities influence the development of students. In reality, from Antonio's story, it is clear to see how individuals undergo formative events in their life prior to arriving at college and outside of the college gates while they are enrolled in postsecondary institutions. Therefore, when student development theorists use the term *context*, they may be focusing solely on events occurring on campus that spur collegians to think about themselves differently. Using this narrow view of context misses an important link to understanding how students' past experiences affect their sense of self, as well as how sociohistorical influences laden with power do the same.

For example, ecological theorists have attempted to draw a connection between individuals and their environments over a given period of time. One of the most notable ecological theorists is Bronfenbrenner (1979, 1993) who suggested that individuals exist within four main ecological systems: the micro-, meso-, exo-, and macro-. The macrosystem in Bronfenbrenner's (1993) model encapsulates the "overarching patterns of micro-, meso-, and exosystem characteristics of a given culture, subculture, or other extended social structure" (p. 25), which can include greater attention to issues of power and oppression. However, scholars such as Renn (2003) contended that macrosystems are "largely missing from traditional student development research" (p. 389). A lack of attention to macroforces of domination severely limits our understanding of student development theory. Specifically, Susan calls attention to this troubling reality in the following portion of our dialogic conversation:

> Who gets privileged in our assumption of context? It's those with more power, those from dominant groups that are privileged by that definition of context because they're benefiting from these larger structures. (S. R. Jones)

If practitioners and researchers only center collegiate contexts, they continue practices that serve majority populations of students. In fact, higher education scholars have routinely drawn attention to the fact that colleges originated for privileged individuals who identified as white men and came from affluent backgrounds (Museus, Ledesma, & Parker, 2015). However, this assumption of context does not fit for many of our students. Antonio's narrative itself functions as an example of how students can be dealing with simultaneous experiences of racism, heterosexism, and other structures of domination. Thus, conceptualizing context from a critical perspective asks us to challenge a collegiate-only container and to understand students' life histories with an explicit focus on how power systems may be affecting students' development (Abes, 2016; Jones & Stewart, 2016). For scholars and practitioners who hope to resist the privileging of certain dominant groups, it is imperative that we expand our view of environments to include local communities, home cultures, and sociohistorical times.

How Does Context Affect Developmental Dimensions Differently?

In Antonio's narrative, he details how his transition to a predominantly white high school was a major transition in his life. Being surrounded by people who came from dissimilar backgrounds led Antonio to retreat in various ways. However, Antonio also credits this experience as one that pushed his ways of thinking and afforded him the opportunity to eventually enroll at New York University. As a result, though his high school environment may have served as a catalyst for cognitive growth, it had negative repercussions on his understanding of self and relationships with others. The complexities in this experience cause us to question how educational contexts may in fact influence developmental dimensions differently, especially for students from historically marginalized backgrounds.

Students with oppressed identities often navigate institutions of higher learning and social structures that were not created with them in mind. For this reason, we see it necessary to explore how these environments affect individuals as it pertains to their cognitive (knowledge construction), interpersonal (relationships), and intrapersonal (understanding of self) domains of development

(Kegan, 1994). Antonio thinks through this point in his narrative by stating, "I wonder if students might be shaped in ways that they can think at higher levels of cognitive complexity, but are they experiencing damaging dissonance in the way that they are seeing themselves?" Though institutions often stress the importance of compositional diversity on campuses (Hurtado, Alvarez, Guillermo-Wann, Cuellar, & Arellano, 2012), colleges frequently fail to create climates that are healthy for collegians with marginalized identities (Chun & Evans, 2016). Thus, a strong focus on cognitive growth may be exposing these students to destructive contexts that adversely affect their interpersonal and intrapersonal dimensions of development. The work of scholars such as Torres (2009), Hernández (2016), and Abes and Hernández (2016) interrogated the taken-for-granted assumptions in what constitutes *development*. Specific to the role of context, Jones and Abes (2013) examined the relationship among meaning-making, identity, and context, suggesting that

> certain contextual influences are more challenging to filter than others, regardless of a person's meaning-making capacity. . . . This realization speaks to how meaning making alone does not shape identity perceptions; it must be coupled with the specific nature of the context. (p. 118)

Consequently, we echo the work of hooks (1994), who warned against educational systems that ask students to enter as "disembodied spirit" (p. 193). When we think about our learning environments without consideration of power and identity, we once again privilege students for whom these contexts were originally created. In the dialogic conversation, Antonio shares, "What does this mean for students as they are developing, growing if they are the ones who constantly have to ask this question for themselves: Was this space meant for me?" Susan articulates that institutions expose individuals from historically marginalized backgrounds to developmental costs, especially in their interpersonal and intrapersonal domains. From this, it is evident that a critical lens requires professionals to question how students' developmental domains are influenced differently by educational and social contexts. In particular, practitioners and scholars must ask themselves how campus programming, classroom environments, and forces outside of the institution may cause students to become disembodied spirits.

How Do You Measure Context?

The questions detailed thus far prompt us to advance our next point of inquiry, a methodological quandary that results from using a critical view on context. Analyzing power structures in students' lives means that the researcher might uncover contextual influences that individuals sharing the stories themselves do not realize. Antonio's narrative serves as a prime example of this reality. Having had years to reflect on his collegiate experience in addition to receiving input from Susan, Antonio could access the impacts of context previously unseen. Thus, methodological complexities exist when understanding context from a critical paradigm.

To begin, we argue that scholars and practitioners must ask more direct questions as they attempt to ascertain the role that contexts play in a student's life, especially as it relates to ideas of power. Susan suggests this as she thinks back on higher education research that explores constructs such as race and racism. As she notes in our dialogic conversation, "Well, one could suggest that the participants didn't see race or that researchers didn't think that they saw race or concluded that they didn't see race because they were never asked about it." Though it appears to be a simple solution, researchers must ask more direct questions of their participants that center the different contexts with which they interact on a daily basis. Moreover, as Nuñez (2014) underscored in her discussion on intersectionality in higher education, researchers must be more explicit about how they define *power*. In student development research specifically, theorists should ask questions about individuals' contexts that align with understandings of power (see Collins, 2009, for an example of domains of power). Nevertheless, asking about context is only the first step in measuring this construct and its relation to student development.

Next, scholars must also wrestle with the challenge of analyzing systems of power from the perspective of an individual inherently entrenched in this structure. For example, using critical race theory (CRT) to understand development, one would subscribe to the belief that racism is engrained in all collegiate contexts, as well as society (Delgado & Stefancic, 2001). This tenet of CRT has led individuals to use air as an analogy for the pervasive existence of racism: "It is in the air we breathe, and we all need to breathe" (Miller & Garran, 2017). Similar to how racism is like air—all around us and difficult to identify—students may also struggle to discuss how their contexts influence them. Individuals can take for granted contextual influences, including systems of power, failing to understand the role that these systems play in their development. The task of critical researchers then becomes analyzing narratives, understanding that they may be uncovering realities that differ from the participants' perspective. Consequently, member-checking, a common method used to ensure trustworthiness in qualitative research, may not make sense when employing critical perspectives (Talburt, 2004).

It is important to note that using context in a study design requires an ethic of care on behalf of the researcher.

> We need to understand that even when we get answers from our partici-
> pants or from our students, there might be levels or other experiences at
> play that might not allow them to make as direct connections between the
> ways that their different contexts are affecting themselves. (A. Duran)
> And I think we need to point out that there are ethical dimensions to all
> research. I guess it goes back to researchers constantly making decisions and
> weighing the benefits and limitations of the challenges, difficulties, of every
> decision. (S. R. Jones)

A critical scholar is alert to the ethical dimensions of analyzing the stories
of others and what the research process itself may mean for an individual's development. Using critical perspectives requires scholars to implicate
themselves in power systems, especially those that result from a research relationship (Denzin, 2010). Hence, when centering context, higher education
professionals must consider the methodological and ethical complexities that
result from investigating power-based understandings of this construct.

Who Can Shape Context? How Does This Happen?

The last section of Antonio's narrative describes how his collegiate experiences have led him to pursue a faculty career, hoping to positively influence students from similar backgrounds. In this statement, Antonio also
communicates the ultimate goal of possessing the ability to shape contexts
positively for those from marginalized populations. This ambition challenges us to question a static understanding of context, a construct that
is immutable to the actions of individuals. Instead, we use this portion of
the chapter as an opportunity to explore the possibilities of shaping context, embracing critical thought around resistance.

> I think about, especially with a lot of critical thought and critical practice,
> this notion of coalition-building. I think in order to really conceptualize
> the changing of context as influenced by hegemonic norms, as influenced
> by all of these -isms, then it would require coalitions across different identi-
> ties, different individuals to do this. (A. Duran)

This quote provides one insight on this question of shaping contexts: the
belief that groups across identities can come together to effectively change
policies and structures at an institution. This line of thinking closely aligns
with the scholarship on critical mass and how larger numbers of underserved populations on campuses can lead to positive change efforts (Museus,
Jayakumar, & Robinson, 2012). By bringing together numerous groups and
collectively advocating for equitable representation and resources, faculty,

staff, and students positively affect the institutional context, as well as the policy arena. Importantly, individuals with privileged identities must also participate in these coalitions in order to mobilize change because of the emotional costs that marginalized populations encounter when exercising their agency.

On a more micro level, Susan offers Tatum's (1997) notion of spheres of influence as another way that individuals can shape their context: "We might not be able to change the world, but we have spheres of influence that we can influence" (S.R. Jones). This concept is particularly powerful in affirming the possibility of people from marginalized backgrounds enacting their own agency in their proximal environments. While enacting larger structural change may require the actions of others, individuals can make intentional efforts to affect the micro contexts in which they reside. Yet, as the perspectives offered in chapter 12 describe, competing forces always exist in society that make it exhausting to constantly be exercising one's agency without assistance from others. In the end, both spheres of influence and coalition-building are needed to truly advance a critical approach to understanding contexts in higher education, a theme that emerged in our dialogic conversation in debriefing Antonio's narrative. Discussing this point, Antonio states,

> It's both–and. We can't be complacent with creating smaller spaces on campus where people can feel their identities affirmed. And these might be the small moves and victories that will take us to shape contexts in a macro sense when it comes from an institutional perspective. (A. Duran)

Thus, Susan and Antonio both indicate that context is not only not a static entity but also can and should be reshaped to generate more equitable systems of education for underserved populations.

Conclusion

In analyzing Antonio's narrative and the issue of context, Susan asks, "What do you do with the individual in these critical perspectives? Is it possible to talk about student development while examining context simultaneously?" These ruminations showcase the issues that emerge when attempting to identify power structures and their influence on college student development. Though these contexts are difficult to potentially measure, it is important that researchers name the contexts in which their students reside beyond the collegiate container, investigate how these environments can affect developmental dimensions differently, and be explicit in their attempt to ascertain context. Notable examples of these types of explorations have emerged (e.g.,

Chun & Evans, 2016; Pizzolato, Nguyen, Johnston, & Wang, 2012; Renn & Arnold, 2003; Stewart, 2015); still, researchers and practitioners must continue to be intentional in their use of criticality when thinking about context. For this reason, in answering Susan's previous questions, Antonio once again asks individuals to embrace a both–and in analyzing identity from a power-based analysis.

> It would need to become a both–and. It would need to become (a) what structures of domination and what power systems affect the ways that our students interact with college and what composes their life? and (b) what effect does this have then on the ways that they understand themselves? Finally, this approach must also presume that students can change context through coalition-building. (A. Duran)

Broadening the focus of context thus allows educators to contextualize the development of students as they navigate inequitable and oppressive structures on college campuses. By framing context using critical theory, higher education researchers and practitioners are better equipped to work with students in the process of creating social change and action.

Discussion Questions

1. How does your present understanding about context influence your practice? How would your approach change with a reconceptualized view of context?
2. How does your current collegiate context privilege and oppress certain student populations? Be specific. How do you see larger societal contexts influencing the development of students?
3. Using the analogy of theoretical waves as discussed in chapter 1, how has the role of context in student development theory shifted across the three waves?
4. Identify two or three strategies that you can use to build coalitions with the purpose of shaping equitable contexts in your department and/or campus.

References

Abes, E. S. (2016). Situating paradigms in student development theory. In E. S. Abes (Ed.), *Critical perspectives on student development theory*(New Directions for Student Services, No. 154, pp. 9–16). San Francisco, CA: Jossey-Bass.

Abes, E. S., & Hernández, E. (2016). Critical and poststructural perspectives on self-authorship. In E. S. Abes (Ed.), *Critical perspectives on student development theory* (New Directions for Student Services, No. 154, pp. 97–108). San Francisco, CA: Jossey-Bass.

Bronfenbrenner, U. (1979). *The ecology of human development: Experiments by nature and design.* Cambridge, MA: Harvard University Press.

Bronfenbrenner, U. (1993). The ecology of cognitive development: Research models and fugitive findings. In R. H. Wozniak & K. W. Fischer (Eds.), *Development in context: Acting and thinking in specific environments* (pp. 3–44). Hillsdale, NJ: Lawrence Erlbaum.

Chun, E., & Evans, A. (2016). Rethinking cultural competence in higher education: An ecological framework for student development. *ASHE Higher Education Report, 42*(4), 7–162.

Collins, P. H. (2009). *Black feminist thought: Knowledge, consciousness and the politics of empowerment.* New York, NY: Routledge. (Original work published 2000).

Collins, P. H., & Bilge, S. (2016). *Intersectionality: Key concepts.* Cambridge, UK: Polity Press.

Delgado, R., & Stefancic, J. (2001). *Critical race theory: An introduction.* New York, NY: New York University Press.

Denzin, N. K. (2010). *The qualitative manifesto: A call to arms.* New York, NY: Routledge.

Hernández, E. (2016). Utilizing critical race theory to examine race/ethnicity, racism, and power in student development theory and research. *Journal of College Student Development, 57*(2), 168–180.

hooks, b. (1994). *Teaching to transgress: Education as the practice of freedom.* New York, NY: Routledge.

hooks, b. (2007). Creating a culture of love. In M. McLeod (Ed.), *The best Buddhist writing* (pp. 40–49). Boston, MA: Shambhala Publications.

Hurtado, S., Alvarez, C. L., Guillermo-Wann, C., Cuellar, M., & Arellano, L. (2012). A model for diverse learning environments: The scholarship on creating and assessing conditions for student success. In J. C. Smart & M. B. Paulsen (Eds.), *Higher education: Handbook of theory and research* (Vol. 27, pp. 41–122). New York, NY: Springer.

Jackson, A. Y., & Mazzei, L. A. (2012). *Thinking with theory in qualitative research: Viewing data across multiple perspectives.* New York, NY: Routledge.

Jones, S. R., & Abes, E. S. (2013). *Identity development of college students: Advancing frameworks for multiple dimensions of identity.* San Francisco, CA: Jossey-Bass.

Jones, S. R., Torres, V., & Arminio, J. (2014). *Negotiating the complexities of qualitative research in higher education: Fundamental elements and issues* (2nd ed.). New York, NY: Routledge.

Jones, S. R., & Stewart, D-L. (2016). Evolution of student development theory. In E. S. Abes (Ed.), *Critical perspectives on student development theory* (New Directions for Students Services, No. 154, pp. 17–28). San Francisco, CA: Jossey-Bass.

Kegan, R. (1994). *In over our heads: The mental demands of modern life.* Cambridge, MA: Harvard University Press.

Kincheloe, J. L., & McLaren, P. (2011). Rethinking critical theory and qualitative research. In k. hayes, S. R. Steinberg, & K. Tobin (Eds.), *Key works in critical pedagogy* (Vol. 32, pp. 285–326). Boston, MA: Sense Publishers.

Miller, J., & Garran, A. M. (2017). *Racism in the United States: Implications for the helping profession* (2nd ed.). New York, NY: Springer.

Museus, S. D., Jayakumar, U. M., & Robinson, T. (2012). Effects of racial representation on the persistence of community college students: An examination of conditional and indirect effects. *Journal of College Student Retention: Theory, Research, and Practice, 13*(4), 549–572.

Museus, S. D., Ledesma, M. C., & Parker, T. L. (2015). Racism and racial equity in higher education. *ASHE Higher Education Report, 42*(1), 1–112.

Nuñez, A.-M. (2014). Advancing an intersectionality framework in higher education: Power and Latino postsecondary opportunity. In M. B. Paulsen (Ed.), *Higher education: Handbook of theory and research* (pp. 33–92). New York, NY: Springer.

Pizzolato, J. E., Nguyen, T.-L. K., Johnston, M. P., & Wang, S. (2012). Understanding context: Cultural, relational, and psychological interactions in self-authorship development. *Journal of College Student Development, 53*(5), 656–679.

Renn, K. A. (2003). Understanding the identities of mixed-race college students through a developmental ecology lens. *Journal of College Student Development, 44*(3), 383–403.

Renn, K. A., & Arnold, K. D. (2003). Reconceptualizing research on college student peer culture. *Journal of Higher Education, 74*(3), 261–291.

Stewart, D-L. (2015). Know your role: Black college students, racial identity, and performance. *International Journal of Qualitative Studies in Education, 28*(2), 238–258.

Talburt, S. (2004). Ethnographic responsibility without the "real." *Journal of Higher Education, 75*(1), 80–103.

Tatum, B. D. (1997). *Why are all the Black kids sitting together in the cafeteria? And other conversations about race.* New York, NY: Basic Books.

Torres, V. (2009). The developmental dimensions of recognizing racist thoughts. *Journal of College Student Development, 50*(5), 504–520.

PART THREE

IMPLICATIONS FOR A CRITICAL STUDENT AFFAIRS PRACTICE

In 1977, Clyde Parker identified the *dilemma, paradox,* and *problem* of translating theory to practice. The dilemma: *Good research and theory building require the abstraction of a few elements from the whole of human experience. Practice requires concrete and specific behavior in complex situations.* The paradox: *Theory dealing with abstractions from the general case cannot be applied in concrete and specific situations. Concrete and specific action flows from the personal theories of the actor.* The problem: *Learning how to transform formal theory into personal theories of action.* The third part of this book seeks to resolve Parker's dilemma, paradox, and problem of applying theories of student development to student affairs practice.

As written in the preface and the introduction to Part One, we assert that critical theories involve critique of "life as it is—within the practices, traditions, values, and beliefs of a particular society" (Jessop, 2014, p. 194). Furthermore, drawing on Martínez-Alemán (2015) we suggest that such frameworks aim to produce social and political action leading to societally relevant practical solutions and transformation. In light of this, we believe it is necessary to engage the practical implications and applications of the critical and poststructural theories (Part One) and critically reenvisioned constructs (Part Two) discussed in this text. As D-L often tells his student development theory classes, "Practice without theory is dangerous. Theory without practice is presumptuous" (D-L Stewart, personal communication, 2008).

The contributors in this part reenvision three core guiding tenets of student affairs practice: involvement and engagement, principles of good practice, and high-impact practices. Anchored in existing perspectives on student affairs practice and scholarship, these chapters transform formal theory into personal theories of action to instigate concrete and specific actions for application in concrete and specific situations. Embedded in these chapters is the assertion that one's worldview and ontological orientation matter for how one does the work of facilitating student learning, meaning making, and development.

In chapter 15, Daniel Tillapaugh considers involvement and engagement through this book's critical and poststructural theorizing. Although involvement and engagement are worthy aspirations, Tillapaugh troubles how those goals have come to be operationalized in student affairs practice to emphasize certain types of involvement and engagement as more worthy than others without considering the barriers students face. Using examples and testimonies from his own and others' professional practice, Tillapaugh reenvisions involvement and engagement as opportunities for inspiring critical consciousness, provocative action, and transformative practice.

In chapter 16, Susan B. Marine explores a foundational document for student affairs practice, the *Principles of Good Practice in Student Affairs* (NASPA: Student Affairs Administrators in Higher Education, 1997), based on Chickering and Gamson's (1987) principles of good practice in undergraduate education. Challenging the profession's values-drift, Marine proposes that we reconsider how we put into practice high expectations, meeting students where they are, and the other principles canonical to student affairs. Marine challenges readers to consider what a "student affairs practice of resistance" (p. 216, this volume) would entail and how we might center dismantling and resisting structural oppression. Ultimately, Marine argues that good practice is critically transformative practice.

In the last chapter in Part Three, Alex C. Lange and D-L Stewart reconceptualize the high-impact practices articulated by Kuh (2008). This set of 11 practices has been promoted as central to achieving student success in college. Lange and Stewart contend that emphasis on these practices likely draws resources away from other practices considered "low impact." In addition, they assert that practices regarded as having "high impact" fail to acknowledge the multiple structural barriers within and external to postsecondary institutions that prevent minoritized students from accessing and fully benefiting from such practices. They encourage student affairs practitioners to consider other ways—through critical and poststructural lenses—that postsecondary education can have highly positive impacts on student learning, meaning-making, and development. Student affairs professionals need to be versatile in their practice, deftly moving from one theoretical location to another to best serve the particular student before them at any given moment.

Critical (re)constructions of student development are not just fodder for heady debates and banter among scholars. The contributors in this part resolve Parker's (1977) dilemma by taking the theoretical frameworks and constructs in Part One and Part Two and directly applying them to concrete situations and issues that student affairs professionals face. To resolve the paradox, the contributors assert the necessity for practitioners to think deeply about their own frameworks and whether those frameworks can serve the liberatory goals of critical theory. The personal theories of the professional should mirror the liberatory frameworks they purport to value. Through these assertions, Parker's problem is resolved: Formal theories—the umbrella of critical theory for our purposes in this text—become personal theories of action through reflexive praxis that centers liberation. These critical perspectives have both epistemic and pragmatic value that can revolutionize student affairs theory and practice to become more liberatory for students and professionals alike.

References

Chickering, A. W., & Gamson, Z. F. (1987). Seven principles for good practice in undergraduate education. *AAHE Bulletin, 3,* 7.

Jessop, S. (2014). Critical theory. In D. C. Phillips (Ed.), *Encyclopedia of educational theory and philosophy* (Vol. 1, pp. 193–196). Thousand Oaks, CA: Sage.

Kuh, G. D. (2008). *High-impact educational practices: What they are, who has access to them, and why they matter.* Washington, DC: Association of American Colleges & Universities.

Martínez-Alemán, A. M. (2015). Critical discourse analysis in higher education policy research. In A. M. Martínez-Alemán, B. Pusser, & E. M. Bensimon (Eds.), *Critical approaches to the study of higher education: A practical introduction* (pp. 7–43). Baltimore, MD: Johns Hopkins University Press.

NASPA: Student Affairs Administrators in Higher Education. (1997). *Principles of good practice for student affairs: Statement and inventories.* Washington, DC: Author. Retrieved from https://www.naspa.org/images/uploads/main/Principles_of_Good_Practice_in_Student_Affairs.pdf

Parker, C. (1977). On modeling reality. *Journal of College Student Personnel, 18,* 419–425.

15

STUDENT INVOLVEMENT AND ENGAGEMENT

Daniel Tillapaugh

P rior to becoming a faculty member, I worked for eight years as a student affairs professional in residence life and then student activities, where I oversaw student clubs and organizations, orientation programs, and student leadership programs. Student development theories, including student involvement and engagement theories, shaped and informed my work. I distinctly remember sharing with students and their families at orientation those talking points informed by research: "It's important to get involved during college to find your niche and passions, but also because research tells us that students who do so perform better, are more satisfied with their college experience, and persist to graduation at higher rates."

As time has gone on, I began to see directly how damaging this mind-set could be and became critical of these talking points. What about the first-generation college student working 2 jobs to put herself through college and prioritizing her finances over getting involved in student clubs? How about the adult learner, a father of 3, coming back to college after a military career, who struggles to connect to many of the experiences dominated by 18- to 24-year-olds on campus? What about Students of Color constantly marginalized by individuals at their historically white institution that perpetuates whiteness and dominant norms through curriculum, campus programming, and policies? Each of these questions provides an essential counternarrative related to students and their engagement or involvement.

When organizing this chapter, I reflected on my time in the field, drawing on and dreaming about what I considered important outcomes for students through their involvement and engagement. This dreaming and this contemplation draw on critical voices and literature to engage in emancipatory or liberatory work aimed at expanding our notions of what it means for students to engage on campus (Tuck & Yang, 2018). In this chapter, I first briefly discuss and define the terms *student involvement* and *student engagement* as they are currently understood. Next, I attempt to reframe the discussion of student involvement and engagement. Last, I highlight the ways that higher education professionals can integrate the praxis of student involvement and engagement from a critical perspective to benefit all students and their development.

Defining Terms

With research spanning almost four decades, higher education scholars (Astin 1984, 1993; Kuh, 2003, 2009; Tinto, 1993; Wolf-Wendel, Ward, & Kinzie, 2009) called attention to the importance of student involvement and engagement as it relates to student success. *Student involvement*, defined by Astin (1984), is "the amount of physical and psychological energy that the student devotes to the academic experience" (p. 297). Astin's (1984) work highlighted the fact that particular environments, such as residence hall communities, and group affiliations, such as honors programs, athletics team involvement, student government, and academic involvement, create positive relationships for student success.

    Student engagement expands on the idea of student involvement to incorporate those meaningful learning opportunities students partake in on campus and the ways institutions promote these opportunities (Kuh, 2003, 2009). Kuh's (2003) work was instrumental to the founding of the National Survey of Student Engagement (NSSE, 2014). The following major benchmarks of student engagement emerged from the NSSE data: (a) level of academic challenge, (b) active and collaborative learning, (c) student–faculty interaction, (d) enriching educational experiences, and (e) supportive campus environment (NSSE, n.d.). Until recently, much of the scholarship on student involvement and engagement has consistently framed these concepts from the perspective of an institutional context. In other words, students are invited and encouraged to find opportunities for involvement based on their personal interests that provide them a stronger connection to their campus community and a network of individuals to support them within that community.

Explorations of Student Involvement and Engagement

As Collins (2000) noted, "Within U.S. culture, racist and sexist ideologies permeate the social structure to such a degree that they become hegemonic, namely, seen as natural, normal, and inevitable" (p. 7). To expand on

Collins's argument, even our notions of student involvement and engagement have been created by centering students who largely fit the dominant culture—those who are white, heterosexual, cisgender, able-bodied, Christian men of wealth—or often demanding students who do not fit that profile to assimilate to the norms of the dominant culture within their institutions. Historically, the collective focus on student involvement and engagement has directed students to participating in campus life. To be sure, many students who participate in student engagement activities find opportunities to engage meaningfully in community, gain a sense of belonging, and develop critical skills that help them personally and professionally (Mayhew et al., 2016; Strayhorn, 2012). Yet, far too often, the dominant narratives in the scholarship on involvement and engagement have focused on those who engage rather than explore why some students do not get involved on campus. By problematizing the concepts of student engagement and involvement, higher education professionals must think critically about how to best support all students rather than continue the status quo.

In their article on student involvement, engagement, and integration, Wolf-Wendel et al. (2009) quoted higher education scholar Frances Stage, who stated, "If you want to do something to change the status quo then we really have to upend the models—we have to change the questions" (p. 422). Stage's words are critical here; we, as higher education professionals, must change our questions and our understandings of student involvement and engagement. In the remainder of this chapter, I frame the discussion using two main questions:

1. How can we reframe our understanding of student involvement and engagement from a critical perspective?
2. What would a critical praxis of student involvement and engagement look like in higher education?

Reframing Student Involvement and Engagement

We know that many students do not find their college or university campuses to be a space in which they wish to involve or engage themselves. In addition, many students, particularly those from historically underrepresented populations, continue to find themselves at institutions with chilly, hostile climates set up to serve those with dominant, privileged identities (Stewart, 2017a). More recently, scholars have examined the connections between student engagement for historically underrepresented student populations, such as Students of Color (Mitchell, Soria, Daniele, & Gipson, 2015; Museus & Quaye, 2009; Rendón

Linares & Muñoz, 2011), student veterans (Kim & Cole, 2013), and transgender students (Dugan, Kusel, & Simounet, 2012). This research has attempted to provide crucial insights on the continued persistence and retention of minoritized students in higher education. This work is meaningful and necessary; however, positivist and constructivist views on student development still ground much of this literature. Therefore, there is a need for deconstructing and reconstructing how higher education professionals come to understand student involvement and engagement using critical lenses, such as those discussed in Part One of this book.

To discuss this further, a critical perspective on student engagement and involvement needs to explore four questions: first, the reasons why students, particularly minoritized students, often reject campus involvement; second, why these students often do not find their campus to be a space or place where they can engage; third, why they are sent messages that they should not engage; and fourth, why these students find the need for community off campus and/or at home in a way that their on-campus community cannot provide. Contemporary scholarship has demonstrated how historically underrepresented students have rejected traditional notions of student involvement and engagement; for example, Indigenous students (Waterman, 2012), Black and Latino students (Solórzano, Ceja, & Yosso, 2000; Stewart, 2017b), and transgender students (Catalano, 2015; Jourian, 2016; Nicolazzo, 2016). Likewise, much of this emergent literature also connects the developmental concepts explored earlier in this text to student involvement and engagement.

Critical Praxis of Student Involvement and Engagement

As a scholar-practitioner who cares deeply about the possibilities of more equitable outcomes of student involvement and engagement for all students, I am instantly drawn to work that helps connect the theoretical to action, which Freire (1970) defined as *praxis*. For some higher education professionals, critical perspectives can be challenging and daunting, especially when grappling with how to best put these concepts into actual practice. As a result, I wanted to forward ideas about critical perspectives on student involvement and engagement as they related to each of the developmental concepts discussed in Part Two of this text. In this section, I offer vignettes from either my personal experiences in the field or those of some trusted colleagues who use critical approaches in their work with students in higher education.

Resilience

When considering my work as an administrator or as a faculty member, I want my students to find their ability to bounce back from difficulties and persist through life challenges. Yet, as Nicolazzo and Carter named in chapter 8, a critical perspective of resilience moves beyond just an individual act of behaviors and instead engages the ways that resilience is a dynamic, ongoing practice of kinship and community that can benefit students. In addition, systemically there are also interlocking power dynamics that institutionally benefit or penalize students based on their multiple social identities that often can affect one's resilience (Abes & Kasch, 2007; Nicolazzo, 2016, 2017).

For instance, CJ Venable, an academic adviser at Kent State University, shared a story of an advisee, who was a Student of Color. She came to CJ's office because she was upset with a faculty member for singling her out during multiple classes because of her race; she felt her grades in the course suffered as a result. CJ recounted,

> She was angry and feeling defeated, with no understanding of what she could do. Helping her to understand what systems exist to file grievances, often hidden from student view until students are expected to use them flawlessly, and to name how a culture of whiteness pervades the department was essential to my work with her. (CJ Venable, personal communication, October 3, 2017)

In terms of student engagement and involvement, there is an onus often on minoritized students at historically white colleges and universities to "fit" and conform into institutions that historically were not created for them. CJ's advisee certainly struggled with understanding how to navigate her department's protocols, but as CJ reflected, "By learning how to use existing systems and structures, the student was able to voice her anger at being targeted while also attempting to address how the department stifles resilience in students of color" (CJ Venable, personal communication, October 3, 2017). Through CJ's work with their student advisee, they were able to partner together as adviser–advisee to engage in resilience that modeled a community strategy of resistance, providing an example of the community-based resilience Nicolazzo and Carter discussed in chapter 8 of this text. In other words, by coming together to discuss how to resist systemic oppression, CJ and the student were able to practice resilience together. In addition, CJ elaborated that Nicolazzo's (2017) work on resilience had been inspirational and prompted them to ask different questions about resilience in students. CJ stated, "Rather than [asking], 'Why don't these students have resilience?',

I ask myself and my colleagues, 'What are we doing to allow students to be resilient?'" (CJ Venable, personal communication, October 3, 2017).

If we continue to examine the notion of resilience in student involvement and engagement, it becomes important to think about how campus structures create problems rather than assume students are the problem. For instance, we often promote student organizations to minoritized students and encourage them to find their niche. Yet, these organizations are typically single-identity focused rather than reflective of one's multiple social identities. The current approach to resilience as individually focused allows a deficit model approach to students' ability to rebound rather than critically interrogating whether institutions are set up for students to persist in the face of multiple moments of failure, resistance, and dissonance, which will be discussed next.

Dissonance

As discussed by Taylor and Reynolds in chapter 9, *dissonance*, from a critical perspective, is defined as "the phenomenon of recognizing lies that societal systems and their authorities tell" (p. 111, this volume). In their chapter, Taylor and Reynolds remind readers that individuals with oppressed identities often experience erasure and invalidation of their lived experiences given the fact that those with dominant privilege control the agents of socialization, such as educational institutions and media. As Reynolds's story of her international service-learning experience in Ecuador in chapter 9 illustrates, dissonance can be experienced quite suddenly and traumatically through experiences of student involvement and engagement.

Given the recent sociopolitical climate within the United States, dissonance, for many students, has been channeled into increased student activism on campus. For example, over the past four years, students protested racial tensions at many institutions, such as the University of Missouri (Izadi, 2015), Ithaca College (Svriuga, 2016), and the University of Vermont (Aloe, 2018). These students engaged across communities, outlined clear demands for justice, and engaged in various forms of protest and direct action. Although the traditional literature on student involvement and engagement does not necessarily name student activism as a high-impact practice, Stewart (2017b) recent work outlined the significance for racially minoritized students, particularly Black students, of protests and demonstrations around social responsibility and engagement with others. Yet, when thinking about the concept of dissonance as discussed in this text, what would have happened if higher education professionals at these campuses had directly named the challenges and issues minoritized students faced in terms of racialized discord on campus rather than promoted potential falsehoods about inclusive communities? This connects to Ahmed's (2012) notion of "institutional whiteness" when she asked, "What would it mean to talk about whiteness as an institutional problem or as a problem of institutions?" (p. 35). How might students experience dissonance differently if we centered whiteness as the problem, particularly in the context of student involvement and engagement? While student protests serve as a spark to important dialogue among students to engage in processing their experiences on campus, finding community with others, and increasing their social support networks, I would argue it is too little, too late for many students. Minoritized students should be able to learn about oppressive environments without having to be the educators about their oppression. This example also connects to the concept of how students come to make meaning of who they are and how the convergence of their identities is constructed.

Social Construction of Identities

In chapter 10, Stewart and Brown expanded on the traditional ways that higher education professionals come to understand the social construction of identities, particularly recognizing the importance of destabilizing identity and centering community, space, and experience as it relates to one's holistic sense of self. When considering this in student engagement and involvement, higher education professionals need to understand that they can create conditions by which students are asked to engage in critical self-reflection of themselves and the systems of which they are a part and how their institutions play a role in how they perform their identities. Salvador Mena, senior associate vice chancellor of student affairs at Rutgers University–New Brunswick, shared an example of this in practice.

Using intersectionality as a framework for his praxis, Mena recounted an example of working with a heterosexual Asian American college man struggling in his adjustment to campus. In particular, the student was struggling with his identity, having been adopted and raised by a white family. During his time on campus, he often felt "othered" based on the small number of other Asian American students at his predominantly white institution; this was particularly salient for the student when discussing his perceived challenges of dating on campus because of commonly held "stereotypes of masculinity and race" about Asian American men (S. Mena, personal communication, December 15, 2017). Continuing on, Mena noted that throughout their ongoing conversations, "we discussed how his identity was formed and shaped in the environment he was raised in before attending the university and how his new environment could further shape his identity"

(S. Mena, personal communication, December 15, 2017). Contemplating this example further, we see that power structures and institutions significantly influenced the social construction of this student's multiple identities. For this student, finding opportunities for connection on campus through student organizations served as a key way of strengthening a sense of social support (S. Mena, personal communication, December 15, 2017).

The ongoing relationship established between Mena and this student created meaningful conditions for critical self-reflection and examination of biases, stereotypes, and assumptions grounded in the ways this student viewed his multiple identities, including his race, gender, and sexuality (S. Mena, personal communication, December 15, 2017). Essentially, these conversations between Mena and the student served as a form of engagement through the use of theoretical praxis. By using intersectionality as a conceptual framework, Mena was able to help this student consider the ways interlocking power structures of privilege and oppression played a role in his life and how that understanding could help him shift his understanding of self and others. In fact, praxis gave the student the tools to explore how others' perceptions influenced his own sense of self and the agency to explore his own language through engagement with peers. This interaction also helped this student gain a better sense of his personal authenticity, which will be discussed in the next section.

Authenticity

Within the context of student involvement and engagement, authenticity is connected to having students engage in meaningful learning opportunities that may connect to their personal interests and network and collaborate with others through these activities. Yet, as Kupo and Oxendine asserted in chapter 11, true authenticity needs to be understood through a critical lens in light of the fact that authenticity is informed by colonization and its role on identity and community. For example, heather c. lou, director of student life and leadership at Metropolitan State University, shared an experience of supporting students who were organizing a sit-in in the chancellor's office to protest social injustice at a former institution. She recalled, "I was able to guide students in their radical praxis through mentorship, coaching, and advising, especially around university politics, policies, health and safety measures, and in building strategic networks" (h. lou, personal communication, November 27, 2017). Through her work, she called "into question the ways that colonialism and white supremacy dictate who is being 'strategic' versus 'manipulative' versus 'authentic' in these highly contested and politicized roles" (h. lou, personal communication, November 27, 2017).

In lou's example here, she names authenticity as a key element that informs students' engagement. As Kupo and Oxendine noted in chapter 11, authenticity from a critical perspective requires an acknowledgment of fluidity, context, and change. lou named that holding her positionality as a "queer, disabled, cisgender, multiracial, Asian womxn of color" (h. lou, personal communication, November 27, 2017) was essential in grounding an understanding of who she is. In addition, her multiple social and personal identities influenced the ways in which she could be authentic in an institution and a system that was not designed for her or for many of her students. In the example of her mentorship to her students, she viewed authenticity as a critical piece of praxis by sussing out one's authentic motives, tactics, and engagement. In addition, lou helped her students understand the systemic flow of power here; there were aspects of power, authority, and privilege that all played out within the larger institutional system, but they did not allow those power structures to dictate their actions. Her work connects to the dialogue between Kupo and Oxendine in chapter 11 when they named that institutions of higher education often are experienced as locations of intense contradiction around identity-based introspection and invalidation. For the students, engaging collaboratively through authentic concern about issues of injustice created opportunities to take action and address these complexities. This scenario provides an example of the various ways that authenticity plays out across individuals and community.

Agency

In the traditional context of student development, *agency* is defined as students acting independently and making their own life decisions and choices. However, a critical perspective interrogates the ways that power, privilege, and oppression play a role in students' sense of agency. As Okello and White noted in chapter 12, the concept of agency is reinforced by Western norms and logic without an adequate examination of the historical and contemporary legacies that colonization and oppression have played on individuals' lives.

Agency is directly connected to, and plays an important role in, student involvement and engagement, particularly when considering minoritized students in higher education. The traditional theories posited by Astin (1984, 1993) and Kuh (2003, 2009) did not take students' multiple social identities into consideration as they directly relate to integration and acculturation into college. Assuming that college students can act autonomously to make their own choices is a fallacy that dismisses systemic issues of power and oppression that play a role in students' lives.

In chapter 12, Okello and White discussed an embodied agency, which takes into account one's social location, an understanding of oppressive factors that contribute to one's subjugation, one's meaning-making process, and an emphasis on taking action. When contemplating embodied agency, I think of one of the undergraduate students I mentored in my first job after graduate school, a young Black man who identified as gay and who was seemingly struggling in his adjustment to campus. He and I connected immediately. What I learned from him was not that he was having difficulties adjusting but that he was engaged in constant questioning about his life choices. He experienced deep tensions about being rejected by his father because of his sexuality and challenges about what it meant to be a queer Black man at a predominantly white liberal arts college; he was certainly engaged in a delicate limbo dance, as Okello and White discussed in chapter 12. As a young man with multiple minoritized identities, he had not only a strong desire to prove himself to others and succeed but also a yearning to please others and not disappoint. He rejected being involved in cultural organizations because he felt a sense of liminality that he was neither Black enough for the Black Student Union nor gay enough for the LGBTQ organization on campus. Instead, his embodied agency led him to find connection and place in studying abroad, peer mentoring programs, and a student programming board, all areas of the cocurricular experience where he could find connection and meaning on his own terms. His story also relates to the importance of understanding how the concept of context is important when considering student development.

Context

As Duran and Jones indicated in chapter 14, a critical approach to centering context creates questions about how individuals are shaped by the context they are in, as well as who gets access to particular contexts. To be sure, context plays a role in understanding student involvement and engagement. Many students' institutional context may not be one where they find belonging, because it was created by and continues to reinforce norms and expectations that do not connect to their culture. Other students' dominant identities have provided them with a privilege of understanding those norms and expectations. In addition, acknowledgment that one context can be experienced and perceived in a multitude of ways by multiple students is necessary.

When considering context as it relates to student involvement and engagement, it is essential to consider *how* students engage rather than merely being engaged. Justin Sipes, coordinator of cocurricular community engagement at the University of North Florida, highlighted this nuance when reflecting on his time working in fraternity and sorority life. He said, "Tradition is the scapegoat when there is failure to critically think about and examine why certain practices and beliefs exist. Too often, chapters do not consider where these traditions stemmed from and never confront why they persist" (J. Sipes, personal communication, September 22, 2017). A student who Sipes advised was actively engaged in a fraternity that had "strong ties to the Confederacy and many local chapters hosted an annual event that harkened to this era in various ways" (J. Sipes, personal communication, September 22, 2017). During the semester, the student leader took a course on the history of the antebellum South, and "he would come and speak to me about what he was learning and we would discuss what that meant for his organization" (J. Sipes, personal communication, September 22, 2017). Through their conversations, "it was clear that his perspective had changed dramatically and he realized that the event hosted, and practices, by the local chapter were antithetical to the values of the organization" (J. Sipes, personal communication, September 22, 2017).

Sipes's example offers an important element of a student's rejection of willful ignorance. Given that the student could no longer reject out of hand the connections of his fraternity's traditions to a harmful, racist practice, he ultimately considered the context of the situation and took meaningful action to create cultural change, both at a local level (his fraternity) and at a larger systemic level (throughout his national fraternity). In addition, the student's actions on local and national levels to end this event were informed by a geographical, a social, and a historical context that was rooted in racism and marginalization. By gaining a clearer understanding of these contexts and the ways they were negatively affecting students' experiences in the fraternity, this student was able to translate his new awareness into positive social change; this also required a new level of knowledge and knowing, which is described next.

Knowledge and Knowing

As Waterman and Bazemore-James discussed in chapter 13, the idea of knowledge and knowing is a contested concept when using critical perspectives. Much of our knowledge is shaped by context and history; yet, history is most often framed from dominant norms and perspectives that promote power and privilege over the subordinated other. As a result, individuals using a critical lens have to interrogate knowledge and knowing, asking, "What is missing from the knowledge I am receiving?" and "What meaning do I make of that information?" In addition, it is important to ask, "Who has the knowledge?"

Recently, I gave a guest lecture in an interdisciplinary first-year honors course on my campus, discussing LGBTQ+ issues in society. Using Freire's (1970) notion of problem-posing education in my pedagogy, I asked students to listen, dialogue, and act to strengthen their critical consciousness around issues of sexuality and gender on campus. One of the students connected with me after the lecture, frustrated because she had wanted to take action after my lecture to create a proposal for a gender and sexuality resource center as her student government project for that year. However, the student government leadership turned down her request to engage on this, saying that they did not think it was necessary or feasible. Not taking that answer lying down, she approached me to see if I could offer her some help on how to move forward.

Since that meeting, she has worked collaboratively with leaders of the campus's LGBTQ+ student organization; built a campus-wide coalition of faculty, staff, and students who are invested in advancing this proposal; and begun to do benchmarking of other peer institutions and their inclusion of such a center on their campus. I would argue that this student's resilience and persistence in the face of dismissal and rejection speaks volumes about the power of transformative learning through student engagement. Her desire to act moved from her hearing a question in the classroom about how each student present could help make change around gender and sexuality issues within their sphere of influence on campus to her finding her own community and coconspirators.

Through this student's actions, she was engaging in questioning forms of knowledge and knowing that continued to reify dominant perspectives. This was a form of disrupting normativity, as the previous example names, by disrupting cisheteronormativity at this specific institution with the hopeful outcome of having a center specifically geared to support sexual and gender minority students. This questioning of knowledge and knowing, done in community through student engagement efforts, can result in transformative possibilities for students.

Concluding Thoughts

Critical theory provides a helpful lens to reexamine how we understand the work of higher education and shift that work. In particular, our thinking on student involvement and engagement in higher education has stayed relatively stagnant, with a great deal of reification and replication of these theories and models since the start of student affairs work in our field. As mentioned earlier in this chapter, student involvement and engagement programs are steeped in traditions and mantras of "we've always done it this way" that uphold the status quo and largely serve students with tradition-ally dominant identities. However, reframing these concepts using a critical approach provides an opportunity to ask why we continue to do this and who is served by these traditions. If any students are excluded in some way by these programs or services for student involvement or engagement, we have to be proactive in critiquing, problematizing, and reshaping these opportunities for engagement. Student affairs professionals must consider how student involvement and engagement theories historically have privi-leged some and marginalized those who do not meet the set outcomes and expectations these theories espouse. As a result, we have to start changing the ways we understand our own professional practices and think critically about the ways we may in fact be harming our students unintentionally. I offer the following discussion questions for readers to consider:

1. Think about the current ways you understand student involvement and engagement as concepts. How can you engage with some emancipatory dreaming from a critical perspective about how these concepts might be reframed on your campus?
2. Many of the developmental concepts discussed in this text connect to the concepts of student involvement and engagement. In what ways do you see these developmental concepts playing a role in either hindering or helping student engagement and involvement for particular student populations on your campus?
3. Critical perspectives are meant to disrupt the status quo and problematize traditions and practices that get reinforced. How can you work collab-oratively with others on your campus to disrupt the traditional notions of student involvement and engagement to create more equitable outcomes for your students?

References

Abes, E. S., & Kasch, D. (2007). Using queer theory to explore lesbian college stu-dents' multiple dimensions of identity. *Journal of College Student Development*, *48*(6), 619–636.

Ahmed, S. (2012). *On being included: Racism and diversity in institutional life.* Durham, NC: Duke University Press.

Aloe, J. (2018, February 22). 5 things to know about the UVM students pro-testing racism on campus. *Burlington Free Press*. Retrieved from https://www

.burlingtonfreepress.com/story/news/2018/02/21/5-things-know-uvm-students-protesting-racism-campus/359146002/

Astin, A. W. (1984). Student involvement: A developmental theory for higher education. *Journal of College Student Personnel, 25*(4), 297–308.

Astin, A. W. (1993). *What matters in college: Four critical years revisited.* San Francisco, CA: Jossey-Bass.

Catalano, D. C. J. (2015). Beyond virtual equality: Liberatory consciousness as a path to achieve trans* inclusion in higher education. *Equity and Excellence in Education, 48*(3), 418–435.

Collins, P. H. (2000). *Black feminist thought: Knowledge, consciousness, and the politics of empowerment.* New York, NY: Routledge.

Dugan, J. P., Kusel, M. L., & Simounet, D. M. (2012). Transgender college students: An exploratory study of perceptions, engagement, and educational outcomes. *Journal of College Student Development, 53*(5), 719–736.

Freire, P. (1970). *Pedagogy of the oppressed.* New York, NY: Continuum.

Izadi, E. (2015, November 9). The incidents that led to the University of Missouri president's resignation. *Washington Post.* Retrieved from https://www .washingtonpost.com/news/grade-point/wp/2015/11/09/the-incidents-that-led-to-the-university-of-missouri-presidents-resignation/?utm_term=.a48c50d03500

Jourian, T. J. (2016) My masculinity is a little love poem to myself: Trans*masculine college students' conceptualizations of masculinities (*Unpublished doctoral dissertation*). Loyola University Chicago, Chicago, IL.

Kim, Y. M., & Cole, J. S. (2013). *Student veterans/service members' engagement in college and university life and education.* Washington, DC: American Council on Education.

Kuh, G. D. (2003). What we're learning about student engagement from NSSE: Benchmarks for effective educational practices. *Change: The Magazine of Higher Learning, 35*(2), 24–32.

Kuh, G. D. (2009). What student affairs professionals need to know about student engagement. *Journal of College Student Development, 50*(6), 683–706.

Mayhew, M. J., Rockenbach, A. N., Bowman, N. A., Seifert, T. A. D., Wolniak, G. C., Pascarella, E. T., & Terenzini, P. T. (2016). *How college affects students* (3rd ed.). San Francisco, CA: Jossey-Bass.

Mitchell, D. J., Soria, K. M., Daniele, E. A., & Gipson, J. A. (Eds.). (2015). *Student involvement and academic outcomes.* New York, NY: Peter Lang.

Museus, S. D., & Quaye, S. J. (2009). Toward an intercultural perspective of racial and ethnic minority college student persistence. *The Review of Higher Education, 33*(1), 67–94.

National Survey of Student Engagement (2014). *Bringing the institution into focus: Annual results 2014.* Bloomington, IN: Indiana University Center for Postsecondary Research. Retrieved from http://nsse.indiana.edu/NSSE_2014_Results/pdf/NSSE_2014_Annual_Results.pdf

National Survey of Student Engagement. (n.d.). Benchmarks of effective educational practice. Retrieved from http://nsse.indiana.edu/pdf/nsse_benchmarks.pdf

Nicolazzo, Z. (2016). "Just go in looking good": The resilience, resistance, and kinship-building of trans* college students. *Journal of College Student Development*, *57*, 538–556.

Nicolazzo, Z. (2017). *Trans* in college: Transgender students' strategies for navigating campus life and the institutional politics of inclusion.* Sterling, VA: Stylus.

Rendón Linares, L. I., & Muñoz, S. M. (2011). Revisiting validation theory: Theoretical foundations, applications, and extensions. *Enrollment Management Journal*, *2*(1), 12–33.

Solórzano, D. G., Ceja, M., & Yosso, T. J. (2000). Critical race theory, racial microaggressions, and campus racial climate: The experiences of African American college students. *Journal of Negro Education*, *69*(1–2), 60–73.

Stewart, D-L. (2017a, March 30). Language of appeasement. *Inside Higher Ed.* Retrieved from https://www.insidehighered.com/views/2017/03/30/colleges-need-language-shift-not-one-you-think-essay

Stewart, D-L. (2017b). Engagement that matters: Exploring the relationship of co-curricular activities to self-reported gains in learning outcomes for racially minoritized students in the United States. In J. F. L. Jackson, L. J. Charleston, & C. K. Gilbert (Eds.), *Advancing equity and diversity in student affairs: A Festschrift in honor of Melvin C. Terrell* (pp. 53–76). Charlotte, NC: Information Age Publishing.

Strayhorn, T. L. (2012). *College students' sense of belonging: A key to educational success for all students.* New York, NY: Routledge.

Svriuga, S. (2016, January 14). Ithaca College president resigns after protests over race issues. *Washington Post.* Retrieved from https://www.washingtonpost.com/news/grade-point/wp/2016/01/14/ithaca-college-president-resigns-after-protests-over-race-issues/?utm_term=.de2b834ccb5a

Tinto, V. (1993). *Leaving college: Rethinking the causes and cures of student attrition* (2nd ed.). Chicago, IL: University of Chicago Press.

Tuck, E., & Yang, K. W. (Eds.). (2018). *Toward what justice? Describing diverse dreams of justice in education.* New York, NY: Routledge.

Waterman, S.(2012). Home-going as a strategy for success among Haudenosaunee college and university students. *Journal of Student Affairs Research and Practice*, *49*(2), 193–209.

Wolf-Wendel, L., Ward, K., & Kinzie, J. (2009). A tangled web of terms: The overlap and unique contribution of involvement, engagement, and integration to understanding college student success. *Journal of College Student Development*, *50*(4), 407–428.

16

PRINCIPLES OF GOOD PRACTICE IN STUDENT AFFAIRS

Susan B. Marine

What does it mean to *practice* student affairs? The concept of practice dates back to the fifteenth century, when it was first associated with the notion of repeatedly performing a specific action in order to gain mastery. According to *Merriam-Webster* (Profession [Def. 1], 2017), practice takes on a very specific meaning when associated with a profession, "a calling requiring specialized knowledge and often long and intensive academic preparation." The concept of practicing a profession, more so than practicing an unfamiliar skill, refers to applying one's learning to a defined set of tasks in a prescribed way toward particular, desired outcomes. Practice, in this sense, implies effort expended toward mastery, and yet mastery eludes the practitioner, as there is always more to learn and better work to do to advance a profession and its aims.

Unspoken but central to the role of any profession are the statements that declare the profession's goals, values, and intentions. These statements provide a compass by which professionals may (and, implicitly, should) direct their practice and to what ends. This chapter explores one foundational document—the *Principles of Good Practice for Student Affairs* (NASPA: Student Affairs Administrators in Higher Education, 1997) (hereafter, the Principles)—and the assumptions that underpin it. It asks us to consider what constitutes the *good* in the principles guiding higher education and student affairs and for whom? Critical analysis, too, begs return to a central question in our work as a field: Does the ongoing project of building a system of U.S. postsecondary education that is truly just call us to reformulate what *the good* might look like, how it is practiced, and how it comes to be?

These, then, are the central questions of this chapter. Do we just know goodness within the student affairs profession when we see it, and when we do,
does it look like justice?

Student Affairs as a Profession

The idea of student affairs as a profession with associated practices has been
in place since the early 1930s, when *The Student Personnel Point of View*
(*SPPV*) (American Council on Education, 1937) articulated both the aims
and the skills requisite for the work of effectively supporting the whole student. The original 1937 iteration of the *SPPV* depersonalized student affairs,
referring to the "work" of student personnel without much reference to the
workers. A council on personnel work was invoked, and various reviews via
professional associations were named essential to do, but no specific reference
to the roles or constitutions of those performing student personnel work was
proposed. The 1949 revision of the *SPPV* referred to "professional personnel
workers" (American Council on Education, 1949, p. 19), whose "professional growth" (p. 31) should be nurtured. They should be "chosen for their
personal and professional competence to discharge their responsibilities" (p.
33). A profession was thus emerging from what otherwise might seem to
be loosely coordinated student services roles, one with explicit foundational
values. These included attention to the whole student's flourishing, including
academic engagement, career preparation, a sense of belonging, and development of both individual and interdependent qualities and sensibilities fitting
for an adult (American Council on Education, 1949).

Much like other professions, such as medicine, law, and teaching, student affairs professionals thus began to articulate a set of values and their
associated tasks to define ourselves. We also began—more intentionally—to
organize ourselves into associations in the 1920s. As Long (2012) noted,
"Deans of men, deans of women, and other staff who were focused on student personnel issues had previously worked in relative isolation, but now
they corresponded and met to share ideas and concerns related to their
work" (p. 4). Issuing statements became a primary role of these associations,
and a deep sense of the collective imbues them. While working toward a
shared understanding of what it meant to attend to the development of the
whole student, these statements declared the worth of student affairs to the
enterprise of higher education. Through the expressions of these values, a
professional identity was forged. Today, student affairs professionals must
demonstrate competence in a wide variety of skill areas and be humble about
the need to keep learning through a consistent commitment to self-awareness
and reflexivity (Arminio & Ortiz, 2017). And where *personnel* refers simply

to those working in an organization, the profession of student affairs had assumed responsibility for shaping it—making a world for the intentional practice of student development.

Since the publications of the *SPPVs*, numerous statements on the student affairs profession and the practice of student affairs have emerged, so it is worth asking if any shared set of values and assumptions guides our notions of ourselves as *practitioners*. What are our foundational *practices*? According to Evans and Reason (2001), in their summary review of the foundational documents of the field, most avow a shared commitment to the development of the whole student, with some attention to individual differences. Context matters, as does ensuring that practice emanates from the sound collection and analysis of data. Education for citizenship is a key role of the profession and is achieved through collaboration and accountability. And although much has changed about higher education as an endeavor, today's student affairs practitioners continue the pursuit of these fundamentals in practice, even as the field as a whole has evolved to engage the use of a competency-based model.

And even as we morph the profession collectively, we also shape it as individuals. I began my career in higher education in a role traditionally dedicated to the fostering of student development: residential life. I soon, however, discovered that my real passion lay in serving students who had survived sexual and relationship violence, many of whom experienced deeply compromised developmental journeys as a result. I spent most of my years in student affairs attempting to influence the policies and practices that directly affected survivors, endeavoring to make the colleges I worked for places designed for the practice of healing, resistance, and resilience. I celebrated firsthand what happens when "good practice" is that which prioritizes students' flourishing, and I lamented deeply when it did not.

Although today I am a faculty member, teaching and conducting research full-time in a graduate higher education program, I continue to practice student affairs—advising students, planning and executing a graduate student admissions and orientation process, creating and promoting developmental cocurricular opportunities, addressing Title IX and other bias-related incidents, and advising graduate student organizations and activities. In my work as a scholar-practitioner, I endeavor to stay abreast of emergent, critical perspectives on student development theories and their applicability to my work. I have "lived the questions," as I reflect on and make meaning of my own college experience as a white, lesbian, able-bodied cisgender woman. Critical theories, and the questions they ask, have been central to my understanding of both my own privileges and experiences with subordination. My insistence on critical scrutiny of accepted truisms in our field often positions me as oppositional and an activist. Colleagues have frequently characterized me as a troublemaker. My deep love for college students and their experiences and for unseating dominance with integrity daily informs my practice, alongside my sense that I remain humbly and avowedly merely a student of the work.

The Context: *Principles of Good Practice for Student Affairs*

I began college in the 1980s, which was coincidentally an auspicious time for the development and refinement of statements regarding the profession of higher education student affairs and its priorities. Evans and Reason (2001) noted that this era brought significant new pressures, including declining state and federal revenues, and increased awareness of the toll of various social challenges such as addiction and poverty. The need to better serve a more diverse student body was also prompting college and university leaders to derive innovative ways of talking and thinking about our work. New attention to the public's waning perception of higher education, and students' dubious engagement with the college experience, led to the emergence of Chickering and Gamson's (1987) seven principles of good practice in higher education. These included attention to increasing (a) student–faculty contact, (b) cooperation among students, (c) active learning, (d) the provision of prompt feedback, (e) time on task, (f) high expectations, and (g) respect for diverse talents and ways of learning.

As the twentieth century approached, U.S. higher education was at a crossroads, as described by Blimling and Whitt (1998). They noted, "Increasing enrollments and increasingly diverse students, increasing competition, and declining funding and public trust" (p. 10) were bearing down on higher education's comfortably numb state. Charged by the then-presidents of ACPA: College Student Educators International (ACPA) and NASPA with considering the impact of these changes on the profession, Blimling and Whitt (1998) created a "principles of good practice" parallel statement for student affairs practice. They described the impetus for the creation of the principles: the ongoing tension between a student development standpoint and a student services perspective. Student development advocates believed the learning and growth that student affairs functions provide should be the driving ethos of the field, whereas the student services sector (mostly emanating from business, human resource management, and Total Quality Management [TQM] acolytes) saw the provision of sound and resource-cognizant student services as a more viable model for the profession.

Eleven distinguished leaders in the field—selected "on the basis of their knowledge and contributions to student affairs research and . . . professional organizations"—were thus appointed to the Task Force to develop these principles (Blimling & Whitt, 1999, p. xiii). The group convened for three days in Chicago in 1996 and pored over numerous foundational documents, including the two *SPPVs* (1949; American Council on Education, 1937) and *The Student Learning Imperative* (ACPA: College Student Educators International, 1994)—described earlier in this text. Three versions of a draft were circulated throughout NASPA and ACPA and vetted for comment at regional meetings, culminating in a complete draft review at the 1997 joint conference in Chicago. Table 16.1 depicts these seven principles of good practice in student affairs. The full-length book project (Blimling & Whitt, 1999) produced from Blimling and Whitt's principles explores each of the seven in-depth and describes specific tools for implementing them in varying campus contexts. A series of inventories for use on campuses with implementing the Principles has also been generated (NASPA: Student Affairs Administrators in Higher Education, 1997).

Examining the Principles reveals that they represent four guiding assumptions germane to the practice of student affairs. First, Principles 1, 3, and 6 suggest that good practice in student affairs is centered on *learning*, specifically learning that is active, that is promoted and fostered collaboratively (by students, faculty, and staff together), and for which high expectations are set and attended to by all involved in postsecondary education. The learning process is stimulated by certain types of activities—active, engaged, and experiential—and certain kinds of relationships—with faculty, with other students in residence, with mentors in one's field—and it is one where students become increasingly more self-directed in their capacity to learn. The *cultivation of values* matters to good practice as well, with emphasis placed on helping students identify and embrace values of learning, as well as responsible citizenship as expressed in Principle 2. Importantly, the authors avoided naming specific values, but instead espoused a process of values clarification, one that hinges on balancing understanding one's self in community with others. Good practice *holds institutions accountable* for their measurement and delivery by insisting on use of evidence to inform decisions and the thoughtful deployment of resources, as described in Principles 4 and 5. Assumptions abound in this directive, regarding what constitutes effective programs and services and responsible administration. And with a nod to the emergent awareness of the shifts in demographics on virtually all campuses, Principle 7 suggests that good practice fosters belonging and inclusion.

Admittedly, there is little to quibble with in the ways the Principles are articulated or in the values embedded within them. Learning, the development of values, accountability, and fostering belonging and inclusion

TABLE 16.1
Principles of Good Practice in Student Affairs

Principle	*Focus area or root assumption*
1. Good practice in student affairs engages students in active learning. Active learning opportunities encourage experimentation, application, involvement, and reflection and advance more complex ways of thinking.	Good practice is centered on *learning.*
2. Good practice in student affairs helps students develop coherent values and ethical standards. Students are challenged to identify, examine, and construct meaningful values for a life of learning and responsible citizenship.	Good practice is centered on *values development.*
3. Good practice in student affairs sets and communicates high expectations for learning. Students hear clear expectations regarding a wide range of experiences and competencies, including academic performance and individual and community responsibility.	Good practice is centered on *learning.*
4. Good practice in student affairs uses systematic inquiry to improve student and institutional performance. Use of current research about students and their learning and rigorous assessment of learning outcomes and environments are essential to effective programs and services.	Good practice is *evidence driven and resource conscious.*
5. Good practice in student affairs uses resources effectively to achieve institutional missions and goals. Financial, material, and human resources are focused on enhancing student learning, as well as on responsible administration.	Good practice is *evidence driven and resource conscious.*
6. Good practice in student affairs forges educational partnerships that advance student learning. Collaboration with students, faculty, administrators, and others provides multiple perspectives on shared commitments and fosters healthy decision-making.	Good practice is centered on *learning.*
7. Good practice in student affairs builds supportive and inclusive communities. Student learning occurs best in safe and caring communities that value diversity and debate, promote belonging, and demand social responsibility.	Good practice is centered on *belonging and inclusion.*

Note. Adapted from *Good Practice in Student Affairs: Principles to Foster Student Learning,* by G. S. Blimling & E. J. Whitt (Eds.), 1999, San Francisco, CA: Jossey-Bass.

are central features of the profession and have been since its inception in the early 1900s, in ways that are generally uncontroversial. One persistent and important critique, echoed by Lange and Stewart in the following chapter, is the puzzling absence of student input into the document or its stated values, a surprising omission given the student-centered spirit of the document.

In summary, the Principles affirmed the notion that student affairs practitioners are called on to use evidence and resources thoughtfully to support the learning, belonging, and values development of diverse groups of students. On the face of it, the Principles seem both appropriate to the field of student affairs and utterly benign in their framing. Who can argue with promoting learning, values development, and fostering of good citizens in a data-driven and resource-conscious manner? And yet when a profession claims a statement of value, it is by necessity leaving other values unstated, other activities unattended to, and thus other outcomes unmet. The Principles are no different, offering an opportunity to examine what is said and unsaid in the priorities they name. A closer look allows us to reconsider the most central question of all: What is the *good* in student affairs practice?

Problematizing "Good" Practice

Any conception of principles of good practice, of necessity, resides in naming how the *good* is defined and operationalized. Underneath the use of words like *good* is the implication that such practices hold greater value and worth than other practices and thus should be advanced and promoted. Western notions of what constitutes the good have been inevitably shaped by philosophy, originating with the ideas of the good advanced by Aristotle, who argued that a life of sustained contemplation of and enactment of particular virtues leads to the greatest good, the choice most likely to lead to genuine human happiness (Kashdan, Biswas-Diener, & King, 2008; Rowe & Broadie, 2002). The focus on learning and the advocacy for reflective values development both show up prominently in the Principles.

Utilitarian concepts of the good also lurk in the Principles. Mill and Bentham (1987) suggested that when deciding between alternative courses of action, we must choose that which entails happiness for the most; this is again echoed in the Principles (Blimling & Whitt, 1998, 1999; NASPA: Student Affairs Administrators in Higher Education, 1997), which suggest that we must endeavor to do good for the most (yet problematically assume that the good is the same for all).

In the 20 years that have passed since the release of the Principles, much has changed in how we conceive of and assert notions of the good within higher education. The good, informed by values, learning, and the appraisal of our actions on others, has been demonstrably decentered in favor of the current decision framework known as neoliberalism, where "ethics reduces to calculations of wealth and productivity" (Fish, 2009, p. 8). Neoliberalism, the predominant value system circumscribing the U.S. economy, posits that the greatest good emanates from policies that amplify the free market and that support maximal production (Harvey, 2007). Ironically, the same economic decline that foreshadowed the emergence of the Principles and their drive to more clearly articulate good practice also led to the embracing of a neoliberal mind-set within higher education. Giroux (2014) characterized this transformation as nothing short of toxic: "Privatization, commodification, militarization and deregulation are the new guiding categories through which schools, teachers, pedagogy and students are defined" (p. 36).

Higher education and student affairs, in turn, has also been deeply affected by neoliberal frames: The profession has been subject to the constant demand for greater accountability, defined only as *cost-benefit ratios* for the work of student development. Current neoliberal logics dictate that good practices are defined by and through measurement and commodification, ranking, and metrics. Those that can be assessed quantitatively are advanced not only as good but indeed as so-called best practices (Murray, Holmes, Perron, & Rail, 2007) or uncritically as high-impact practices, as Lange and Stewart describe in the following chapter. They are good, and because they are sellable, they are also goods. And although the Principles appear to be aligned in some sense with this value set—referencing, again, the emphasis on "rigorous assessment of learning outcomes and environments"—they implicitly resist it also, retaining equal emphasis on nonquantifiable goods such as "meaningful values," "high expectations," and "supportive and inclusive communities." Their insistence on sameness of outcome, while neglecting differences in input, should give us pause. In chapter 17, Lange and Stewart also note that assuming that specific practices are beneficial for all—and have equal impact for all—is an idea that should hasten skepticism, given higher education's specious history regarding those who are marginalized.

Thus, the Principles both reflect and refute historical and current regimes of "goodness." As referenced in previous chapters of this text, taken-for-granted concepts such as "learning," "values," "community," and indeed "education" are heavily overlaid with the dominant culture's values and priorities. As noted by Okello and White (chapter 12) and Nicolazzo and Carter (chapter 8), students' agency, resilience, authenticity, and knowledge are contextually influenced and socially constructed and contested, surfacing the reality that such concepts elide solidity for any one student or even community. In addition, in chapter 15, Tillapaugh contended that concepts like "student engagement" and "involvement"—constructs we've long used to envision and enact good practice—ethically must take into account the differing levels of entitlement and familiarity students possess in any campus context. Taken as a whole, this text's compelling assertion of the lack of universality in the college experience should be less troubling than it is enlightening, prompting us instead to return to the original question: How might we reenvision goodness as a function of *advancing full human flourishing for all?*

To do so begins with acknowledging that neither higher education nor student affairs have ever operated within a system where all students are equally valued and cherished and their flourishing equally advanced. The history of U.S. higher education is replete with a centuries-long legacy of centering the experiences of white, cisgender, male, Christian, affluent students, faculty, and staff. This legacy, reconsidered, requires us to examine the heart of both the enterprise and our profession within it to excavate and reclaim its power for those least well served historically. This also means troubling long-held assumptions about what constitutes meaningful challenge and support, dissonance and consonance, in the student experience. And it requires us to ask whose growth and development is accelerated, versus retarded, through the ways we approach good practice. This requires also reengaging with student affairs' legacy of social justice advocacy (Gaston-Gayles, Wolf-Wendel, Tuttle, Twombly, & Ward, 2005). In the spirit of my belief that "another world is possible" (Pitcher, 2015, p. 1), I assert that critical theories offer an alternative framework for both conceiving of the good and enacting it.

Reconceptualizing "Good" Practice Through a Critical Social Justice Lens

As the profession propels headlong into the twenty-first century, our thinking about the good in student affairs can and must evolve beyond notions of a single, universal human good (embedded in Aristotelian and Utilitarian thinking), as well as beyond the sellable good(s) of the neoliberal U.S. university. When we examine the outcomes of such practices, two truths are revealed. First, higher education continues to disproportionately serve the interests of the white, affluent establishment for whom it was originated (see Harris & Poon, chapter 2 in this book). Second, as argued by Lange and Stewart in chapter 17, to truly enact the good in higher education, a courageous, critical stance to reformulate the principles that undergird practice is both timely and overdue.

The evidence for the first statement is abundant. Over the past two decades while the Principles were ostensibly "put to work" in student affairs, college outcomes for those historically least well served continued to be substandard at best. As described by Harris and Poon in chapter 2, Black, Latino, and Native American students continue to apply to and complete college in grossly underrepresentative numbers (Tate, 2017), a fact that is even more starkly noticeable at the most prestigious colleges (Ashkenas, Park, & Pearce, 2017). They continue to experience college as a persistently hostile environment as a result of racist macro- and microaggressions (Solórzano, Ceja, & Yosso, 2000), rendering higher education in need of reformation through critical race theory frames (see Harris & Poon, chapter 2). Trans* and nonbinary students are targeted by transphobic peers, faculty, and staff, and their experiences too are clouded by hostility and indifference (Nicolazzo, 2017). Salis Reyes and Tauala described in chapter 5 the ways that Indigenous students, surviving colonization, must expend needless energy to maintain self-determination on stolen land, the site of much of U.S. higher education. Those who are undocumented, or DACAmented, face great uncertainty and the stressors that accompany it in the current presidential administration's aggressive policies of enforcement (Gonzales & Terriquez, 2013). And one in five cisgender women and trans* students experience sexual violence during their time in college (Cantor, Fisher, Chibnall, & Bruce, 2015). In these ways and innumerably more, minoritized students experience college as a labyrinth of obstacles. The investment of energy to overcome them suggests a failure of our charge to ensure learning, growth, development, and healthy and empowered values formation for all students. Thus, we must examine new ways to envision the principles by which we do our work and the impact it has.

As argued throughout this text, critical theoretical practices and principles signal the ways we can and must reformulate these principles for the good of students and their development. Alongside other ideas, a reconceptualizing of professional purpose emanating from Black feminist scholars offers a viable alternative for thinking about the work we are called to do and the ways we are called to do it. Describing her relentless experiences with subjugation, erasure, and minimization as a Black woman in a predominantly white profession—the law—Harris (1992) first proclaimed the development of a "jurisprudence of resistance" (p. 351). Harris argued that from collective awareness of these hostile acts, awareness of practices of resistance emerges; practices that can define a profession, insisting that the profession must be, indeed, *constituted of* that resistance. Alexander-Floyd (2010) named the ways that Black feminist jurisprudence has changed the practice of law and the academy alongside it, including centering personal experiences (and one's stories) in both illuminating injustice and developing legal remedies for it. A commitment to intersectional thinking, action, and policy development—fully seeing and honoring the complex experiences of those of minoritized races and genders—typifies this resistance as well. Black feminist jurisprudence resistance foregrounds the histories that shape current practice and demands reckoning with the ways they continuously dispossess. It is, then, a set of professional practices that emanate from a set of principles—principles that assert the goodness of Black feminist ways of knowing, surviving, and transforming a profession, and its professionals, beset by white dominance.

What, then, might we understand to be a student affairs practice of resistance? In place of the guiding assumptions underpinning the Principles, a critical theoretical lens grounded in resistance would assert the following as foundational assumptions: (a) Good practice for student affairs centers *naming and dismantling* these persistent injustices and inequities; (b) good practice centers *education for empowerment, agency, and voice*; (c) good practice centers *naming and resisting administrative violence* (Spade, 2015); and (d) good practice requires *reenvisioning notions of knowing and learning* that resist neoliberal logics (Zepke, 2016).

By naming and resisting persistent injustices and inequity, student affairs professionals would appropriately resume their civil rights–era roles as advocates for students and for the work of advancing justice (Gaston-Gayles et al., 2005). We would use data and evidence not to defend the worth of our work or the so-called products of our labor but to unmask the persistent marginalization of those without voice and status in higher education, unseating the policies and practices that promote hegemony. We would partner with our colleagues in the faculty to enact critical pedagogies, advanced by Freire (1972) and hooks (2014), both within and outside of the classroom, dissolving the boundaries of learning spaces and abandoning the triteness of teachable moments for deeply engaged teaching and learning. We would doggedly seek and deconstruct the ways in which ingrained yet invisible policies and practices exert what Spade (2015) called *administrative violence*—erasure, marginality, and reduced life chances—for those least well served. And we would aggressively decry neoliberal knowledge acquisition practices, including the incessant metricizing of higher education, instead enacting assessment models that integrate multiple forms of expression of mastery, knowledge, and wisdom, including the wisdom of lived experience.

In short, we would lift up multiple ways of knowing and learning, valuing, and community formation. We would delimit the notion that what counts can always (only) be counted. We would center the advancement of those whose college experiences least reflect the bounty neoliberalism has offered the dominant classes, and we would define policy and practice by the extent to which they proliferate liberatory futures. A student affairs practice of resistance would create where there has been destruction, would amplify where there has been voicelessness, and would illuminate where there have been shadows. It will, in turn, require of us to attend wholeheartedly to the "task beyond survival" (Harris, 1992, p. 351)—social transformation.

Conclusion

Twenty years on, the Principles have provided a framework for articulating the goals of the student affairs profession and the ways it will be accountable to its publics. The profession of student affairs has a deep and abiding ethical responsibility to declare a set of guiding principles that can serve as bright beacons in the miasma of the neoliberal academy. The critical and poststructural scholars in this text, and in previous research, have passionately argued the essential nature of centering social justice within the profession and, indeed, within all of higher education (Pitcher, 2015; Saltmarsh & Hartley, 2011). The opportunity to critically examine the Principles is both essential and enlightening to this goal. As with all statements of values, the passage of time and the shifting sands of the economic and political contexts in which higher education operates provides an opportunity to revisit and reframe our work and to fearlessly consider how our sense of ourselves as a profession ought to continually evolve. And as Arminio and Ortiz (2017) so eloquently stated, "Professionalism is where the personal and professional intersect. This is integrity: The intersection of obligations and 'oughtness'" (p. 389).

Throughout this text, we affirm student affairs' role as both the guardians and the catalysts of student agency, resilience, and authenticity, wrought through multidimensional learning in an unfinished democratic project. The relentless press of neoliberalism on the academy demands an equally steadfast path of resistance, one offered through critical theories and their fearless commitment to reframing the terms of professional effectiveness. Otherwise enduring constructs such as values, learning, and community seem relatively impotent in the face of unfettered marketization of postsecondary education, calling for more inventive and courageous stances. As Evans and Reason (2001) noted,

> We believe that the next major philosophical statement of the student affairs profession—the one that will guide practice in the 21st century—must address the need for student affairs professionals to view their role on campus through a critical lens, to interject their professional values into their work, and to become change agents. . . . Student affairs professionals should seriously examine critical theory as the lens through which to view the world. (p. 376)

The Principles invoked a historically specific call to action among our colleagues and our field. Yet, the spoils of their labor have yet to result in the goodness that matters most: justice. The time has thus come to revisit, reframe, and rearticulate a vision of the good within the student affairs profession and, in so doing, spark a recommitment to transforming higher education in the years to come. I hope readers will consider the following discussion questions about good practice in student affairs:

1. Are there timeless values in student affairs practice? If so, which of the root assumptions underpinning the Principles are still most salient, and why? Good practice is centered on *learning, values clarification, being evidence driven and resource conscious*, and/or *belonging and inclusion*.
2. What is the role of professional associations and their members in fostering complacency or resistance to the current neoliberalism dominating higher education?
3. Can we dream and enact a "student affairs practice of resistance?" What possibilities does approaching practice as resistance hold for the work we do alongside students?

References

ACPA: College Student Educators International. (1994). *The student learning imperative*. Washington, DC: Author. Retrieved from http://www.myacpa.org/files/acpas-student-learning-imperativepdf

Alexander-Floyd, N. G. (2010). Critical race Black feminism: A "jurisprudence of resistance" and the transformation of the academy. *Signs: Journal of Women in Culture and Society, 35*(4), 810–820.

American Council on Education. (1937). *The student personnel point of view: A report of a conference on the philosophy and development of student personnel work in colleges and universities* (American Council on Education Study, Series 1, Vol. 1, No. 3). Washington, DC: Author.

American Council on Education. (1949). *The student personnel point of view.* Washington, DC: Author.

Arminio, J., & Ortiz, A. (2017). Professionalism. In J. H. Schuh, S. R. Jones, & V. Torres (Eds.), *Student services: A handbook for the profession* (6th ed., pp. 377–392). San Francisco, CA: Jossey-Bass.

Ashkenas, J., Park, H., & Pearce, A. (2017, August 24). Even with affirmative action, Blacks and Hispanics are more underrepresented at top colleges than 35 years ago. *New York Times.* Retrieved from https://www.nytimes.com/interactive/2017/08/24/us/affirmative-action.html?_r=0

Blimling, G. S., & Whitt, E. J. (1998, March–April). Principles of good practice for student affairs. *About Campus,* 10–15.

Blimling, G. S., & Whitt, E. J. (Eds.). (1999). *Good practice in student affairs: Principles to foster student learning.* San Francisco, CA: Jossey-Bass.

Cantor, D., Fisher, B., Chibnall, S., & Bruce, C. (2015). *Report on the AAU campus climate survey on sexual assault and sexual misconduct.* Rockville, MD: WESTAT.

Chickering, A. W., & Gamson, Z. F. (1987). Seven principles for good practice in undergraduate education. *AAHE Bulletin, 3,* 7.

Evans, N. J., & Reason, R. D. (2001). Guiding principles: A review and analysis of student affairs philosophical statements. *Journal of College Student Development, 42*(4), 359–377.

Fish, S. (2009). Neoliberalism and higher education. *New York Times.* Retrieved from https://opinionator.blogs.nytimes.com/2009/03/08/neoliberalism-and-higher-education/

Freire, P. (1972). *Pedagogy of the oppressed.* New York, NY: Continuum.

Gaston-Gayles, J. L., Wolf-Wendel, L. E., Tuttle, K. N., Twombly, S. B., & Ward, K. (2005). From disciplinarian to change agent: How the civil rights era changed the roles of student affairs professionals. *NASPA Journal, 42*(3), 263–282.

Giroux, H. A. (2014). *Neoliberalism's war on higher education.* Boston, MA: Haymarket Books.

Gonzales, R. G., & Terriquez, V. (2013). *Preliminary findings from the national unDACAmented research project* (pp. 33–58). Washington, DC: Immigration Policy Center.

Harris, C. I. (1992). Law professors of color and the academy: Of poets and kings. *Chicago-Kent Law Review, 68*(1), 331–352.

Harvey, D. (2007). *A brief history of neoliberalism.* London, UK: Oxford University Press.

hooks, b. (2014). *Teaching to transgress.* New York, NY: Routledge.

Kashdan, T. B., Biswas-Diener, R., & King, L. A. (2008). Reconsidering happiness: The costs of distinguishing between hedonics and eudaimonia. *Journal of Positive Psychology, 3*(4), 219–233.

Long, D. (2012). The foundations of student affairs: A guide to the profession. In L. J. Hinchliffe & M. A. Wong (Eds.), *Environments for student growth and development: Librarians and student affairs in collaboration* (pp. 1–39). Chicago, IL: Association of College & Research Libraries.

Mill, J. S., & Bentham, J. (1987). *Utilitarianism and other essays*. London, UK: Penguin.

Murray, S. J., Holmes, D., Perron, A., & Rail, G. (2007). No exit? Intellectual integrity under the regime of "evidence" and "best-practices." *Journal of Evaluation in Clinical Practice, 13*(4), 512–516.

NASPA: Student Affairs Administrators in Higher Education. (1997). *Principles of good practice for student affairs: Statement and inventories*. Washington, DC: Author. Retrieved from https://www.naspa.org/images/uploads/main/Principles_ of_Good_Practice_in_Student_Affairs.pdf

Nicolazzo, Z. (2017). *Trans* in college: Transgender students' strategies for navigating campus life and the institutional politics of inclusion*. Sterling, VA: Stylus.

Pitcher, E. N. (2015). Another world is possible: Envisioning an intersectional social justice student affairs praxis. *Journal of Critical Thought and Praxis, 4*(1). Retrieved from http://lib.dr.iastate.edu/jctp/vol4/iss1

Profession [Def. 1]. (2017). In *Merriam-Webster Online*. Retrieved fromhttps:// www.merriam-webster.com/dictionary/profession

Rowe, C., & Broadie, S. (2002). *Nicomachean ethics*. Oxford, UK: Oxford University Press.

Saltmarsh, J., & Hartley, M. (2011). *To serve a larger purpose: Engagement for democracy and the transformation of higher education*. Philadelphia, PA: Temple University Press.

Solórzano, D., Ceja, M., & Yosso, T. (2000). Critical race theory, racial microaggressions, and campus racial climate: The experiences of African American college students. *Journal of Negro Education, 69*(1–2), 60–73.

Spade, D. (2015). *Normal life: Administrative violence, critical trans politics, and the limits of law* (2nd ed.). Durham, NC: Duke University Press.

Tate, E. (2017, April 26). Graduation rates and race. *Inside Higher Ed*. Retrieved from https://www.insidehighered.com/news/2017/04/26/ college-completion-rates-vary-race-and-ethnicity-report-finds

Zepke, N. (2016). *Student engagement in neoliberal times: Theories and practices for learning and teaching in higher education*. London, UK: Springer.

17

HIGH-IMPACT PRACTICES

Alex C. Lange and D-L Stewart

S tudent affairs practitioners facilitate students' learning and educational outcomes during postsecondary education. To understand which practices have maximal effects, researchers have studied particular practices and the net effects of their contributions to student success (Kuh, Kinzie, Schuh, & Whitt, 2005, 2010). The outcome of this research has been the promulgation of a set of 11 high-impact practices (Kuh et al., 2010) that have gained national attention in setting practice and policy agendas (Finley & McNair, 2013). In this chapter, we introduce these high-impact practices and why they should be critiqued from a critical theoretical lens. In addition, we focus on the implications of these critical reformulations for student affairs practice, taking into consideration the theoretical constructs discussed in Part Two of this volume. To begin, we acknowledge how we each enter this conversation.

Entry Points

Patel (2016) discussed the responsibility of researchers to be not only "fluent in existing research" but also responsible for "our ontological entry-points and impacts" (p. 57): Why us? Why this? Why now? We extend this to practitioners as well, whose work—whether consciously or unconsciously—is grounded in one's personal assumptions and informal theories about education, students, and development (Parker, 1977).

Critical and poststructural theorizing has been the place I (Alex) continue to find myself. Like hooks (1994), when I was without a sense of home or of myself growing up, I found "sanctuary" in theorizing. It was a place where possibility existed more so than in my lived experience. As I am someone at the border of identities both dominant and contested, theorizing in the borderlands

(Abes, 2009; Anzaldúa, 1987) allows me to imagine, name, and dream about my epistemologies, modes of being, and professional work in life-giving ways. My queerness, transness, and multiraciality continue to be contested objects of discourse and reality. For me, critical and poststructural paradigms frame my positionality as a scholar and practitioner who dares to make bold, public disruptions of "established" knowledges in postsecondary education. I want to trouble how we as a field come to amass knowledges (Gonzalez & Pasque, 2017) for a greater goal beyond intellectual exercises.

These modes of thinking have helped me destabilize dominant ideas of student development work. My time as an LGBTQ+ resource center professional helped me use critical and poststructural theories to *critically queer* my work. Critically queered praxis helps me trouble ideas of student success metrics, which are often limited to persistence and graduation. For me, student success also includes dimensions of wellness, connection, and support. Rather than being unidirectional in application from educator to student, educational practice should be versatile, blurring the dualities of educator and student, such that practitioners might occupy multiple roles over time rather than be limited to one particular positioning (Sheldon, 2016).

Like Alex, I (D-L) have found critical and poststructural theory to be a site of liberation, empowerment, and visibility. Growing up in Harlem, New York City, provided me early exposure to beauty salon and street corner critical race theorizing. I was encouraged to see oppression as a structure by the Afrocentrists selling books on 125th Street. I heard the rallying cry of Black feminism through the biblically intoned wisdom of my pastoring and church-founding grandmother and the Black women who ran the holiness churches in which I grew up. It would be years later, during undergraduate and graduate school at Kalamazoo College and The Ohio State University, respectively, that I would be introduced to the formal academic language defining my childhood experiences. I committed myself to pursuing a radically democratic vision (West, 2017) of education that centered minoritized peoples' experiences and their inherent wisdom and possibilities.

Through such paradigmatic frameworks, I seek to push the boundaries of what can be and what can be done in higher education. Moreover, I join Alex in unlearning dominant ideals of educational practice and destabilizing presumably fixed knowledges. Embracing my Blackdisabledqueertrans* identities, as a valid standpoint and critical poststructural lens on the world, has led me to unflinchingly engage a critical praxis that asks "why" as an entry point to alternative vision(s) and release of assumptions that reinscribe oppressive structures and systems. I giddily turn things on their head out of the dogged belief that we are not tied to what we once knew to be true or to one vision of truth. From these standpoints, we turn to our examination of high-impact practices.

High-Impact Practices

Kuh et al. (2005) broadly defined *student success* as inclusive of "satisfaction, persistence, and high levels of learning and personal development" (p. xiv). According to Kuh (2008), there is one practice that institutions can do to enhance student learning and success:

> Make it possible for every student to participate in two high-impact activities during his or her [*sic*] undergraduate program, one in the first year, and one taken later in relation to the major field. The obvious choices for first-year students are first-year seminars, learning communities, and service learning. (p. 21)

These high-impact activities comprise 11 institutional initiatives that Kuh et al. (2010) determined were tested across a broad variety of institutions and found to be applicable to students of many backgrounds (Kuh, 2008). These practices are (a) first-year seminars and experiences, (b) common intellectual experiences, (c) learning communities, (d) writing-intensive courses, (e) collaborative assignments and projects, (f) undergraduate research, (g) diversity and global learning, (h) ePortfolios, (i) service-learning and community-based learning, (j) internships, and (k) capstone courses and projects.

Kuh has noted, independently (Kuh, 2008) and with colleagues (Kuh et al., 2010), that these practices have been practiced by *some* postsecondary institutions for *some* groups of students at *some* times. Instead of this haphazard, unsystematic approach, these scholars argued that a systematic, institution-wide approach is necessary to support the learning and success of the majority of students within and across institutional sectors. Based on their research with institutions, including two- and four-year colleges, public and private universities, and predominantly white and minority-serving institutions (Kuh et al., 2010), these 11 practices demonstrated the highest impact on student learning and success in college and the capacity for scaling up to the general population of students (Kuh & O'Donnell, 2013).

These practices are mobilized differently across institutions based on their unique norms and climates—they are not meant simply to be adopted cookie-cutter style from one institution to the next. However, there are some common foci and identifiable emphases across the set. The greatest emphasis is on written expression. From the different styles of coursework to undergraduate research and other documentation of learning (e.g., ePort-folios, credit-bearing internships), writing is the dominant mode of expression. Following the emphasis on writing is a strong focus in more than half of the high-impact practices on cognitive and intellectual development, as well as on problem-solving and practical application. Of notable emphasis is the synthesis or integration across the formal curriculum. Receiving little explicit attention are curricular and cocurricular collaboration, learning about diversity and inclusion (and no focus on equity or justice), and community engagement.

Critiques of High-Impact Practices

What the 11 high-impact practices do and do not emphasize is itself worthy of critique. The focus on cognition and intellectualism that has become entrenched in U.S. postsecondary education has been bemoaned by Kuh, Shedd, and Whitt (1987). To emphasize written expression so heavily leaves us wondering about the place of the arts in such a curriculum. In addition, higher education scholars have critiqued institutions' consistent and persistent lackluster attention to and recognition of the import of the cocurricular experience (i.e., student affairs) (ACPA: College Student Educators International, 1996; Kuh et al., 1987); the lack of integrated and explicit focus on issues of diversity and inclusion, let alone equity and justice (Stewart, 2017); and the uncritical heralding of the benefits of service-learning (Gilbride-Brown, 2008; Jones, LePeau, & Robbins, 2013; Jones, Robbins, & LePeau, 2011, Spring).

A host of institutions employ high-impact practices, making decisions to implement these particular programs and practices over others (Johnson & Stage, 2018). If other practices are not empirically proven to work like high-impact practices, institutions may not equitably fund them, and those practices may receive less attention from practitioners and policymakers. Though the quality and method of implementation of high-impact practices are essential (Kuh & Kinzie,), the exclusion of what are then perceived as non–high-impact practices may close off researchers and practitioners to new possibilities of educational strategies that may also have high impact.

We note that there are other questions about high-impact practices: *For whom* are these practices high impact (Kilgo, 2016), and *how* are these practices enacted in ways to benefit *all* students? In the initial conceptualization of high-impact practices, Kuh (2008) noted a "compensatory effect" (p. 19). This compensatory effect suggested that high-impact practices may be particularly beneficial to those who are Black, Latinx, and academically unprepared (as defined by low ACT scores) regarding GPA and persistence from first year to second year (Finley & McNair, 2013; Kuh, 2008). Although some research has supported these findings (Finley & McNair, 2013), other scholars have suggested that racism and classism can be at play in the delivery of high-impact practices, which may lead to lower participation from these groups (Kilgo, 2016; Kilgo, Sheets, & Pascarella, 2014).

Bringing Critical Theory to Bear on High-Impact Practices

Though these practices were developed to play a part in addressing the opportunity gap (Pendakur, 2016) among subsets of students in higher education, we assert that a critical theoretical review of the practical implications of high-impact practices reveals other concerns related to student development. This approach requires that practices always be under examination and about the "process rather than a singular point of" success (Spade, 2015, p. 2). Therefore, we now analyze high-impact practices through a critical and poststructural paradigmatic lens. We invoke four tenets from critical and poststructural theoretical scholarship in this analysis: (a) decolonization (Patel, 2014), (b) redistribution of power (Fraser & Honneth, 2004), (c) validation of multiple forms of knowledge and counternarratives (Ladson-Billings & Ladson-Billings, 1998), and (d) pervasiveness of power and oppression (Foucault, 1980; Giroux, 1983).

Decolonization

When used uncritically and exclusive of Native peoples, decolonization rhetoric "recenters whiteness, it resettles theory, it extends innocence to the settler, it entertains a settler future" (Tuck & Yang, 2012, p. 3). As discussed by Salis Reyes and Tauala in chapter 5, Indigenous and decolonizing paradigms require material change and disruption of settler constructs. These settler constructs include the attitudes, dispositions, and decision-making frameworks that guide theory in modernist constructs (Patel, 2014).

The focus on cognition and written expression in the high-impact practices as noted previously reflects settler constructs that deprioritize a holistic approach to people and their relationship to each other, to nature, and to the land. Although some institutions may allow oral performances in students' ePortfolios, the emphasis on writing and cognitive engagement is carried throughout the high-impact practices regardless. These skills are unquestionably valued in the cultural and economic marketplace. However, the uncritical promulgation of these values maintains settler coloniality. For example, knowledge transmitted orally by Indigenous peoples, instead of in writing, has been disregarded as less meaningful and less intelligent than the written knowledge of colonial empires.

The settler colonial disposition of the high-impact practices is even more apparent in its cursory attention to community-based engagement. As our earlier discussion noted, scholars have critiqued some enactments of service-learning and community-based learning (Gilbride-Brown, 2008; Jones et al., 2011; Spring, 2013). An anticolonial approach (Patel, 2014) to community-based learning would prioritize relationship building with the community and then center the knowledge and wisdom that preexists in the community. This approach would put students in the position of the ones who learn and receive assistance from the community. There is no more egregious display of settler colonialism than to enter a community and presume to be able to assist and help. Service-learning and community-based learning have been recommended as a high-impact practice without the requisite critique of what it means to position those with more access, higher status, and greater privilege as the doers of service to those positioned as lesser and in need. As the letter from the Indians of the Six Nations (1744) to the College of William and Mary illustrated, useful and practical education is taught by the people whose lived experiences have procured them wisdom.

Despite a heavy emphasis on synthesis and integration of knowledge, the high-impact practices say little about the responsibilities of people in community with each other. As Salis Reyes and Tauala noted in chapter 5, Indigenous and decolonizing paradigms emphasize relationality and stress wholeness and balance. Rather than merely promoting cognitive connections, practitioners can promote connections between students and the land and nonhuman animals. This is where student affairs professionals—nearly absent from the high-impact practices—have expertise that academicians often do not (Magolda, 2005). Practitioners can assist students in making connections to how they are part of a whole system that wants to support them and that helps them find a balance between their needs and others' needs.

Redistribution of Power

Critical race theories (Harris & Poon, chapter 2), intersectionality (Wijeyesinghe, chapter 3), and critical feminist theories (Robbins, chapter 4) draw attention particularly to power between individuals and systems. These and other power-conscious frameworks discussed by Linder (2018) can assist practitioners in thinking through various forms of their power and how practitioners are gatekeepers of that power. However, as a whole, the 11 high-impact practices do little to nothing to acknowledge or disrupt the power imbalance between the institution and its students.

High-impact practices reflect institutional power in two fundamental ways. First, data *about* students but not data *from* students informed the designation of high-impact practices. Using a postpositivist paradigm, researchers have solely used quantitative data to support the inherent value and effectiveness of high-impact practices. Data from students—collected through qualitative methodologies, such as phenomenology, narrative, ethnography, and case study—could either support, challenge, or nuance the effectiveness of high-impact practices and students' access to them during their undergraduate years. Power is at work here in that institutional administrators and researchers have determined that the evidence of effectiveness and value lies wholly in the repositories of institutional databases instead of in the lived experiences of students.

Second, the entirety, save one (internships not taken for credit), of the activities proposed as high-impact practices are determined, structured, and assessed by faculty, not students. How can faculty work with and alongside students to structure courses and curriculum, as well as to assess and evaluate students' work? Such a redistribution of power would invest in students as knowers, forming valuable learning partnerships that have been shown to enhance student learning (see Baxter Magolda, 2009; Baxter Magolda & King, 2004). In undergraduate research (a high-impact practice), faculty can model redistribution of power by conceptualizing research as working with and alongside participants rather than using them to advance a scholarly agenda (Jourian & Nicolazzo, 2017). Through the curricular and cocurricular collaborations that are recommended to produce common intellectual experiences (another high-impact practice), student affairs professionals can conceptualize a student affairs praxis that requires working with and alongside students in curriculum development, program planning, individual and group advising, and organizational decision-making processes that complement the academic program.

Validation of Multiple Forms of Knowledge and Counternarratives

As Jones discussed in chapter 1, student development research, theory, and practice have been informed primarily by positivist, postpositivist, and constructivist paradigms that either ignore or fail to critique the ways power, identity, and systemic oppression affect students' lives. These paradigms rely heavily on whiteness and its desires to reduce knowledges and peoples into quantifiable, comparable data points (Zuberi & Bonilla-Silva,

2008). Such paradigms also inform the development and operationalizing of Kuh et al. (2010) 11 high-impact practices.

As Waterman and Bazemore-James (chapter 13) pointed out, and discussed earlier, orientations toward knowledge must be (re)considered and (re)conceptualized. The (in)visibility of Indigenous "storying" (Waterman & Bazemore-James) and other cultures based in oral traditions illustrates how an institution perceives folk traditions and Indigenous knowledge orientations (Kirkness & Barnhardt, 1991). Silencing the counternarratives that such forms of knowledge can enunciate starves the institution of valuable perspectives that can be transformative to institutional systems, policies, and practices.

Although often excluded, multiple knowledge frameworks can be leveraged in the assessment and evaluation processes of high-impact practices. For instance, when designing new living-learning communities (a high-impact practice), these communities can honor different knowledge orientations. Programs can be designed to encourage multiple forms of knowledge to emerge throughout the semester or academic year that break down the preeminence of decontextualized, specialized, and literate knowledge on campus.

Diversity and global learning, a high-impact practice, is often dependent on the use of dissonance in the name of furthering learning despite counternarratives to the contrary from minoritized students, particularly Women of Color and others with multiple marginalities in our experience. Common awareness-raising activities like privilege walks often center majoritized students' learning at the expense of minoritized students, especially those who experience multiple marginalities. Minoritized students must then reckon their position with those with the most privilege, reminding students of their social position so that those most ahead ostensibly can learn just how ahead they are. This was also discussed by Taylor and Reynolds in chapter 9.

Moreover, few people realize or note that Belenky, Clinchy, Goldberger, and Tarule (1997) called into the question the role of dissonance in their research. Although they acknowledged that resolving conflict can lead to growth, they also pointed out that for the women in their study, the experience of being doubted—the introduction of dissonance—was debilitating, not energizing (Belenky et al., 1997). These scholars made the point that belief and connection need to play a more prominent role than doubt and separation.

Such activities can be flipped on their head by engaging students in demonstration and consideration of counternarratives and alternative perspectives on disadvantage. Jones and Abes (2016) discussed such an approach specific to the privilege walk. D-L has used a class activity that portrayed poor and working-class youth as skilled and resourceful instead of as victims of circumstance. Alex has found value in using individual reflections and race caucuses to provide space for exploring students' feelings of dissonance. This process allows deeper learning about power and privilege to occur, while not asking minoritized students to put the tangible outcomes of their societal oppression on display. Diversity and global learning are better realized when those who have been afforded privilege recognize the resilient and resistant practices developed by minoritized communities in response to oppression.

Power and Pervasiveness of Oppression

A key tenet of critical theory is a recognition of the pervasiveness of oppressive power relations in society (Giroux, 1983). As such, practitioners and researchers must interrogate the context of social identity development for students rather than just focus on how students articulate their identities in the midst of oppression. Such an awareness of the pervasiveness of oppression also means interrogating institutional systems that create barriers for full engagement by students in their collegiate experiences.

One way to begin to interrogate these systems is by examining spaces, like learning communities, that create boundaries around who does and does not belong in a space, reinforcing systems that continue to keep the same bodies and identities in the space that have always been there (Johnston-Guerrero, Pizzolato, Johnston-Guerrero, & Pizzolato, 2016; Nicolazzo & Marine, 2015). For example, learning communities for queer and trans* students are consistently occupied mainly by white queer and trans* students. As a result, queer and trans* People of Color (QTPOC) perceive that they do not belong in the space, the white students in the space treat interested QTPOC as though they do not belong in the space, and the result reinforces that QTPOC do not occupy the space. Practitioners can take a step back and examine how conceptions of who uses services create ideas of who can use these services and be involved in particular offices.

This has relevance for how we consider high-impact practices generally. Using data to inform practice is essential in diversity work, as discussed by Sundt, Cole, and Wheaton (2017). High-impact practices are said to be accessible to most students, but what data inform this narrative? It is not enough to review data of the students accessing a service or set of services as broadly representative of the campus. This is particularly faulty when those data are not disaggregated and contextualized using intersectional analyses that can make visible students within and across groups who are not accessing a high-impact practice or set of practices. Moreover, upon noting that certain groups are not making use of a practice or set of practices, researchers and professionals must be cognizant of the narrative they tell about those data. Is it presumed that all students could access a certain practice and those who do not are simply choosing to not do so? An acknowledgment of the pervasiveness of oppression, even in purportedly benign systems, must initially consider what unacknowledged barriers exist that prevent certain groups of students from engaging in certain otherwise high-impact practices.

Implications of Student Development for High-Impact Practices

Now that we have critically interrogated high-impact practices, we turn to considering these practices through the lens of development. Kuh et al. (2005, 2010) did not explicitly consider student development; however, as Mayhew et al. (2016) concluded, students do experience psychosocial development during their college experience. This development is not isolated to any one facet of students' experiences in college, but rather the whole of the experience contributes to student development. Therefore, the developmental constructs discussed in Part Two can provide insight and implications for critically deploying high-impact practices. We focus here on those constructs not already incorporated in the previous discussion.

As Nicolazzo and Carter (chapter 8) cautioned, *resilience* is borne of students' experiences with adversity. Many minoritized students come to college having already developed resilience strategies for negotiating oppressive institutional systems. High-impact practices need to be implemented with a consciousness of how students may feel they have to be resilient in order to navigate their college experience.

In chapter 9, Taylor and Reynolds complicated the practice of invoking *dissonance* in students in order to facilitate their development. Their chapter uses Reynolds's experience in a study abroad program, a high-impact practice related to diversity and global learning, to make the necessary distinction between dissonance and trauma. Students come to higher education with various experiences. For minoritized students, those experiences may include already negotiating the dissonance of living among unjust systems. Their engagement in high-impact practices should not reproduce that traumatic dissonance in the name of facilitating developmental goals.

Stewart and Brown unpacked the *social construction of identities* in chapter 10, pointing out in their discussion the vital role that othermothering and mentoring can play in helping minoritized students find support in their identity journeys. High-impact practices like first-year experiences with faculty and undergraduate research need to be designed with this potential in mind. Faculty need training and development in this level of mentorship so that the burden of fulfilling these roles does not fall inherently to minoritized faculty .

Kupo and Oxendine confronted the challenges of *authenticity* for some students in chapter 11. They noted that not all students can show up authentically in institutional spaces. This is especially important to consider in all high-impact practices, but especially those that involve and expect deep sharing of personal histories in settings before rapport has been established.

Agency is the subject discussed by Okello and White in chapter 12. They proposed "embodied agency" as a means of reckoning with the material and psychic effects of oppression. By acknowledging the many facets of the realities facing minoritized students (i.e., existential situation, competing forces, historical memory, meaning-making capacities, and creativity), their engagement in high-impact practices can be nuanced. This is key for practices like internships, which challenge authenticity, the social construction of identities, and agency. Internship coordinators must acknowledge and work to support students' meaning-making capacities and creativity in the face of competing forces and historical memories of employment discrimination affecting People of Color, queer and trans* people, people with disabilities, and formerly incarcerated people.

Conclusion

In this chapter, we discussed high-impact practices and critical theory challenges to and of those practices and considered the student development implications of those practices. We offered ways to more mindfully offer high-impact practices on campuses, disrupting the neutrality narrative associated with high-impact practices as an inherent good. We hope that through this analysis, practitioners are able to think more deeply about the ways student affairs praxis can support and redirect academic affairs' applications of high-impact practices as elements of students' postsecondary experiences. As a field committed to transformational practice, practitioners should see student development work as one that requires critical reflection, discussion, planning, and action. We encourage readers to consider the following discussion questions:

1. Beyond what the authors offer, how can established high-impact practices be modified to better account for critical and poststructural concepts of student development?
2. How have you seen high-impact practices implemented in ways that did not take into account the critical theoretical perspectives espoused here? How have you seen high-impact practices implemented in ways that did?
3. As a student affairs practitioner, how can you operate within your sphere of influence to bring a critical consciousness to bear on how high-impact practices are used at your institution?

References

Abes, E. S. (2009). Theoretical borderlands: Using multiple theoretical perspectives to challenge inequitable power structures in student development theory. *Journal of college student development, 50*(2), 141–156.

ACPA: College Student Educators International. (1996). *The student learning imperative: Implications for student Affairs.* Washington, DC: Author. Retrieved from http://www.myacpa.org/sites/default/files/ACPA%27s%20Student%20Learning%20Imperative.pdf

Anzaldúa, G. (1987). *Borderland/La frontera: The new mestiza.* San Francisco, CA: Spinsters/Aunt Lute.

Baxter Magolda, M. B. (2009). Promoting self-authorship to promote liberal education. *Journal of College and Character, 10*(3).

Baxter Magolda, M. B., & King, P. M. (2004). *Learning partnerships: Theories and models of practice to educate for self-authorship.* Sterling, VA: Stylus.

Belenky, M. F., Clinchy, B. M., Goldberger, N. R., & Tarule, J. M. (1997). *Women's ways of knowing: The development of self, voice, and mind.* New York, NY: Basic Books. (Original work published 1986).

Finley, A., & McNair, T. (2013). *Assessing underserved students' engagement in high-impact practices.* Washington, DC: Association of American Colleges and Universities.

Foucault, M. (1980). *Power/knowledge: Selected interviews and other writings, 1972–1977* (C. Gordon, Ed., Trans.). New York, NY: Pantheon Books.

Fraser, N., & Honneth, A. (2004). *Redistribution or recognition: A political-philosophical exchange* (J. Golb, Trans.). New York, NY: Verso Books.

Gilbride-Brown, J. K. (2008) (E)racing service-learning as a critical pedagogy: Race matters (*Unpublished doctoral dissertation*). The Ohio State University, Columbus, OH.

Giroux, H. (1983). *Theory and resistance in education.* New York, NY: Bergin and Garvey.

Gonzalez, LD., & Pasque, PA. (2017). *Interventions in higher education research and practice: Confronting epistemic oppression.* Paper presented at the 2017 Annual Association for the Study of Higher Education Conference, Houston, TX.

hooks, b. (1994). *Teaching to transgress: Education as the practice of freedom.* New York, NY: Routledge.

Indians of the Six Nations. (1744). *Letter to the College of William and Mary.* Retrieved from https://www.ancestry.com/boards/topics.ethnic.natam.intertribal.six-nations/58/mb.ashx

Johnson, S. R., & Stage, F. K. (2018). Academic engagement and student success: Do high-impact practices mean higher graduation rates? *The Journal of Higher Education, 89*(5), 753–781.

Johnston-Guerrero, M. P., & Pizzolato, J. E. (2016). The utility of race and ethnicity in the multidimensional identities of Asian American students. *Journal of college student development, 57*(8), 905–924.

Jones, S. R., & Abes, E. S. (2016). The nature and uses of theory. In J. H. Schuh, S. R. Jones, & V. Torres (Eds.), *Student services: A handbook for the profession* (6th ed., pp. 137–152). San Francisco, CA: Wiley.

Jones, S. R., LePeau, L. A., & Robbins, C. K. (2013). Exploring the possibilities and limitations of service-learning: A critical analysis of college student narratives about HIV/AIDS. *Journal of Higher Education, 84*(2), 213–238.

Jones, S. R., Robbins, C. K., & LePeau, L. A. (2011, Spring). Negotiating border crossing: Influences of social identity on service-learning outcomes. *Michigan Journal of Community Service Learning,* 27–42.

Jourian, T.J., & Nicolazzo, Z (2017). Bringing our communities to the research table: The liberatory potential of collaborative methodological practices alongside LGBTQ participants. *Educational Action Research, 25*(4), 594–609.

Kilgo, C. A. (2016). An epistemological revolution: Using quantitative data to critically interrogate high-impact educational practices *(Unpublished doctoral dissertation).* Retrieved from Iowa Research Online.

Kilgo, C. A., Sheets, J. K. E., & Pascarella, E. T. (2014, April). *Do high-impact practices actually have high impact on learning for all students?* Paper presented at the 2014 Annual Meeting of the American Educational Research Association, Philadelphia, PA.

Kirkness, V., & Barnhardt, R. (1991). First Nations and higher education: The four Rs—respect, relevance, reciprocity, responsibility. *Journal of American Indian Education, 30*(3), 1–15.

Kuh, G. D. (2008). *High-impact educational practices: What they are, who has access to them, and why they matter.* Washington, DC: Association of American Colleges and Universities.

Kuh, G. D., & O'Donnell, K. (2013). *Ensuring quality and taking high-impact practices to scale.* Washington, DC: Association of American Colleges & Universities.

Kuh, G. D., & Kinzie, J. (May 1, 2018). What really makes a "high-impact" practice high impact? Retrieved from https://www.insidehighered.com/views/2018/05/01/kuh-and-kinzie-respond-essay-questioning-high-impact-practices-opinion

Kuh, G. D., Kinzie, J., Schuh, J. H., & Whitt, E. J. (2005). *Student success in college: Creating conditions that matter*. San Francisco, CA: Jossey-Bass.

Kuh, G. D., Kinzie, J., Schuh, J. H., & Whitt, E. J. (2010). *Student success in college: Creating conditions that matter* (new preface and prologue). San Francisco, CA: Jossey-Bass.

Kuh, G. D., Shedd, J. D., & Whitt, E. J. (1987). Student affairs and liberal education: Unrecognized (and unappreciated) common law partners. *Journal of College Student Personnel, 28*(3), 252–260.

Ladson-Billings, G., & Ladson-Billings, G. (1998). Just what is critical race theory and what's it doing in a NICE field like education? *International Journal of Qualitative Studies in Education, 11*(1), 7–24.

Linder, C. (2018). *Sexual violence on campus: Power-conscious approaches to awareness, prevention, and response*. Bingley, UK: Emerald Publishing.

Magolda, P. M. (2005). Proceed with caution: Uncommon wisdom about academic and student affairs partnerships. *About Campus, 9*(6), 16–21.

Mayhew, M. J., Rockenbach, A. N., Bowman, N. A., Seifert, T. A., Wolniak, G. C., Pascarella, E. T., & Terenzini, P. T. (2016). *How college affects students: 21st century evidence that higher education works* (Vol. 3). San Francisco, CA: Jossey-Bass.

Nicolazzo, Z, & Marine, S. B. (2015). "It will change if people keep talking": Trans* students in college and university housing. *Journal of College and University Student Housing, 42*(1), 160–177.

Parker, C. (1977). On modeling reality. *Journal of College Student Personnel, 18*(5), 419–425.

Patel, L. (2014). Countering coloniality in educational research: From ownership to answerability. *Educational studies, 50*, 357–377.

Patel, L. (2016). *Decolonizing educational research: From ownership to answerability*. New York, NY: Routledge.

Pendakur, V. (2016). *Closing the opportunity gap: Identity-conscious strategies for retention and student success*. Sterling, VA: Stylus.

Sheldon, J. (2016). Versatility. In N. M. Rodriguez, W. J. Martino, J. C. Ingrey, & E. Brockenbrough (Eds.), *Critical concepts in queer studies and education: An international guide for the twenty-first century* (pp. 445–452). New York, NY: Palgrave Macmillan.

Spade, D. (2015). *Normal life: Administrative violence, critical trans politics, and the limits of law* (2nd ed.). Durham, NC: Duke University Press.

Stewart, D-L. (2017, March 30). Language of appeasement. *Inside Higher Ed.* Retrieved from https://www.insidehighered.com/views/2017/03/30/colleges-need-language-shift-not-one-you-think-essay

Sundt, M. A., Cole, D., & Wheaton, M. (2017). Using data to guide diversity work and enhance student learning. In K. M. Goodman & D. Cole (Eds.), *Using data-informed decision making to improve student affairs practice* (New Directions for Student Services, No. 159, pp. 93–103). San Francisco, CA: Wiley.

Tuck, E., & Yang, K. W. (2012). Decolonization is not a metaphor. *Decolonization: Indigeneity, Education, and Society, 1*(1), 1–40.

West, C. (2017). *Race matters.* New York, NY: Beacon Press. (Original work pub-
lished 1993).
Zuberi, T., & Bonilla-Silva, E. (Eds.). (2008). *White logic, white methods.* Lanham,
MD: Rowman & Littlefield.

PART FOUR

CONCLUSION

18

RETHINKING
STUDENT DEVELOPMENT

Elisa S. Abes, Antonio Duran, Susan R. Jones, and D-L Stewart

In this final chapter of *Rethinking College Student Development Theory Using Critical Frameworks*, we return to the core construct under investigation: student development. What can be said about *student development* when employing critical perspectives? In this book, we engaged this question by first providing brief overviews of critical theories such as critical race theory, intersectionality, decolonizing/Indigenous theories, queer theory, and crip theory. We then provided examples of how a number of central student development constructs may be reimagined when these critical frameworks and others are put to work. These constructs included resilience, dissonance, socially constructed identities, authenticity, agency, knowledge and knowing, and context. Finally, we considered how student affairs practice might look different when critical perspectives are used to interrogate several prevailing tenets that are presumed to produce positive student development and learning outcomes such as student involvement, principles of good practice, and high-impact practices. Taken together, these chapters prompt a good deal of reflection and leave us with important questions relative to what we call student development. In this chapter, we take up some of these ideas, pose new questions, and offer some of our thinking about future directions in student development.

Personal Narratives

Theories reflect the assumptions and beliefs of those who develop them, so we begin this chapter with our own academic genealogies. That is, we each offer a brief statement about how we came to know student development theory, which is then followed by our individual reflections on the relationship between *how* we came to know and *what* we believe about student development. In providing these reflections, we try to model the importance of both appreciating and scrutinizing what we were taught and learned about student development. We suggest that to *rethink* student development, we need to know what we think in the first place. And this careful rethinking may indeed lead to reimagining something entirely new. This is the liberatory and transformational potential of theory.

Elisa

I am from Susan R. Jones, who introduced me to ways of thinking and bodies of knowledge that I had not known existed. I found a kindred research spirit.

"I study identity," she said.

"Why would someone do that?" I skeptically wondered.

Identity steeped in systems of inequality is now the lens through which I view life.

I am from Rob Rhoads's critical service-learning research; Beverly Daniel Tatum's *Why Are All the Black Kids Sitting Together at the Cafeteria*; Pat King's *Reflective Judgment*; Bob Rodgers's student development transparencies; and Susan R. Jones and Marylu McEwen's Model of Multiple Dimensions of Identity. I am from Marcia Baxter Magolda's research on self-authorship that provided clarity when making my own professional and personal transitions as a graduate student.

I am from Susan, who encouraged me to "keep going" when I was working through my questions around these new ideas. I am from Marylu McEwen, who invited me to present my own ideas, an invitation that made me feel like I belonged.

I am from Deborah Britzman and queer theory before I knew I was from queer theory. Am I still from queer theory? (Yes, in conjunction with critical perspectives.)

I am from Marcia Baxter Magolda, my long-time colleague who guided my early teaching of student development theory. And I am from Marcia, who graciously supported my emerging critical voice that challenged her research.

I am from my nephew, Harrison Abes, whose extra 21st chromosome signaled me to continue challenging the norm and am now from Mia Mingus's disability justice.

I am from my students—Bianca Zamora, Lisa Combs, Michelle Wallace, Mika Karikari; a few among so many—whose intersectional stories teach me to never stop challenging the norm and how much I still need to learn.

My perspective on development comes from my story. I am a mix of significant privilege and early socialization of constructivist worldviews intersected with multiple forms of marginalization and justice-oriented sensibilities. I am a "heterosexual" corporate lawyer turned "lesbian" critical academic. Equally true, my perspectives on development have evolved because of how I continuously learn from the diverse students with whom I am in community and have continued to evolve by listening to the voices in this book. Indeed, it is my responsibility to truly listen to and believe these diverse voices as I consider the meaning of a critical perspective on development. Through their description and analysis of theoretical perspectives and from their rethinking of student development constructs, the voices in this text offer key ideas about the ways in which critical and poststructural theoretical perspectives can be used to rethink student development theory. I glean from some of these key ideas my critical perspective on the construct of development.

Development is situated in, forms in response to, and reshapes historical, political, and social contexts and is dependent on how students are positioned within intersecting systems of oppression. The nature of development is therefore different across students. Development is nonnormative; there is no standard against which it is measured. Development is therefore not only about meaning-making complexity.

Development is fluid. It is the process of becoming and emerging in no precise direction and at an inclusive pace as a whole, as fully human, and as tentatively free despite forces that feed lies to marginalized populations; police their bodies, minds, spirits, and voices; and present a range of constraining inequities.

Both hopeful and realistic, development embraces failure as positive. Failure is often a result of navigating oppressive systems and creating realities not typically named and valued and sometimes not entirely feasible. Failure opens up new possibilities for the self that others try to deny. Maybe then failure transformed into possibilities is the new developmental complexity.

Development is grounded in and occurs within community, family, and kin. It is about connection rather than separation and is rooted in experience and wisdom. We need each other to become whole, fully human, and tentatively free in a world telling us otherwise.

This reconceptualized understanding of development does not erase the constructivist perspective on developmental complexity. It puts caution tape around it though, which for some students should never be crossed. For some students, constructivist developmental theory describes their experiences. But it does not describe the experiences of all students or the entire experience of individual students. We need to be able to use multiple perspectives on development—and sometimes simultaneously despite their contradictions. Both critical and constructivist perspectives are valuable; neither is an alternate to the other. We must be able to appropriately put both into practice.

Antonio

I am from three phases of my educational career when I have asked the questions, *Who am I,* and *Why am I here?* I am from an undergraduate course where I first learned about student development, embracing the theories presented in this course as my doctrine. I am from a class project on *A Hope in the Unseen* (Suskind, 1998), a rudimentary attempt to fit stories into theories and theories into stories. I am from my first graduate course on student development centered largely on self-authorship. I am from moments of dissonance when I realized Kegan's (1994) orders of consciousness didn't align with my emerging critical consciousness. I am from an awareness that existing theories and models regularly failed to account for culture, power, and intersections. I am from a doctoral education that exposed me to critical perspectives on development while reminding me that earlier research should never be forgotten. I am from Matt Mayhew, Marcia B. Baxter Magolda, and Susan R. Jones—three educators who approached the study of student development in different yet equally enriching ways. I am from Patricia Hill Collins, Kimberlé Crenshaw, Roderick Ferguson, bell hooks, and E. Patrick Johnson—influences that continuously inform my scholarship. I am from a constant cycle of awakening, fueled by those who came before me and the brilliant individuals who are a part of my academic community. I am from this very project and a gratitude to Elisa S. Abes, Susan R. Jones, and D-L Stewart for providing me with this opportunity.

Though potentially idealistic, I still believe that college students *can* develop and grow as a result of participating in higher education. This claim most likely stems from the first student development theory course I took as an undergraduate student at New York University (NYU) during my senior year. This class challenged me to think about how I had changed throughout my time at NYU. Ultimately, I came to the conclusion (and still assert) that the experiences that I had in this environment, together with the people whom I met, provided me with a new lens with which to view myself and my identities. Nevertheless, my subsequent explorations into student development theory paired with an emerging personal sense of criticality have led me to question how higher education professionals engage with the concept of development.

Critical frameworks ask scholars to shift their analytic lens from solely examining the individual to also considering the systems of power that shape lived experiences. Thus, using a critical perspective on development necessitates a focus on how postsecondary institutions reproduce systemic inequalities and reinforce dominant norms. In reflecting on Knefelkamp, Widick, and Parker's (1978) seminal work on the nature of development in college, a text introduced at various points of my academic genealogy, the authors encouraged individuals to isolate the "factors in the particular environment of a college/university [that] can either encourage or inhibit growth" (p. x). Throughout my educational journey, I have witnessed professionals center their thinking on the ways that institutions can positively affect development without critically interrogating how our universities can also negatively affect students. It is in this reading that I ground my critical view of development.

As represented through the previous book chapters, the manner in which practitioners and faculty preference certain ways of knowing or specific populations of students in their practices can cause collegians to struggle with their cultural histories in relation to these new ideas. Our institutions may not be the best settings to get students to achieve a complexity of thought and behaviors, because colleges were not created for those who are not white, able-bodied, heterosexual, cisgender men. What does this mean for development? With an attention to historical and contemporary legacies of oppression on college campuses, educators must be prudent in their approach to working with students from marginalized backgrounds when they have a goal of development in mind. For this reason, my ideas about development have led me to create specific questions that professionals on college campuses must ask themselves: How do I engage an ethic of care when attempting to foster environments that contribute to the growth of students, especially those with marginalized identities? How will I cause harm to individuals in this process, and how will I respond in these moments? It is only when educators acknowledge their potential for harm and violence that we can reshape practices, interactions, and policies to better assist in the development of students.

Moreover, as we continue to rethink development from critical perspectives, we must also remain attentive to the affective dimensions of a student's journey. Development is not linear. Development is not always easy. Development does not occur without very real emotions happening along the way. *Hate, love, disgust, pride*—these are a few words that might describe how college students feel as they grow in their ways of knowing and connecting with others and their views of themselves within the context of higher education. Therefore, how do we prepare ourselves and others to support students in these emotions as they move through institutions? Though I do not believe that development occurs only within colleges and universities, when experiences and environments are designed appropriately, with an ethic of care, and with a critical eye, these institutions can still be places where development occurs.

Susan

I am from a long-standing fascination with the question "Who am I?" I am from an eighth-grade paper on Erik Erikson and psychosocial moratorium written during the same year as a field trip to Washington, DC, when a national protest against the Vietnam War (also called Moratorium) was being held. I am from a college experience in which I was highly involved and fashioned a love of the book *Zen and the Art of Motorcycle Maintenance* and this quote:

> We're living in topsy-turvy times, and I think that what causes the topsy-turvy feeling is inadequacy of old forms of thought to deal with new experiences . . . you have to stop and drift laterally for a while until you come across something that allows you to expand the roots of what you already know. (Pirsig, 1974, pp. 163–164)

I am from a master's degree education that focused on Perry, Kohlberg, and Chickering and theories in which I did not see myself but sparked in me a love of theory and a drift laterally. I am from a doctoral education that surrounded me with scholarly inspiration from people like Marylu McEwen, Bonnie Thornton Dill, Patricia Hill Collins, and Ruth Fassinger; people who encouraged me to create a theory in which I saw not only myself but also others left out of theories of college student development and to expand the roots of what I already knew. I am from great students and collaborators who stretch my thinking, people like Elisa Abes, D-L Stewart, Antonio Duran, Vasti Torres, Jan Arminio, Charmaine Wijeyesinghe, and Sherry Watt. I am from continuing to live in topsy-turvy times and an interest in both drifting laterally and expanding roots that grow something new. This is what animates my interests in rethinking college student development using critical frameworks.

In some ways I have come full circle and continue to evolve in my thinking. In short, I started my fascination with theory with Erik Erikson, became a fierce critic of anything developmental and stage based, and then emerged as someone who believes that development can be *both* developmental *and* dynamic and *always* contextual. That is, *something* happens to individuals along the way, and context matters. I still think that the question of "Who am I?" is an important one and that college students should be different as a result of their time in collegiate environments. I also appreciate that answering the question of "Who am I?" is not always easy and that our student development theories don't always equip us to understand the ways in which development is socially, historically, and culturally constructed. I also know that the college environment places barriers to development in front of some students more so than others and that what constitutes support for some will surely challenge others. I also believe that what we call *development* is a process that is not limited to college campuses and that individuals may thrive in many different spaces (which curiously then raises a possibility of something that is more universal than not!).

Beginning with my dissertation research (Jones, 1997), where the core category of the grounded theory I developed was titled "contextual influences on the construction of identities," I have always been fascinated by *context*. My early explorations into context were driven by the experience of difference and the juxtaposition of identity (sameness and coherence according to Erikson) and difference (or otherness as discussed by philosophers such as Heidegger and Derrida). I used this juxtaposition of identity and difference to investigate the influence of larger contextual influences—in other words, how might experiences of *difference* along dimensions of race, culture, ethnicity, gender, religion, and sexual orientation influence one's sense of self? I drew from standpoint theory and Patricia Hill Collins's idea of outsider-within status as providing a special angle of vision that one on the outside looking in develops. I understood from my experiences of feeling different that the way in which my own development proceeded was both because of and in spite of my sense of not fitting into normative expectations. I learned how to manage others' expectations of me, my own tightrope of self-doubt and authenticity, and the varying contexts in which I moved. I came to locate the phenomenon of difference in larger structures of power and privilege, mostly through my early introduction to the literature on race, class, and gender and then intersectionality. In so doing, I realized that the conversation about *development* needs to meaningfully integrate these larger societal contexts into an understanding of individuals' experiences of themselves and others. In other words, an individual cannot be understood outside of these power relations and social locations. And when what we call development is understood as deeply contextual, then the emphasis needs to move away from development as a noun, with an implied directionality, and more so as *developing*, which suggests a dynamic process inexorably bound up in shifting contexts.

So, I am not ready to wholly give up on the concept of development, but there does exist an "inadequacy of old forms" that no longer serves us well. And even if we are interested in investigating developmental pathways, we can't impose theories (e.g., developmental positions) that were empirically derived on samples of white students on minoritized social groups. We must account for shifting contexts and structures of inequality and systems of power in understanding developing individuals.

D-L

I am from Beverly Daniel Tatum, Joy James, Kaylynn Sullivan TwoTrees, Patricia Hill Collins, Lorene Cary, William E. Cross, Nikki Giovanni, Cornel West, and bell hooks—I am from Black intellectual thinkers who contextualized development and identity in, through, and despite racial oppression. I am from overcoming as past, present, and future.

I am from Bob Rodgers's essential questions and three classes on student development theory. I am from *internalize* as a praxis and kinetic expression. I am from before the *Student Development in College* books. I am from reading the original scholarship from the theorists themselves. I am from having to digest, analyze, and interpret extant theory on my own with instructional mentoring and supervision.

I am from Marigene Arnold, Karen Kitchener, Susan Robb Jones, Linda James Myers, Cynthia Dillard, Patti Lather, and Mary Leach—I am from women whose pedagogy pushed me to make myself known in theory and through theorizing.

I am from leaving homeplace (hooks, 1991); cleaving to structured and well-manicured houses of thought; and returning, finally, back to where I started. I am from critical theory and constructivism and from critical theory again.

I am from others' validation that I am a theorist. I am from thinking my way into being. I am from community networks of thinking and being. I am from socially constructed knowledge with critically minded kin. I am from legacies of kinship who have thought each other and therefore themselves into being, into (the) wor(l)d. I am from continually becoming.

Development is a false signpost. I know this is rather heretical coming from someone like me, whom others in this field regard as a student development theorist. I once believed strongly in the idea of development as envisaged in constructivist developmentalism—that understanding of the self is dependent on increasing complexity (Jones & Stewart, 2016). Given this, student development theory asserted that increasing complexity was essential to answering Bob Rodgers's core questions of student development theory:

Who am I? What do I believe? Who will I love? What do I want to do with my life? And what does it all mean anyway? I was once fervently committed to college being the best context for students to explore these questions and for their answers to emerge, having been appropriately challenged and supported by dedicated, skilled, theoretically grounded student affairs professionals. I spent years in others' academic houses; I drank the Kool-Aid. I believed. What changed?

Deep considerations of what counts as knowledge and knowing disrupted the ease with which I had been considering what happens for students in college. I became grounded in epistemological questions: How do I know who I am? How have I known whom to love? Whose knowledge am I relying on for deciding what I believe? What knowledges tell me what is worthwhile to do? How will I know meaning; will I recognize its form? I do not believe that answering these questions effectively is a matter of increasing complexity but rather believe that it is a matter of reflection, homeplace, and community.

Being from such diverse and sometimes conflicting lineages has produced a bricolage of epistemology, methodology, and praxis. My current critical theoretical and cynical views of and on development and constructivist notions of how students come to be and to know in college are shaped as much by my formal academic training as it is by my grounding in Black, femme, trans*, and queer (and Blackfemmetrans*queer) kin communities. I have returned to honoring the complexity of lived experience beyond the academy, laypersons' meaning-making, and streetwise knowledges. Consciously living in, among, and in resistance to oppression formulates expressions of knowing and meaning-making that are not captured by models informed by constructivist developmentalism. As I discussed with Shaunda Brown in chapter 10, oppression is not merely the milieu in which development happens. Rather, oppression (in)forms a critical consciousness through which people negotiate their movement through the world around them, a negotiation that happens in and beyond the academy.

I do think that college students become more sophisticated in how they articulate their thinking. College assuredly teaches people a new language, new modes of expression, and the capacity to perform all of this as required to persist in college. (This is admittedly a rather cynical view of college. It is also not necessarily untrue.) I no longer believe that sophistication is a signpost of development or that development is a signpost of meaning-making complexity. The association of college with development as an indicator of complexity and fitness for participation in a democratic society has come to trouble me. What of the knowing of those for whom college is inaccessible? Florid language does not signal complexity; neither do theoretical musings indicate that one has developed capacity for integrating complex and conflicting ideas. Development as a matter of increasing complexity suggests there is an endpoint, a singular, final arrival as illustrated by the linear, hierarchical stage models that inundate first-wave student development theory: "I am complex (enough)!" I have come to believe that is a false signpost. Individuals are continually becoming, arriving to, and departing from consciousness. Meaning-making to enable a liberated life is (must be) fluid, dynamic, and contextual but not inherently linked to what student development theory has constructed as development.

Concluding Thoughts

The four of us (Elisa, Antonio, Susan, and D-L) discussed and shared more about our narratives, written independently of each other. We responded to each other's narratives, and in so doing, we talked through thorny questions with which we were still wrestling. We'll share those questions next and how we are currently working through them. Ultimately, we embraced that we had arrived at different places by the time we reached the end of our journey with this book. We believe this is good and appropriate—and likely aligned with how readers of this text may be thinking and feeling upon reaching this final chapter as well. We recognized that readers (and we) may be hungry for definitive answers. So what does this all mean? What is development? Should we keep it, ditch it, or find some way to keep and ditch? If we ditch development as a construct, what do we put in its place? We are choosing to resist providing definitive answers to these and other questions in place of allowing the questions to motivate readers' and our own continued reflection. As Parker (1977) wrote over 40 years ago, "Concrete and specific action flows from the personal theories of the actor" (p. 419). In other words, it is the sense you make of the discussions and dialogues in this text that will inform what you do in your theorizing and practice more than any further theorizing we might offer. Therefore, instead of offering answers, we offer our readers continued musings about the "what if" questions this book and our personal theories keep us coming back to concerning the meaning of the words we use, the feasibility of retaining earlier formulations of development, and the utility of constructivism for some students.

What if words matter? What if we can reclaim words? D-L asserts in his narrative that *development* has a specific meaning in constructivist developmentalism—increasing complexity—and rejects it. Yet, Susan, Elisa, and Antonio each offer different conceptualizations of what development can mean and hold on to it. Must a word—in this case, *development*—retain a singular meaning over time and place? Theoretical perspectives and personal histories play a central role in shaping individual views on development. D-L often uses the metaphor of taking pictures with a camera to illustrate that different paradigms result in seeing the image in the camera in different ways: One lens may be used to see in the dark; adjusting the shutter may help capture moving subjects; producing sepia tones, black-and-white, or color photographs depends on the filters used. Likewise, the meaning of development shifts if one considers it from the vantage point of differing theoretical perspectives and life experiences.

If some change its meaning while others do not, what effects are wrought for those in conversation and practice with each other about student development, and what happens for students in college? What does it look like to reclaim a word that has perhaps caused harm for some? We have examples of this in contemporary U.S. culture. *Queer* has been reclaimed (by some) from its roots as a slur against those who defied conventional norms of sexuality and gender to a proclamation of pride in being unconventional, counterconventional, and beyond the confines of convention. Yet, as we noted parenthetically, not all have accepted or adopted this reclamation, including those who hold minoritized identities of sexuality and gender, and the meaning of *queer* is not uniformly agreed on. These debates remain unsettled within and beyond queer communities but have not prevented advocacy and activism for liberation on behalf of LGBTQ+ people.

For our discussion of development, perhaps similar issues must be brought to bear. Can development be both constructivist and critical? Must we assume that development is inherently constructivist? Who is included and who is excluded in discussions of development? How do we have conversations about translating student development theory into practice if we all don't define development in the same way and others of us are not using *development* at all? These are debates that will likely remain unsettled for quite some time and perhaps never be resolved. Asking this question—What does development mean?—has implications for how we approach teaching, research, and practice with students in college. Understanding development as increasing complexity, as challenging the origins of what is known and believed, or as a mix of the two affects how we do programming and trainings from diversity orientation sessions to anti-hazing workshops. No matter where we stand on development, its meaning, and its utility, we believe we can still be advocates and activists for liberatory praxis.

What can we retain here? Are there some things that we should retain? We believe we have learned important ideas from some branches of first- and second-wave student development theory that are worth holding on to. The questions that D-L reframes in his personal narrative are—as he describes them—epistemologically oriented. These are the kinds of probing questions that epistemological development theorists, going back even to William G. Perry, have affirmed need to be asked if one is to know anything about how another person defines truth and knowledge. These probing questions may be worth continued use even if one decides to reject the construct of development and/or the guiding questions of constructivist developmental theories. One might then ask how the probing questions and concerns from theories about different domains of development (e.g., epistemological, moral, and existential [faith]) might better inform the kinds of questions and concerns asked by intrapersonal and interpersonal (psychosocial) and social identity development.

Doing such epistemological work is why we anchored this book in constructs, not particular theories or models of development. We believe this allowed the authors in Part Two the ability to draw outside the lines and reconceptualize these ideas without being confined to how they are used within a particular model or paradigm. The constructs of authenticity, context, and agency—for example—have meaning both inside and outside constructivist paradigms and models.

Are constructivist models of development just fine for some kinds of students? This question asks us to consider the goals of our epistemological paradigms. How far can we stretch their utility, and when do they become no longer useful? In our discussions we acknowledged that constructivist models of development have been very useful for understanding some groups of students—namely, white, heterosexual, cisgender, middle-class, and able-bodied students—and perhaps to varying degrees even parts of the stories of some students who do not fit each of these privileged identities. These models may have continuing utility, but they should not be used for all. As Elisa noted in her narrative, we must put "caution tape" (p. 239, this volume) around them.

Upon reading this, some might raise Audre Lorde's (1984) contention that "the master's tools will never dismantle the master's house" (p. 112). If the house is white supremacist cisheteropatriarchy, are its tools the aims and goals of constructivist theories of student development? Are the tools of white supremacy inherent to constructivist models or merely an issue of how they have been applied?

When we considered the goals and aims of constructivist and critical paradigms, we began questioning whether putting caution tape around constructivism was enough (without giving up on constructivism entirely). Constructivism is not intended to dismantle oppressive systems. Critical theory is meant to do exactly this. The outcome of constructivism is not intended to be liberation. The outcome of critical theory is. As Susan noted in chapter 1, bell hooks (1994) asserted, "Theory is not inherently healing, liberatory, or revolutionary. It fulfills this function only when we ask it to do so and direct our theorizing towards this end" (p. 61). If we are to take hooks seriously, then the aims of our research paradigms should matter. If our goal through student development theory is liberation, then we must use research paradigms and theoretical frameworks that are aimed in that direction. Moreover, if white supremacist cisheteropatriarchy is left intact after our theorizing, is this really good for anyone—even students who are white, cisgender, heterosexual, middle class, and able-bodied? We think not. Who needs theory informed by critical theoretical perspectives? Everyone.

And it's possible to hold firmly to this critical, liberatory stance while still resisting throwing it (constructivism and constructivist developmentalism) all away. Some of us continue to take this position, even if with some lingering hesitancy. These multiple perspectives we offer here and the nondefinitive answers we provide to our own questions reflect differences in perspectives among the four of us based on our own lived experiences. Where does this leave you, our readers? We hope that your journey through this book has also left you with more questions than perhaps you have answers and that you are inspired to continue to search them out. Your personal theories—the ones that will guide your scholarship and practice—are rooted in the twin histories of what you have lived and what you have been taught. We encourage you to dive deep within those personal theories by evaluating your worldviews through the lenses of those presented by the contributors in Part One. Then, consider how the constructs in Part Two have shown up in your own narratives of learning, growth, and development and how your testimony about those constructs—and the testimonies of those with narratives different from your own—inform what development means to you. Finally, broach the questions raised in Part Three for your own practice with college students. Our theories-in-use are directed toward particular ends, even if we are not conscious of them. It is our responsibility to question our theorizing and our practice and see whether they are aligned with the values we espouse. That, then, is the journey of this book and of being student development practitioners: To look at ourselves as we look at our students.

Discussion Questions

1. Consider your own journey in understanding the study of student development theory. If you were to write your own narrative, what major academic and personal influences would you identify as being critical to your view of student development? How did these influences inform

your thinking? If you have challenged any of these influences, in what ways have you done so?

2. What is your perspective on the meaning of development? What constructs (as highlighted in Part Two) do you believe are particularly relevant to student development, and why?

3. If many people have different perspectives on development, what does this mean for research, practice, and teaching? How do we engage with others across our differing ideas about development?

4. In keeping with critical theory's liberatory aims, how can you use critical and poststructural conceptualizations of student development theory in your practice to advance goals of equity?

References

hooks, b. (1991). *Yearning: Race, gender, and cultural politics*. London, UK: Turnaround.

hooks, b. (1994). *Teaching to transgress: Education as the practice of freedom*. New York, NY: Routledge.

Jones, S. R. (1997). Voices of identity and difference: A qualitative exploration of the multiple dimensions of identity development in women college students. *Journal of College Student Development, 38*, 376–386.

Jones, S. R., & Stewart, D-L. (2016). Evolution of student development theory. In E. S. Abes (Ed.), *Critical perspectives on student development theory* (New Directions for Student Services, No. 154, pp. 17–28). San Francisco, CA: Wiley.

Kegan, R. (1994). *In over our heads: The mental demands of modern life*. Cambridge, MA: Harvard University Press.

Knefelkamp, L., Widick, C., & Parker, C. (Eds.). (1978). *Applying new developmental findings* (New Directions for Student Services, No. 4). San Francisco, CA: Jossey-Bass.

Lorde, A. (1984). *Sister outsider: Essays and speeches*. Freedom, CA: Crossing Press.

Parker, C. (1977). On modeling reality. *Journal of College Student Personnel, 18*, 419–425.

Pirsig, R. M. (1974). *Zen and the art of motorcycle maintenance*. New York, NY: Bantam Books.

Suskind, R. (1998). *A hope in the unseen: An American odyssey from the inner city to the Ivy League*. New York, NY: Broadway Books.

EDITORS AND CONTRIBUTORS

Editors

Elisa S. Abes, PhD, is an associate professor at Miami University (Ohio) in the student affairs in higher education program in the Department of Educational Leadership. Over her 15-year faculty career, her research and teaching have focused primarily on student development theory, in particular critical approaches to identity development. Along with peer-reviewed journal articles and book chapters, Abes is the coauthor (with Susan R. Jones) of *Identity Development of College Students: Advancing Frameworks for Multiple Dimensions of Identity* (Jossey-Bass, 2013). She is also the editor of *Critical Perspectives on Student Development Theory* (Jossey-Bass, 2016). Abes is currently researching disability identity among college students, including college students with physical and intellectual disabilities. In doing so, she interrogates intersectional ableism and explores antiableist intersectional practices. Abes has earned multiple university and professional association awards for her teaching, research, and service. Above all, Abes is a proud mother of two kind children, ages 10 and 8 years, both of whom have social justice sensibilities and creative minds that will no doubt contribute to a more just world.

Susan R. Jones, PhD, is a professor in the higher education and student affairs program in the Educational Studies Department at The Ohio State University (Ohio State). Prior to rejoining the faculty at Ohio State, she was an associate professor and director of the college student personnel program at the University of Maryland–College Park. She began her faculty career at Ohio State, where she served as an assistant professor and director of the student personnel assistantship program after a number of years as a student affairs administrator, including as the dean of students at Trinity College of Vermont. Jones's research focuses on psychosocial perspectives on identity, intersectionality and multiple social identities, service-learning, and qualitative research methodologies. She has published over 25 journal articles, mostly in top-tier journals including the *Journal of College Student Development* and the *Journal of Higher Education*; over 26 book chapters; and 5 books. She is the coauthor (with Elisa S. Abes) of books titled *Identity Development of College Students: Advancing Frameworks for Multiple Dimensions of Identity* (Jossey-Bass, 2013) and *Negotiating the Complexities of Qualitative Research: Fundamental Elements and Issues* (with Vasti Torres and Jan Arminio)

(Routledge, 2006, second edition published in 2014). Jones is one of the coeditors of the fifth and sixth editions of *Student Services: A Handbook for the Profession* (Jossey-Bass, 2011, 2017). Jones is the recipient of a number of awards, including the Contribution to Knowledge Award from the American College Personnel Association (ACPA, 2015); the Thomas M. Magoon Distinguished Alumni Award (2012) and the Outstanding Scholar Award (2011), both from the University of Maryland; NASPA's Robert H. Shaffer Award for Academic Excellence as a Graduate Faculty Member (2010); The Ohio State University Alumni Award for Distinguished Teaching (2002); and ACPA's Emerging Scholar (2001) and Senior Scholar (2009) awards.

D-L Stewart, PhD, is professor in the School of Education and cocoordinator of the student affairs in higher education unit at Colorado State University. Stewart is a scholar, educator, and activist focused on empowering and imagining futures that sustain and cultivate the learning, growth, and success of minoritized groups in U.S. higher education institutions. His work is motivated by an ethic of love grounded in justice and informed by an intersectional framework that recognizes both the lived experiences of individuals with multiple marginalities and the material effects of interlocking systems of oppression. Over the course of their 18-year faculty career, Stewart has focused most intently on issues of race and ethnicity, sexuality, and gender, as well as religion, faith, and spirituality in his research, teaching, and service to professional organizations and institutions across the nation. Stewart is the author of over four dozen journal articles and book chapters, as well as either editor, coeditor, or author for three books covering multicultural student services, gender and sexual diversity of U.S. college students, and the historical experiences of Black collegians in northern liberal arts colleges in the middle of the twentieth century. Stewart has also provided professional service and leadership to a number of scholarly and professional associations, most substantively through a variety of roles in ACPA: College Student Educators International, as well as for the Association for the Study of Higher Education.

Contributors

Nya:weh s:geno. My name is **Cori Bazemore-James**, PhD. I am Turtle Clan of the Seneca Nation of Indians and I work in the Graduate School Diversity Office at the University of Minnesota-Twin Cities. I acknowledge that I currently live and work on the original homelands of the Dakota and Ojibway nations.

Shaunda Brown is a proud first-generation college student and product of Detroit, Michigan. She received her bachelor's degree in liberal studies and master's degree in college student personnel from Bowling Green State University. Brown is now the director for student inclusion and involvement at Edgewood College in Madison, Wisconsin. Her professional interests include multicultural affairs, residence life, and fraternity and sorority life. Brown is committed to creating equitable educational environments that center the experiences of minoritized student, staff, and faculty populations. She centers her work on creating institutional transformation toward realizing justice and equity.

Riss Carter identifies as QTPOC (queer, transgender, Person of Color). Carter does not use pronouns and instead uses Riss's name as a pronoun. Carter is an undergraduate student at Northern Illinois University. Carter is passionate about intersectionality, centering QTPOC identities, and living a life that would make Marsha P. Johnson proud.

J. Michael Denton, PhD, is a faculty member of the higher education and student affairs program at the University of South Florida. His research interests include using queer, affect, and poststructural frameworks with narrative and arts-based methods to examine the intersections of collegians' sexuality, gender, bodies, and/or illness, especially HIV/AIDS.

Antonio Duran is a doctoral candidate in higher education and student affairs at The Ohio State University. His research interests include using intersectional frameworks to understand how queer and transgender Students of Color explore their intersecting identities at historically white institutions.

Jessica C. Harris, PhD, is an assistant professor of higher education and organizational change at the University of California, Los Angeles. She earned her master's degree in college student affairs from Pennsylvania State University and her doctoral degree in higher education from Indiana University. Through her research, Harris focuses on multiraciality in higher education, Women of Color and campus sexual violence, and the possibilities of using critical race theory to interrogate race and racisms in postsecondary contexts.

V. Leilani Kupo, PhD, (*Kānaka Maoli*) was raised on the U.S. continent away from her ancestral land of Ukumehame, Maui. Kupo received her PhD from Bowling Green State University in higher education administration. She currently serves as associate dean of students at the University of California, Merced.

Alex C. Lange is committed to a vision and reality of promoting education as transformative, ongoing learning within and outside of schooling. They are currently a graduate fellow at the University of Iowa, working on their PhD in higher education and student affairs.

Susan B. Marine, PhD, is an associate professor and program director of the higher education master's program at Merrimack College. Her teaching, scholarship, and activism seek to center feminist, queer, and antiracist pedagogies in the service of transforming student affairs practice to advance human flourishing and liberation.

Z Nicolazzo, PhD, is an assistant professor of trans* studies in education in the Center for the Study of Higher Education at the University of Arizona. Nicolazzo's research focuses on discourses of gender in higher education, with a particular emphasis on affirmative and resilience-based research alongside trans* students.

Wilson Kwamogi Okello, PhD, is a visiting assistant professor in the department of global and intercultural studies at Miami University (Ohio), where he teaches Black Studies. Bridging the scholar–artist divide, his research employs Black feminisms to critique and advance student development theory and pedagogical praxis in higher education.

Symphony Oxendine, PhD, (*Cherokee/Choctaw*) is an assistant professor in higher education at the University of North Carolina, Wilmington. Oxendine received her PhD in educational studies with a concentration in higher education from the University of North Carolina at Greensboro, where she also received her master's of education.

OiYan A. Poon, PhD, is an assistant professor of higher education leadership in the School of Education at Colorado State University. Her research focuses on the racial politics and discourses of college access, higher education organization and policy, affirmative action, and Asian Americans.

Danyelle J. Reynolds is an assistant director for student learning and leadership at the University of Michigan's Ginsberg Center for Community Service and Learning. She amplifies positive community impact through student leadership development and community engagement. Her interests include applying justice-oriented frameworks to leadership education and community engagement.

Claire Kathleen Robbins, PhD, is an assistant professor of higher education at Virginia Tech. Her research explores graduate students' development, identity (re)construction, socialization, and perspectives on equity, diversity, and inclusion. Using primarily qualitative methodologies and critical theoretical perspectives, Robbins problematizes intersecting systems of oppression, especially racism, in graduate education.

Nicole Alia Salis Reyes, PhD, (*Kānaka Maoli*) is an assistant professor of higher education at the University of Hawai'i at Mānoa. Her research broadly considers how communities of color, especially Indigenous peoples, define postsecondary success for themselves and how institutions of higher education can better support these forms of success.

Maria Tauala earned her bachelor's degree from Portland State University, where through various student leadership positions she developed an interest in student affairs and multiracial identity development. She is now a master's student, studying educational administration at the University of Hawai'i at Mānoa.

Kari B. Taylor, PhD, is an assistant professor in residence and director of the University of Connecticut's higher education and student affairs program. Her research contributes to theoretical and methodological issues concerning college student development by conceptualizing developmental processes as both psychological and sociocultural in nature and by investigating development through multiple methods.

Daniel Tillapaugh, PhD, is an assistant professor and chair of the Department of Counselor Education in the Graduate School of Education at California Lutheran University in Thousand Oaks, California. His research centers on intersectionality in higher education, particularly college students and their development in different contexts.

Nya weñha Skannoh. My name is **Guy yon di saye, Stephanie J. Waterman**, PhD, Onondaga, Turtle Clan. I acknowledge that I am a guest of the Mississauga of the Credit River, in territory that is subject to the Dish with One Spoon Wampum covenant between the Haudenosaunee and Anishnaabek, the Huron-Wendat, Petun, and other First Peoples.

Kiaya Demere White is a second-year graduate student in the student affairs in higher education program at Miami University (Ohio). Her research interests explore student development theory through the critical lens of Black feminist thought and consider the possibilities of engaged pedagogy in higher education.

Charmaine L. Wijeyesinghe, EdD, is an independent author and consultant in the areas of intersectionality, social identity and inequality, and organizational change. Her background includes positions in student affairs administration, program and board development, and over 30 years working with institutions on social justice issues. She resides in Delmar, New York.

developmental dimensions
  differences from, 179–80
Duran narrative, 174–77
Duran positionality, 173
in involvement and engagement,
  200–201
Jones on, 180, 245
Jones positionality, 173–74
measurement of, 180–82
positionality and, 172–74
privilege and, 178–79
shaping of, 182–83
contextual influences, on identity, 245
Cooks, L. M., 38
Cornell, S., 48
counternarratives
  on disadvantage, 228
  in high-impact practices, 227–29
  IKS and, 228
Creating Change conference, for
  LGBTQ+, 86
Crenshaw, Kimberlé, 28, 31, 152, 242
crip failure, 68
crip identity, contested, 66–67
cripistemology
  Johnson, M., and McRuer on, 67
  knowledge through, 67–68
crip relationships
  access intimacy in, 69
  forced intimacy in, 68
crip theory, xiii, 5
  ableism in, 1, 64, 65, 68–69
  claiming crip in, 66–67, 68
  community-based practice and, 78,
    82–84
  compulsory able-bodiedness and
    able-mindedness, 65–66, 69
  contested crip identity and, 66–67
  crip failure and, 68
  crip relationships intimacies and,
    68–69
  knowledge through cripistemology,
    67–68
  limitations of, 69–70
  McRuer on, 67, 82

poststructuralism, queer theory and,
  64
crisis, theorizing in wake of, 149
critical
  defined, 2
  Tierney and Rhoads on, 12
critical conceptualization, of
  dissonance, 99–100
critical constructivist perspective,
  116–17
critical feminist theories (FemCrit), xiii,
  4, 35
  art of failure and, 39–40, 68
  defining of, 36
  differential consciousness and, 38–39
  gender as starting point, 40–41
  knowing, being, and doing in, 37–38
  student development theory from
    perspective of, 40–42
  tenets, as student development
    framework, 37–40
  Zaytoun on, 40
critical frameworks, x, xi, 1, 3, 129–31
*Critical Perspectives on Student
  Development Theory*, ix
critical-poststructuralist paradigm, 117,
  121
critical praxis, of involvement and
  engagement, 195–202
critical questions, about context,
  177–83
Critical Race Feminism: A Reader
  (Wing), 36
critical race theory (CRT), xiii, 2, 4,
  159
  ahistorical narratives challenges, 18
  on differential racialization, 18,
    21–22
  Hernández on self-authoring
    processes, 19
  on racism as endemic, 18, 19
  student development theory and,
    17–22
  on whiteness as property, 18, 20
critical reflection, Brookfield on, 106

(Continued from previous page)

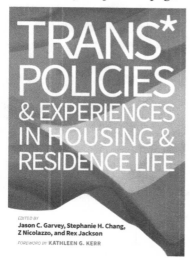

Trans* Policies & Experiences in Housing & Residence Life

Edited by Jason C. Garvey, Stephanie H. Chang, Z Nicolazzo, Rex Jackson

Foreword by Kathleen G. Kerr

"From storytelling to practical application, *Trans* Policies & Experiences in Housing & Residence Life* is a necessary text for residential life professionals across all levels."—***Van Bailey***, *Director, LGBTQ Student Center, University of Miami*

"Cultural change does not happen suddenly and completely. Instead, within our sphere of influence, we must remove those structural artifacts that support a gender binary and are not gender inclusive. Our students deserve all of our focus and energy to dismantle those artifacts, piece by piece. Making sure every student has a residence hall 'home' to return to at the end of the day is the least we can do. This book gives us the tools needed to accomplish that."—***Kathleen G. Kerr***, *Associate Vice President for Student Life and Executive Director of Residence Life & Housing at the University of Delaware*

22883 Quicksilver Drive
Sterling, VA 20166-2019

Subscribe to our e-mail alerts: www.Styluspub.com

(Continued from previous page)

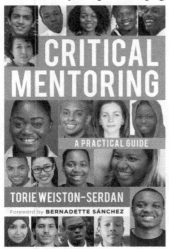

Critical Mentoring

A Practical Guide

Torie Weiston-Serdan

Foreword by Bernadette Sánchez

"Sustained by extensive theoretical and practice-based research, *Critical Mentoring: A Practical Guide* equips the reader with effective strategies to provide youth development programs with tools necessary for critical mentoring and critical consciousness. While the foundations of oppression are deeply seated in contemporary society, Weiston-Serdan presents an avenue along which mentors, protégés, and their respective communities can bring to light crucial issues and stride toward a new paradigm."
— ***Mentoring & Coaching Monthly***

"*Critical Mentoring* offers an unwavering and accessible answer to the age-old question: What constitutes the status quo? It brings contemporary struggles within youth mentoring work to full resolution. This book deconstructs the ways in which the social algorithm of mentoring has historically materialized into deficit lenses of Black youth and other dehumanized populations. Torie Weiston-Serdan's trove of wisdom is imperative for educators who believe that justice can only be achieved by continual self-reflection and courageous interrogation of current practices. Weiston-Serdan's exhaustively researched work provides a much needed and foundational service to scholar-activists, education policy makers, and practitioners alike."— ***Arash Daneshzadeh***, *Associate Director, Urban Strategies Council*

(Continues on preceding page)